If at All Possible, Involve a Cow

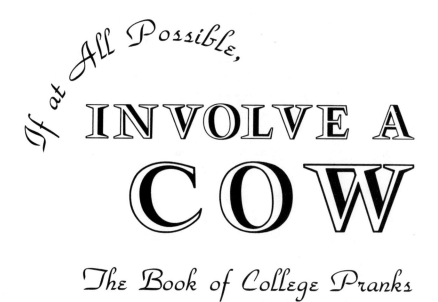

If at All Possible,

INVOLVE A COW

The Book of College Pranks

NEIL STEINBERG

ST. MARTIN'S PRESS • NEW YORK

To my father, Robert Steinberg

Who, when quitting a frat
At Ohio State University
Punctuated his resignation speech
By grinding out a cigarette
In the palm of his hand
Where, conveniently,
He had tucked a quarter
So as not to get burned.

It is to that spirit
And to my father
This book is lovingly dedicated.

IF AT ALL POSSIBLE, INVOLVE A COW: THE BOOK OF COLLEGE
PRANKS Copyright © 1992 by Neil Steinberg. All rights
reserved. Printed in the United States of America. No part of
this book may be used or reproduced in any manner
whatsoever without written permission except in the case of
brief quotations embodied in critical articles or reviews. For
information, address St. Martin's Press, 175 Fifth Avenue,
New York, N.Y. 10010.

Library of Congress Cataloging-in-Publication Data

Steinberg, Neil.
    If at all possible, involve a cow: the book of college pranks
/ Neil Steinberg.
        p.   cm.
    ISBN 0-312-07810-2 (pbk.)
    1. Student activities—United States. 2. College students—
United States—Humor. 3. College wit and humor. I. Title.
    LA229.S63 1992
    378.1'98'0207—dc20   92-6117
                                                              CIP

First edition: July 1992

10 9 8 7 6 5 4 3 2 1

CONTENTS

You've disgraced yourself, sir;
you've disgraced your family;
you've disgraced your college;
and tomorrow it will all be in the New York papers
and the next day in the Philadelphia papers.

—Dr. James McCosh
Princeton University president,
reprimanding a student prankster

ACKNOWLEDGMENTS

Many people helped me with this book. I'd like to first thank three who had particularly crucial roles: journalist Andrew Patner, who knows everyone in the world and put me in touch with his extraordinary agent, David Black, who did not dither at all but whipped my proposal into professional shape and sold it right away to Bill Thomas, my enthusiastic, skillful editor at St. Martin's Press. Thanks guys.

Then there were the strangers across the country who I imposed on, out of the blue, and who got into the spirit of what I was doing and helped out. Thanks to: Dennis Bitterlich, archivist at UCLA and generous with his copying card; Frank Lockwood, my research assistant at Harvard, ages ago; David Rothman at the University of Wisconsin; John Updike, for allowing me to quote from his work; David Halberstam; Northwestern University archivist Patrick Quinn; Paula Martin, proud representative of the University of British Columbia; Boston attorney George S. Abrams; Washington psychologist Michael Maccoby; the staff of the *Harvard Lampoon,* a nice bunch who threw open the gates and archives of their sacred castle and let me use their copier; Brian Liebowitz, for his insight and the tour of MIT; Bob Di Iorio, friendly MIT spokesman; Dr. Kenneth Russell, zealous metallurgist at MIT; Sally Beddow, at the MIT Museum; Jay Kennedy at King Features Syndicate; Jim Mallon at Best Brains; the genius Leon Varjian; historian Judith Schiff at Yale, who took her sweet time about it but always came through; Boston cabbie Mark Green; Cornell's venerable E.T. Horn; Ginette Blumner; the patient, burdened staff of the New York Public Library; John Loengard, famed *Life* photographer; Karen Bartholomew, harried editor of the *Stanford Observer;* Curt Slepian, who accepted my original pranks article at *Games;* Jonathan Napack, for his delightful index; Los Angeles sports writers Mal Florence and Joe Jares; broadcasting legend Mel Allen; prankmeister Dick Tuck; Pat McClenahan, for generous use of his excellent video "Crosstown: The USC-UCLA Rivalry!"; Jeff Bliss at Pepperdine; Diana Perron at Wesleyan University; J. Elias Jones, archivist emeritus at Drake University, and Richard Klin, production guru.

The people at the California Institute of Technology are so wonderful they deserve a paragraph of their own. Deep thanks to Bill Swanson, '91, senior class president who spilled the beans about the date of Ditch Day in time for me to get a cheap airplane ticket; able PR guy Bob Finn; good-natured mathematician Dr. Tom Apostol; humble engineer Lyndon Hardy (Class of 1962 and a former resident of Lloyd House, *n'est pas?*) Mark Montague, Virgil to my Dante during Ditch Day preparations, and the the Caltech Alumni Association, which labored to assemble two fine collections of Caltech pranks and permitted me to quote from them as much as I liked, provided I mumbled the following comma-riddled legalism: "Reprinted, with permission, from *Legends of Caltech,* and (or) *More Legends of Caltech,* published by the Alumni Association of the California Institute of Technology." Keep it in mind whenever you see the name "Caltech."

On a personal note, I'd like to thank Richard Roeper, my constant friend at the *Chicago Sun-Times;* college pals Kier Strejcek, Cate Plys and Rob Leighton; buddy in absentia Jim Sayler;

my brother Sam and sister Debbie; my mother June, the Queen Bee of Boulder, Colorado; and, finally, a special, kiss-laden thanks to Edie Steinberg—a damn good editor, damn good lawyer, damn good wife.

INTRODUCTION
What Makes a Prank Great?

I asked around to some people,
but they said they didn't know
of any pranks at Brandeis
and wouldn't tell you if they did.
—Barbara Blumenthal,
Brandeis PR flack

*T*he startled residents of Washington, D.C. awake one morning to find the red banner of Soviet communism flapping proudly from a tall flagpole in front of the U.S. Supreme Court Building. The Rose Bowl halftime show is taken over on national television by mischievous California science students. The library dome at the Massachusetts Institute of Technology is transformed, overnight, into a giant breast.

There is something glorious about a college prank. A really good prank brings not just laughter, but a visceral satisfaction and a kind of awe that does not fade with time nor diminish with retelling. In the narrow world of university life, so routine, so programmed and often—like life in the real world—too dull to tolerate, a prank shakes things up, breaks the tedium, and gives hope for a life filled with hidden, delightful possibility.

When I began collecting stories about college pranks, I assumed it was a matter of time before I stumbled upon the "Time-Life College Prank Series" or "The Oxford Book of College Pranks."

It never happened. I kept being struck by the echoing void when it came to pranks. Not only are there no books about college pranks, there are very few newspaper or magazine articles. The concept of a prank itself is rare. In the New York Public Library's exhaustive computer listing of 900,000 doctoral dissertations written since 1861, the word "college" brings up 31,170 citations. The word "prank" brings up none.

The reasons for this conspicuous silence are clear. First, people associate pranks with hazing, and feel an understandable shiver of disgust at the thought. The idea of locking somebody in a car trunk with a quart of grain alcohol and a cat in a bag does not resonate with humor. Due to a steady drip-drip-drip of horrific hazing tragedy stories, many people react negatively when they hear the words "college prank."

Hazing is not what this book is about. For me, the very definition of a prank is something that is pleasurable to retell. A prank must have some sort of wit, some sort of sense of hubris punctured or justice restored. Cruelty ruins a prank. Slyly tricking a stern temperance leader into visiting a notorious drinking club is a prank. Leading a procession of blindfolded pledges into the path of a speeding truck is not. To confuse the two is the same as thinking of those pouty clown paintings on black velvet whenever someone mentions the word "art."

And a great prank is like art, in that there is some concept underlying the work itself. Ideally, a prank makes a statement. It is instructive. In the fall of 1938, a group of freshmen at the University of Michigan circulated a petition asking that a psychology lecture, held on Saturday afternoon, be shifted to Wednesday so students could attend football games. Many upperclassmen signed. Only the next day, when they picked up the student newspaper, did they discover the full text of what they had put their names to:

> We, the undersigned, hereby petition that the lecture in Psychology 2 be changed from Saturday to Wednesday afternoon. By signing this document without reading it we cheerfully disqualify ourselves as candidates for any degree conferred by this university. We furthermore declare that the freshmen are our superiors in wit and wisdom, and that our stupidity is surpassed

only by the mental lethargy of the underpaid faculty that teaches us.

Not only is it a good prank, it was probably more educational than some of the classes that year.

Even people who grasp the meaning of pranks sometimes shy away from them—what I call the Brandeis reflex. A prank is a rebellion to the system, albeit a small one, and to the PR-damaged mind-set, rebellion is misbehavior and therefore bad.

For every college official who was at all interested in helping ferret out her school's pranks, there were three or four who blew me off with a noncomprehending shrug or a bland dismissal. A professor at Columbia University, referred to as a sage of Columbia lore, told me in utter sincerity that, in his 46 years at Columbia, nobody pulled any pranks.

In their minds, I'm sure, they are protecting their schools from being associated with gleeful undergraduate mischief. (Some of it might be simple laziness. I never actually heard a ripping, comic yawn come from the other end of the phone line, but there are times I imagined one—particularly with archivists, whose standard response is often a flabbergasted "Well, I'd have to look that up!" as if searching for information is an unimaginable doom).

This blinkered view is particularly strong among authors of college histories. The average college history is the size of a phone book and bears a numbing resemblance to every other college history. Turgid and lifeless, these volumes document the tiniest personal habits of their deans and presidents, their tiffs with faculty and debates over which arcane educational philosophy to employ when grinding students into a uniform powder. The provenance for every brick ever placed upon another brick on campus is given, along with spread sheets to account for every dollar spent paying for those bricks.

The students are nowhere to be seen. They appear, like a drowning man breaking the water's surface, every 90 pages or so, take a few short gasps—sports! fashions! clubs!—then down they go again for another league of icy tedium.

Anyone familiar with college administrations will recognize, of course, that the histories are only giving past students the same due that colleges grant the living students populating their campuses today.

"Students have strangely always had to insist that they are human beings," Frederick Rudolph wrote in his engaging 1966 essay, "Neglect of Students as a Historical Tradition." Rudolph argues that not only are student pranks often "undergraduate imagination at its best" but "might more properly be considered for the insights they provide to the collegiate experience and to shadows they cast across the history of higher education."

Sadly, the shadows are much shorter than they should be. Pranks, when they arise, are given the backhand. Few college histories list "pranks" in their indexes. Rather they can be found, if at all, under "discipline." There they are scantily sketched, usually without names or dates. Often, the focus of the story is not the prank, but how a certain president handled the matter.

Yet colleges are also very historically minded. Several people have asked me why *college* pranks as a subject, and I point out that there have probably been good pranks at steel mills over the centuries, but how would you learn about them? Even colleges that completely lack an understanding of their pranks still record them, somewhere. You often have to crack through smug, auto-erotic officialdom, particularly at a place like Harvard or Princeton. They won't help you, but the pranks are there, somewhere—*everything* is there, somewhere. The beauty of a college, to those with a taste for history, is they are dreams of documentation, fantasies of preservation and order. At the *Harvard Lampoon* the day-to-day jottings of the staff—phone messages, idle notes, graffitti—are preserved in a big book which, when filled, is added to a shelf jammed with other big books, holding the idle jottings of the staff over the past 115 years. Immortality in an instant.

While the material may be there, the perspective usually is not. Rare is the chronicler of school history who cuts through official squeamishness and sees value in a school's pranks.

"The resourcefulness of the students in finding occasion for pranks and the labor which they often expended on their schemes merit sincere admiration," James F. Hopkins wrote about the University of Kentucky of the 1890s. "Apparently nothing was overlooked, no man nor thing was immune."

That zeal, that all-encompassing energy students put into pranks will quickly become clear to readers of this book. In a sense, a good prank is like Alfred Hitchcock's universal plot device, which he called the "MacGuffin" and defined as the thing everybody wants and cares about.

Whatever a prank is—whether constructing a huge mock-up of the Statue of Liberty or publishing a fake edition of the *New York Times*—it is cared about. A prank is never the product of apathy. Perhaps this sets pranks apart from hazing even more clearly, since notorious hazing episodes are always the result of inertia, drunkenness, or stupidity, while pranks become known because of their cleverness, their planning, and the energy required to bring them to being.

The purpose of writing this book was to find these stories, lost at a hundred lonely colleges, scattered across the country, and pin them down. To look hard at them and see if they are real and what, if anything, they mean.

I've tried to make this book an act of historical research. An essential aspect of pranks is that they are *true*. Often this distinction escapes people, especially those from the old school, the cracker-barrel humorists who have written about pranks in the past, but in a vague "there was once an undergraduate at a large midwestern college who . . ." manner that is more infuriating than anything else.

Such material is suffocating. I wanted to drag these stories out of the basement of myth and rumor, into the daylight, where I think they belong.

In doing so, I found many famous pranks to not be true, or at least not to have happened in the way they are said to have happened. Many legendary pranksters exist more on reputation than on the basis of having actually done a specific prank.

But just because a prank is found to be untrue, does not mean it ceases to be of interest. The way the myth developed about why Eugene O'Neill was kicked out of Princeton turns about to be more interesting than had the playwright actually hurled a beer bottle through Woodrow Wilson's bedroom window, as generations of Princetonians believed.

One side benefit of looking at pranks is that they illuminate the times in which they occurred. To understand the pranks of 100 years ago you need to know that seniors carried canes and classes battled each other in bitter rivalries. You need to know that, even 35 years ago, freshmen wore beanies and had to do whatever the upperclassmen said. Twenty years ago colleges agonized over whether to permit men and women to go to school together.

I also give some background because, having struck upon it, I just had to pass it along. No one really needs to know that the design on the Campbell's soup cans was inspired by Cornell football jerseys, or that in the beginning you could pay your Harvard tuition in sugar. But it would be selfish to uncover this sort of thing and keep it to myself.

In these times of somber self-righteousness, it is worthwhile to note that, just a generation or two back, students kidnapped each other, wrestled with policemen, and in general treated the day's pieties in a less-than-respectful manner. Yet their parents did not sue one another. The heavens did not crack.

And who knows, perhaps pranks are important, in a larger sense. Rudolph credits them with no less than the entire positive development of secondary education, an engine of change forcing stubborn and short-sighted academics into growth.

"They took what were pale imitations of English residential colleges, given over to what was certainly more religion than most students could bear, and they simply reformed them," Rudolph writes. "And what is remarkably instructive about what they did is how much more effective they were than the would-be reformers in the ranks of the presidents and the professors."

In her splendid book about women's colleges, *Alma Mater,* Helen Lefkowitz Horowitz points to the commencement of pranks as the pivotal moment when women students broke away from the tight control of overseers and began asserting their own identity.

"High jinks were serious business," she writes. "They signal at Vassar the beginnings of college life for women. Like their brothers at the men's colleges, Vassar students began to see themselves as separate from the college authorities."

But I don't want to bog down in scholarliness. If pranks changed the world, that's nice, but I'm interested in them because pranks are fantastic. The world needs more pranks, more whimsy, more presidents settling their fat behinds onto whoopie cushions, more droning intellectuals rudely interrupted with elaborately staged hoots of ridicule.

I hope that this book will remind students that they are abandoning a precious birthright of mischief and wickedness by viewing college just as a chance to buff their resume. Responsibility, like crow's feet, will come in time.

And for those readers who, like myself, have left our college days and are trudging through the desert of adulthood, I hope these pranks convey a degree of hope. The way life is served up may be a bland, steaming bowl of tasteless gruel, but that shouldn't prevent the intrepid spirit from spicing it up a bit, so the thing can be consumed with a measure of gusto and satisfaction.

—Neil Steinberg
Dec. 16, 1991
Chicago

EARLY PRANKS

Wicked Acts of Sacrilege

When I was asked to come to this university, I supposed I was to be at the head of the largest and most famous institution of learning in America. I have been disappointed. I find myself the submaster of an ill-disciplined school.
—Edward Everett
Harvard president, 1847

A heavy, flat stone, pried from the frozen mud of the Massachusetts countryside, flies through the chill December air and shatters the windowpane of a hated professor's house. The glass—cheaply made, flawed with air bubbles and sand—explodes nicely into a shower of glittering shards.

Several dozen teenagers, already beginning to sweat in the May fog of South Carolina humidity, sleepily drag themselves into a plain wooden chapel for 8 A.M. services. The sun, peeking over the horizon, is already angry and hot. From the pulpit, where Dr. Cooper is expected to appear any second, grins a stuffed raccoon, frozen on its hind legs, as if caught in an antic dance.

The pranks of the early days of American colleges, in keeping with the lives of the students, were simple and physically direct. They were immediate acts—students had scant free time to plan complex pranks and even less privacy in which to carry them out.

Pranks were unsubtle little rebellions of an unsubtle time, and most of them would fall below our horizon of interest if they happened today.

But early pranks are worth noting for two reasons. First, they illustrate how far pranks have developed from those initial flying stones and stolen Bibles. Second, and more important, they grant us a peek at a time in student life now largely forgotten.

It was before the famed universities of today boasted their ivy-dappled Gothic towers, their lushly-landscaped Yards, their weird geometric concrete libraries, glass-walled student centers or neo-cathedral administration buildings. They were instead pathetic collections of clapboard shacks—or, in some cases, solitary barnish wood-frame buildings—attended by a few dozen students and taught by a handful of sour visionaries.

Curriculum focused on the classics. Students had to be fluent in ancient languages before they were even let in the door. Math consisted of grinding over rote trigonometry tables. History meant Thucydides and literature was the Bible and, later, Shakespeare (which of course, had it been taught to Harvard's first graduating class, would have constituted modern literature, *Hamlet* being only 30 or so years old at the time).

Student life was, to say the least, different. Cows roamed the campus, grazing their way deep into the collective psyche of college life, where they remain to this day. There was mandatory daily chapel in the places where it wasn't held twice daily. College laws governed every aspect of existence—what students wore, how they took their meals, when they must study, even when they could speak in their native tongue—at Brown in 1783, there was a rule requiring students to speak to each other in Latin during study hours, which took up the bulk of the day.

And unlike today, these laws were no flapdoodle spelled out to placate parents and avoid legal vulnerability. They were rigorously enforced by zealous professors and tutors, unaware that their slavish belief in rules undermined the very discipline they were trying to maintain.

Any student bold and foolish enough to stand up directly to the grip of repression was certain to find himself with a one-way ticket home. So pranks became an important way to react against the confining net of discipline, and the anonymity of pranks in those early years was a crucial part of their appeal.

SIX RIDICULOUS COLLEGE RULES

If colleges and universities were actually as open and liberal as they pretend to be, there would be less need to rebel and fewer college pranks. Happily, colleges have constantly devised new ways to restrict inquisitive youth, who invariably react with pranks. Here are a few of the more memorable university laws:

1. Perhaps the sorest point between students and schools were their provisions for meals. Students were usually required to eat at some sort of commons or designated boarding house, whose service was often substandard due to the forced monopoly. Students frequently rebelled and, rather than improve the food, colleges found it easier to pass laws. At Brown University in 1774, every aspect of mealtime was codified, down to the stipulation of who "shall carve; this being done in Alphabetical [sic] order, the next to him shall distribute the Meat, & Sauce; no one else being allowed to take them him-self; and the same Person, for the Day, shall pour out Cofee, [sic] Tea, &c and put in a proper Quantity of Sugar."

2. The University of South Carolina in the mid-19th century was, evidently, a loud place. In 1860 senior Charles Woodward Hutson wrote to his sister complaining of "the diabolical noise of a banjo in the room overhead, which will effectually prevent my sleeping for some time to come." Other letters mention "yelling in the Campus" and "a tremendous volley of crackers" outside his window. This cacophonous state no doubt inspired law number 219:

If any student shall be convicted of having or blowing any horn or trumpet, or beating any drum, or of disturbing the quiet of the institution by riding any horse or mule within or near the College enclosure, or of making any loud or unusual noise by any other means, within or about the same, he shall be punished by admonition, or suspension, at the discretion of the Faculty.

3. An 1899 volume on Yale College lists the following freshman restrictions: "The Freshman is not allowed by college custom:"

(a) To smoke a pipe on the street or campus.
(b) To carry a cane before Washington's Birthday.
(c) To dance at the Junior Promenade.
(d) To sit on the college Fence.
(e) To play ball or spin tops on the campus.

4. Universities have always faced the problem of banning practices which, to the delicate sensibilities of those making the laws, are too horrible even to articulate. How do you ban something you can't bring yourself to mention? The University of Georgia, in its catalog of 1870, skirted around that problem with the following ingenious rule:

All those things are forbidden which tend to deteriorate moral character, to prevent intellectual and moral advancement—in short, all those wicked and immoral practices and habits which would be forbidden in good and cultivated families, and which tend to prevent preparation and training for good citizenship.

5. Ohio Wesleyan, a Methodist college, had a variety of quaint guidelines and amusing rules. For years, a notice in the catalogue told parents "young men at college have very little need of pocket money" and "earnestly advised" them to entrust their children's allowances to the safekeeping of a professor. Then there was the "walking rule." Having become coed in 1871, educators worried over the pernicious effect of permitting the sexes to stroll together, unrestricted. The practice was allowed only "provided their duties call them in the same direction," and students were forbidden to walk together after 11 o'clock recitation, or afternoon chapel. The ban was for all students "except in case of brothers and sisters."

6. Some of the most extreme rules come from women's colleges, which were in several cases founded by people with experience establishing lunatic asylums and shared a similar goal of total control over the inmates. In 1865 at Vassar

College, it was ruled that while "no general restraint" was to
be placed on students' correspondence, it was "understood to
be the duty of corridor teachers to carry all letters to and from
the office for students on their corridors, and to notice so far as
they may be able, the extent and apparent character of such
correspondents, and to report to the Lady Principal such cases
as seem to them to need attention, and that it be the duty of all
to inculcate right principles on the subject of correspondence."
(Vassar's policy was relatively lenient. All letters to women at
Alabama College at the turn of the century were opened and
censored, and they were forbidden to receive any mail at all
from the local post office, for fear of their developing local
beaus. This was such a great concern to school authorities that
the students were forbidden to hold conversations with people
on the street during their visits to nearby Montevallo, a hardship
for girls who came from the area and were forced to snub clerks
and passersby they'd known all their lives. Women were not
alone in having their mail scrutinized. In the 1860s Fordham
University "carefully censored" students' letters, both sent and
received, not out of Victorian horror of romance, but rather to
stem their vociferous complaining to their parents about the
inadequacy of the school. "Lies and misrepresentations" were
causing parents to remove their students in droves, and some
students beat them to the punch. In December, 1868, 3 boys
were expelled for convincing 30 others to pretend to go home
for the holidays, then register en masse at Xavier).

Like any skilled art, it took a while for pranks to develop.

To be completely thorough, we probably should trace college
pranks back 700 years, to the first universities, jelling together in
Europe out of guild unions and the church.

They were wild places, these early European universities, but
their pranks weren't really much. While complete order will cut
back on good pranks, so will utter chaos. Not too many good
pranks are mixed in with the muck of early university life because
students already had license to do whatever they wanted. They

didn't need pranks. Why concoct a prank when you can spill into the streets and slaughter people?

Consider this description of your average Dark Ages undergraduate, at Paris and Oxford no less:

> The typical student was a drunkard, a frequenter of taverns, a gambler, addicted to roaming the streets in gangs, shouting, singing, quarrelling, throwing stones, breaking down doors, and smashing heads, ready with his dagger, and given to playing practical jokes of the most brutal kind . . . Respectable citizens and their wives complained of taunts and insults, of the throwing of filth on their sober finery, the slicing of noses in drunken pranks, the picking of pockets in jest or in earnest, the ravishment of wives and daughters, the eruption into houses in the dead of night.

No student would need to dream up a creative way to get back at a professor when it was easier to respond to a flaw in the lecture by "shouting, hissing, groaning, or the throwing of stones . . ."

To keep this book from starting out with a grim recitation of niceties like the Battle of Saint Scholastica's Day (February 10, 1354, when scholars from England's Merton College found fault with the wine in a nearby town and ended up butchered by several thousand armed peasants) it is best to wait for the Reformation to kick college life across the ocean, to the fertile soil of America, a place where pranks could really take hold.

America had the perfect blend of Puritanical desire for restraint with the ad hoc limitations of Colonial life. A handful of founding fathers could get together, make all the ponderous pronouncements they wanted, force everybody to speak Greek while standing on their heads, but eventually the sun would go down, the fires would ebb, and the reality that they were a group of a few dozen boys and men in the middle of some wild nowhere studying archaic disciplines would manifest itself.

Then came the pranks.

In order to have American college pranks, we must have American colleges. The first American college was started in Rhode Island in 1619, and may have had some fine pranks, not to mention taken down Harvard a notch or two, had not the entire

BOOTING A BARD

$\mathcal{P}$ercy Bysshe Shelley is remembered chiefly as being one of the more prominent English Romantic poets, author of "Prometheus Unbound" and other rhymes. But he was also a notorious early British college prankster.

Known both as "Mad Shelley" and "Shelley the Atheist" before he left Eaton, he arrived at University College, Oxford, in October, 1810, and wasted no time in establishing himself. "There were few, if any," recalled a Mr. Ridley, who was a junior fellow at the time, "who were not afraid of Shelley's strange and fantastic pranks."

He used a galvanic battery to electrify the doorknob of his room and demonstrated acid's corrosive effect by pouring it over the carpet of a tutor. "Once," according to Gribble's history of Oxford, "it is said, by pretending to be a woman, he lured a bishop into controversy, and handled him as the impertinent have delighted to handle the pompous from the beginning of the world."

With the goading of his buddy, Thomas Jefferson Hogg, Shelley lasted an entire five months in Cambridge before they both got the boot for their cage-rattling pamphlet, "The Necessity of Atheism." Though general consensus is the pamphlet was more of a practical joke than a sincere expression of belief— Shelley hand-inscribed the document to the various bishops and dons at Oxford, and personally stacked them in the window of a local bookseller—Oxford never forgave him. Years after his death, when a monument to Shelley was finally permitted on campus, it was located, in Gribble's words, "in a dark corner of those precincts, only to be reached by way of an obscure passage which looks as if it led to a coal-hole wherein an unwary visitor would run a serious risk of being arrested and charged with loitering with intent to commit a felony."

student body been killed by Indians in a massacre that shut down the school.

Which paved the way for Harvard to claim the stage as the oldest college in the United States, formed in 1636 when the Massachusetts Bay Colony voted 400 English pounds toward "a schoale or colledge."

It wasn't called Harvard then, but "Cambridge," after the mighty university in England. The "Harvard" came in 1639 when a minister named John Harvard died and left half his estate—780 English pounds and 260 books—a staggeringly generous behest at the time. The budding school took his name in gratitude.

The place was difficult to get into, even then. You had to know both Latin and Greek. On the other hand, it was not what we would consider expensive. You could pay for your education in sugar, or bacon, or grain, and a majority of students did. Nor did you have to turn over a huge amount of goods. A quarter's tuition to Harvard in 1650 could be settled with a bushel-and-a-half of wheat. Room and board for a year could be paid with a fair-sized hog. (Compare that to the price paid by Elena Carter Percy, who in 1932 drove nine head of Hereford cattle to the president's office at Louisiana State University and traded them for her school tuition).

The earliest pranks were not particularly clever. In Harvard in the middle 1600s, the thing to do was break windows. During the winter quarter of 1651–52, at least ten students were charged a shilling or more for "mendinge Chamber windoes."

Breaking glass was in vogue for centuries.

"One Scott, a youth under my tuition, some time ago riding through Smithfield . . . rode up to, and, in a most audaciously wicked manner, broke the windows of the Friends' meeting house in said town," reads an apologetic note from Brown President James Manning, written on December 12, 1770. "When this is settled, we shall discipline him with the highest punishment we inflict, next to banishment from the society . . . I am sorry for his friends, and that it happened to fall to my lot to have such a thoughtless, vicious pupil."

Elaborate pranks were extremely rare, but they were not unknown. Historian Samuel Elliot Morison recounts a prank played during the reign of Harvard's first president, Henry Dunster, citing two centuries of Dunster family tradition as his source:

> The President was at Concord visiting his kinsman Simon Willard when a messenger came post-haste to say that he was urgently wanted at Cambridge, for the scholars had literally raised the Devil! The role of exorcist was a new one for Dunster, but he was quite equal to the emergency. Hastening back to Cambridge, he found the College in a turmoil.
>
> Some of the scholars had tried a bit of black magic, and it had succeeded only too well; old Nick, impersonated no doubt by some practical joker, had materialized, and the young boys were thoroughly frightened. The President solemnly emptied his horn of gunpowder in the Yard, laid a train, touched it off with a live coal, and literally "blew the Devil out of Harvard College!"

If Harvard graduates often act as if Harvard is the only school in the country, they may be displaying some sort of collective race memory dating back several centuries. Harvard had a monopoly on American colleges—and college pranks—for 57 years, until the College of William and Mary was founded in Williamsburg in 1693.

Like Dunster's exorcism, William and Mary's earliest pranks are a reminder of just how involved college presidents were with the routine, day-to-day operations of the school. Most students of today rarely set eyes on the human form of their college presidents, who shun the company of those who are not apt to whip out a checkbook and donate vast sums.

But for the first 250 years of American college life, small size dictated that the president was an active presence on campus. He knew each student, was involved in their lives and, sometimes, their misdeeds. When a pair of students were whipped at Harvard in June 1644 for breaking into homes, it was President Dunster who laid on the lashes. When students barricaded themselves in their rooms at William and Mary in 1702, it was the president, Rev. James Blair, himself, who threw his shoulder against the barred door. Blair writes:

I made haste to get up, & with the assistance of two servant men, I had in the College, I had almost forced open one of the doors before they sufficiently secured it, but while I was breaking in, they presently fired off 3 or 4 Pistols & hurt one of my servants in the eye with the wadd as I suppose of one of the Pistols. While I press'd forward, some of the Boys, having a great kindness for me, call'd out "For God's sake sir, don't offer to come in, for we have shot, & shall certainly fire at any one that first enters." Upon hearing of this, I began to think it was something more than ordinary in the matter . . .

In addition to battering down doors and braving undergraduate gunplay, Rev. Blair, like his modern brothers, still had to worry about fund-raising. He showed some modern flexibility at locating revenue sources, once arranging for a trio of captured pirates to donate 300 English pounds' worth of booty to aid his fledgling school.

If the reference to pistol-firing seems startling now, it was also an average occurrence during the first several centuries of college life. Many students came to their remote colleges bearing pistols, swords, knives, and rifles, and almost every college in existence before 1880 has stories of guns being fired at members of the faculty, in jest or anger.

The president of the University of South Carolina, Dr. Thomas Cooper, wrote a letter to his friend Thomas Jefferson describing the riot of February 8, 1814. He related how professors "were threatened, pistols were snapped at them, guns fired near them, Col. John Taylor (formerly of the Senate from this place) was in company with myself burnt in effigy: the windows of my bedroom have been repeatedly shattered at various hours of the night, & guns fired under my window."

"At evening prayers the lights were all extinguished by powder & lead, except 2 or 3," Harvard Professor Eliphalet Pearson wrote in his "Journal of Disorders" on Dec. 9, 1788.

"The Faculty met in the evening and a pistol was fired at the door of one of the tutors," Princeton President Ashbel Green noted in his diary on April 6, 1815. "I ought to be very thankful to God for his support this day."

Tutors in President Green's day were not the tutors we think of today—brainy kids who pick up pocket change helping football players keep their eligibility. Rather tutors were like grad students, but held in even less respect by the underclassmen, if such a thing is possible. The thankless role of monitor and disciplinarian fell to the tutors, and many pranks were directed against them.

"The Old Brick resounds very frequently with the breaking of glass bottles against Tutor T's door, if he can be called a Tutor," a Brown resident wrote in 1799. "We have given him the epithet of Weazle. He is frequently peaking through the knot holes & cracks to watch his prey."

While a young tutor at Brown, Horace Mann, "the father of American public education," was once hissed out of a room.

The barrage of misbehavior facing tutors is captured in a sarcastic broadside written anonymously by a Harvard student in 1823. Published in a local newspaper and intended to shame his riotous classmates into goodness, (without success—almost the entire senior class was expelled) he provides an unintentional laundry list of the rather mean pranks of the time:

> To plague or insult a Tutor, is always considered a good joke—knocking at his door when nothing is wanted—putting a stick of wood against his door, so that when he opens it the log may fall and hurt his feet—making a general shuffling with your feet in the Chapel, when any officer who is disliked comes in—provoking your tutor by noise and riot in your room, and when he comes to still you, break a chair against the door as he opens it, or throw your wash-bowl or boot-jack at his head, &c.—Breaking the plates and dishes in the dining hall, or gapping the knives, or ending the prongs of the forks by sticking them into the table—then if the pudding should be disliked, or the beef not cooked to suit the fastidious taste of some of the fault-finders, throw slices of it about the hall, &c. All these are species of practical wit which have an excellent effect . . .

Ironically, relatively few contemporary accounts of pranks are written by students themselves, compared with the volumes of official disciplinary records—letters to parents, faculty meetings, black books, and the like—immortalizing the smallest student infractions, again many against tutors.

"Your son," an angry President Asa Messer wrote to the parents of a Brown student in 1819, "since his return has thrown a stone through the window of one of the Tutors, and has put into his bed a shovel of ashes; though the Tutor had given him no Provocation; nor did even know him."

"Bisket, tea cups, saucers, & a *knife* thrown at the tutors," Professor Pearson set down in his "Journal" for December 9, 1788. The winter of 1788–89 was particularly lawless at Harvard, due in part to the "stiff and unbending" rule of the president, Rev. Joseph Willard.

Pearson's journal provides a glimpse of the common pranks of the day; most of them, again, spontaneous acts against unpopular overseers:

> D E C . 5 . A snowball was thrown at Mr. Webber, while he was in the desk at evening prayers.
>
> D E C . 9 . The President read the confession of Sullivan . . . but there was such a scraping, especially in the junior class, that he could not be heard. He commanded silence, but to no purpose.
>
> D E C . 1 5 . During lecture several pebbles were snapped, certain gutteral sounds were made on each side [of] the chapel, besides some whistling.
>
> J A N . 2 . Mumbling noise & whispering at morning prayers, chiefly among the juniors on the north. Bible taken away at evening prayers.
>
> J A N . 3 . Bible taken away at morning prayers & concealed at evening prayers . . .
>
> J A N . 4 . Bible concealed at eveng. prayers, & several squares of glass found broken in the window of the desk.

The reference to hiding the Bible points to the odd connection between pranks and chapel. The solemnity of chapel, and its enforced nature, made it an enticing target for pranks. Moreover, chapel was the one time of day when the entire student body, faculty and president would be all together in one room, so an ample audience was guaranteed.

This led to some wicked acts of sacrilege. Bibles were nailed to the pulpit, pulpits adorned with cadavers or stuffed animals taken from the taxidermic "museums" found at every early college.

Chapel pranks were continuing and universal. In 1819, Brown students carried away the chapel doors. Toward the end of the 19th century, at Purdue, the president's chair in chapel was, one morning, found entombed in railroad ties from floor to ceiling. At Ohio Wesleyan, pigeons were released. At Ohio's amusingly-acronymed College of Wooster, a chipmunk was let loose, earning the perpetrator a three-week suspension. At Syracuse University in 1886, a mocking caricature was lowered behind Chancellor Sims while he was conducting services. At the University of Illinois at Champaign-Urbana, science students in the early 1890s manufactured stink bombs in the school laboratory and placed them under the woven chapel mats. Students stepping on the mats broke the stink bombs, forcing early adjournment.

At Knox College, in 1889, a young poet named Edgar Lee Masters, "the leading prankster" of his day, hitched the janitor's cow in the chapel (one of Masters's earliest poems is about kidnapping the janitor's rooster).

One of the most elaborate chapel pranks took place in 1867 at Miami of Ohio. The legislature had voted to establish a state agricultural college and Miami was vigorously lobbying for the plum. To lampoon this desire, students placed a haystack, a harrow, a plow, and a farm wagon in the school chapel, along with a cow, two horses, pigs, ducks, and chickens. Chapel was cancelled, and the ag school was established in Columbus, laying the beginnings of Ohio State University.

Even after schools burst out of their single buildings and into campuses, they were still small communities. While the undergraduate of today is lucky to see the inside of his or her eccentric Marxist English professor's paperback-strewn home, students back then knew where their teachers dwelled and took their pranks home to them.

THE CHLORINE BANQUET

The most notorious prank of the 19th century was the infamous "Chlorine Banquet" at Cornell University.

It was the height of interclass warfare, and though the class of '98 had tried to keep their February 20, 1894 banquet a secret, word leaked out and the location was discovered ahead of time. By the time the freshmen, protected by a vanguard of 30 juniors, arrived at the Masonic Hall where the banquet was to be held, the street was filled with sophomores "ready to pounce upon them and use every endeavor . . . to spoil the freshmen's evening," according to the next day's *New York Times*. Though the entire Ithaca police force was at hand, a riot ensued as the freshman tried to enter the building, "faces were punched, hats smashed, and there was a general melee, in which the officers were tossed about like chaff." The freshmen eventually gained entrance to the hall, and the banquet went ahead, graced by such talks as "Our Noble Selves" and "Where Men of Muscle Win their Way."

Shortly after 11 P.M., an overpowering odor began to permeate a room that was being used as a kitchen by the caterer. Several waiters and two juniors who went to investigate were overcome by fumes and had to be taken outside. The cook, Henrietta Jackson, died. Contrary to early lurid *Times* reports, which fantabulized two dozen freshmen rushed outside at the point of death, the banquet proceeded normally and the freshmen were not informed of what was going on in the kitchen. An investigation showed that someone—presumably a group of sophomores—had intended to pump gas into the banquet hall, but misjudged, and bored holes through the floor of the kitchen instead, piping in chlorine gas they created in a large glass jug. There was a huge outcry, and a grand jury met to consider charges against several suspects, who fled the campus. But guilt was never determined and no one was indicted. The negative publicity surrounding the Chlorine Banquet did not prevent foolish students at other universities from replicating Cornell's mistakes. At Montreal's McGill University, in March 1907, sophomores doused the lights at a freshman concert and poured ammonia down the ventilation shafts. Several freshmen were burned and some nearly blinded.

"Fowl houses and gardens have always been regarded as the student's legitimate prey, especially those of the professors," reads a history of the trouble-bound University of South Carolina. "Dr. Cooper's horse was often painted, her tail shaved . . . Professors' benches were tarred."

(Perhaps calling the college "trouble-bound" is unfair. The prominence of a school like the University of South Carolina in the early history of pranks raises the question as to whether it had an unusual discipline problem, or just more candid historians. I imagine the latter is true, simply because the pranks whose stories survive to this day must be a tiny fraction of those that took place. As Morison writes: "It is only by accident that we hear anything of these brawls and pranks. They seldom get into the Corporation records; for aught we know they may have been matters of frequent occurrence.")

Either way, the South Carolina faculty was not entirely without cunning in combating student exuberance.

"One of the presidents hearing that his coach was to be dragged off hid himself inside behind the tightly fastened curtains," a school history records. "When the students had pulled it to the bottom of the hill and were about to leave it, he stepped out and politely informed them that they had better drag it back to the carriage house, which they did." (The embarrassingly-initialed College of Wooster records an almost identical episode, with students on Halloween unhitching the president's buggy and dragging it "to the top of a hill a mile and a half from town" before the president thanked them for the ride and asked to be taken back).

Relocating wagons—just as relocating cars today—was always a popular prank. At Ohio Wesleyan in the 1840s, a wagon loaded with lumber was disassembled and dragged, piece by piece, up

the winding stairways of Elliot Hall to the roof, where it was put
back together, lumber and all.

The ferocity of student pranks was also directed toward fellow
students who, through scholarly disinterest or courageous independence or mere awkwardness, held themselves aloof from undergraduate carousing.

Thomas Hill entered Harvard in 1839 and was an instant
target for his classmates because of his independent mind and
sharp tongue. His letters home are filled with tales of the abuse
heaped upon him; in August, 1839 while he was in the very act
of putting pen to paper:

> Many of the students however care nothing either for health or
> economy. There is nothing but mischief in their heads from morn
> till night. While I am writing some of the wise fools are amusing
> themselves by throwing shot into my open windows. I advised
> them not to waste their lead so, for it was silly to be so extravagant.
> They have now gone. Perhaps some of them may want the cost of
> the shot ere long, to buy a halter to hang themselves.

After tattling on some classmates who were throwing stones at
windows, Hill found himself the recipient of swift undergraduate
justice:

> . . . the next night, I unguardedly going to bed with the door
> unlocked, some ruffians came in, dragged the mattress from under
> me and emptied several pails of water on me. I immediately ran
> yelling out of doors and when I waked up I was dancing on the
> frosty grass in the bright moonlight, dripping with water . . . A
> young man lost his life in this way a few years ago, the shock and
> the chill bringing on a cold which soon killed him.

The willful if undiplomatic Hill did not die. Though he was
hissed and laughed at, pelted with bottles and his windows broken so often he moved to the third floor of his rooming house to
better challenge his classmates' aim, Hill survived and apparently

bore Harvard no ill will over his ordeal since, during the Civil War, he became president of the university.

Frugal students such as Hill could not be expected to own as expensive a piece of modern equipment as a timepiece. So it was vital that colleges have a bell system to let students know when classes were beginning and ending. Assaults upon the bells were universal.

When Brown students became upset at how officials had divided up the speaking parts for the commencement of 1798 (permission to deliver the endless, arcane addresses at commencement was a coveted honor) "the next night after; the locks that are on the doors that lead to the bell were filled with lead so that we had a long morning before the ringing of the bell," a student wrote.

In March, 1864, enterprising students first scaled the outside of Princeton's historic Nassau Hall and stole the clapper out of the bell. Until a new one could be ordered, the only way the bell could be rung to signal classes and prayers was for the janitor to climb up with a ladder and strike the bell with a hammer. In years to come, stealing the clapper became such a common prank at Princeton that the college kept a supply of extra clappers on hand. At the University of Missouri, the president reported that the bell clapper was stolen three times in 1861. He finally decided not to replace it, despite the inconvenience to teachers and students.

The mordantly-monogrammed College of Wooster offers this delightful yet vague bell clapper incident. The bell clapper disappeared and Wooster president Dr. Archibald Taylor received an anonymous note telling him the clapper could be found that spring just "north of the Barux." A few days later a spelling test was held and, as usual, Dr. Taylor gave out the 100 words personally from the rostrum of the chapel. Shortly thereafter, he summoned a certain sophomore to his office and asked him to do him a favor and go get the clapper. The shocked student did, and afterward a laughing Dr. Taylor showed the chagrined sophomore the letter and the spelling test, both with the odd spelling of barracks.

ONE STUDENT'S VIEW

$\mathcal{B}$enjamin Crowninshield's private journal is a candid description of Harvard life in the mid-1850s. He plays billiards and cards almost daily, shops incessantly, drinks a good bit, walks out on the great Shakespearean actor Edwin Booth performing *Hamlet,* and records an episode of cheery, uninhibited bulimia after a hearty meal.

Like most undergraduates of his day, Crowninshield was a shameless breaker of glass. "I filled my pockets with apples before I left the table and on the way out broke 2 gas lamps and some windows," he notes, matter-of-factly.

He also records a novel twist on the steal-the-clapper prank.

"Somebody last night got into Harvard Hall and took the clapper out from the bell and upset the bell and filled it full of acid, and clamped all the doors in the building," he writes, on March 23, 1856. "Mills next morning had to ring the bell with a hammer."

Shameless Harvard diarist Crowninshield

Before schools were financially solvent enough to afford a piece of advanced technology like a bell, they used horns to signal classes and prayers. Students also carried horns, for hailing over distance, and these early communications devices seem to be the precedent for the practice of "horning" or "horn-sprees," one of the more vexing expressions of student ill will.

Dartmouth students expressed their displeasure at the preparations for a St. Johnsbury Fourth of July celebration in 1851 by drowning out the speech of the local congressman with their horns.

On March 9, 1864, Princeton students used their horns to call an assembly on campus. The massed students' "riotous procession moved into the streets of the village, shouting, breaking windows, and making off with fences and gates."

Student ire at fences and gates perhaps was rooted in their dislike of cows. At Dartmouth, the cows that farmers pastured on the college green were a constant source of provocation to the students. Historians credit Dartmouth students with perhaps the first bovine-centered prank. One night in the 1790s, the students drove "the whole offending herd three or four miles up the Connecticut, then into the river and across into Vermont. Another time they herded the cows into the cellar of Dartmouth Hall, barricaded the doors and held them as hostages in exchange for promises from the farmers that in the future they would pasture them elsewhere."

Cow abuse, as will be seen, is a thread woven throughout college life, from the earliest days until the present time.

Horses too, caught students' devious attentions, particularly if the horse happened to belong to a professor or college president.

Samuel G. Howe, later to gain fame as an educator of the disabled, was "more noted for pranks and penalties than for scholarship" while at Brown University in the early 1820s. He once led the president's horse to the top floor of University Hall and left it there overnight, a prank from which he derived satisfaction for the rest of his life.

"There was no keeping the twinkle out of his eye," his daughter, Laura Richards, recalled in a memoir, "as he told how funny the old horse looked, stretching his meek head out of the fourth-story window, and whinnying mournfully to his amazed master passing below."

DAMN, THE TORPEDOES

The fact that Samuel G. Howe graduated from Brown at all is something of a miracle. Several times he was "rusticated"— sent to the country to study with a minister—as a form of discipline, once after the horse incident, a second time after he squirted ink through a keyhole into the eye of a curious tutor who was spying on him. He no doubt also set off a contact firework or two—known in Howe's day as a "torpedo."

But the best Howe story happened years after he distinguished himself as a premiere American educator and performer of good works. Once again it is told by his daughter, quoting a story Howe loved to recount "with great relish:"

My father, being in Providence at Commencement time, went to call on his old president, Doctor Messer, then living in retirement, for the express purpose of apologizing to him for the "monkey shines." The old gentleman received him with a look of alarm, and motioning him to a chair, took his own seat at some distance, and kept a wary eye on his former pupil. My father began his apology, but Doctor Messer interrupted him.

"I declare, Howe," he cried, moving his chair still further back, "I am afraid of you now! I'm afraid there will be a torpedo under my chair before I know it."

Many schools have tales of the president's horse being abandoned on the upper floors of a college building. The University of Delaware records not only a horse being led into the dorms, but also a white bull. Those unfamiliar with the ways of horses may miss the zest of this prank—horses are reluctant to climb staircases and even more loath to go down again. Often an animal, once gotten to an upper floor, could only be returned to the ground by means of a rope and pulley.

The most famous prank at Connecticut's Wesleyan College occurred on October 20, 1837, when a Southerner named Benjamin Britt, angry at having been reprimanded, took the president's horse and, after shaving the mane and tail to the skin, left the beast tied up to the chapel pulpit with a "wicked and blasphemous notice" affixed to its side. Even fellow students found the prank "too serious and too deeply tinctured with malice to be passed over with a mere smile," according to a letter by classmate Daniel Harris. Students voted to aid in the investigation, and Britt, once caught, was given 48 hours to get out of town.

At least students didn't shoot the horses, or blow them up. Students intimate with guns could also be expected to concoct their own fireworks. In another letter (to his brother; history has yet to record a student discussing pranks in a letter to his parents) Harris describes a novel prank at his residence. One night, he wrote, several "wild fellows . . . blew out the lights in the halls and amused themselves by putting quills loaded with powder into the keyholes. They then touched fire to the quills. Of course, this sent them with an explosion into the room."

James Fenimore Cooper was expelled from Yale in 1806 for a similar prank—pushing a rag dusted with gunpowder through the keyhole of a friend's room and touching it off. Cooper was another person destined to be expelled. "The wonder is not so much that Cooper was asked to leave Yale in his Junior year," wrote biographer Robert E. Spiller, "but rather that, with such a liberal attitude toward authority, he was permitted to stay so long."

The keyhole pyrotechnics were mild compared to the more powerful fireworks, some of which were practically bombs. One memorable firework *was* a bomb.

The night of January 9, 1814, a school year at Princeton already grown stormy with mischief, was capped by the ignition of what became known as the "Big Cracker"—two pounds of gunpowder inside a hollow log, placed behind the central doors of Nassau Hall.

The device caused a "tremendous explosion," cracking walls and blowing out windows throughout the historic building. That no one was killed was credited by Princeton's president to "the merciful providence of God."

An intense faculty manhunt tracked down the two perpetrators of the "infernal machine." One was let off the hook because of youth, the other tried in the civil courts and expelled, which led to more crackers, more protests, and more expulsions, in a turmoil that lasted for some time.

Perhaps it was the cathartic impact of the bloodiest and most wrenching trauma this nation has every experienced. Perhaps it was coincidence. But after the Civil War, more sophisticated and carefully executed pranks appear with greater frequency.

At Denison College, in Ohio, a prank held the small town in its thrall for a few days in January 1871, after Bob Stone, the son of the principal of the Young Ladies' Institute, was thrilled to discover oil in an abandoned well situated behind the college. "For a time the whole town rocked with the news," a college history recounts. But eventually it was discovered that several Denison students had spiked the well with two gallons of oil and tricked young Bob into making his startling discovery.

The University of Kansas records a number of interesting late 19th–century pranks. Among the usual gate-stealers and outhouse-tippers there was a secret society called the Turkey Catchers, whose members wore badges with the initials "T.C." and whose sole purpose appeared to be dining on stolen roasted turkey. (Kansas was not alone. Mississippi State had the "Pick-'Em-Up Club," which in 1907 issued a public thanks to the professors at Christmastime for "keeping such nice fat turkeys and chickens and allowing them to roost in such convenient locations.")

Two Kansas episodes stand out. One occurred at the commencement ceremonies of 1873 when, according to a history:

> Wags lowered a skeleton on a rope through a hole in the unfinished roof of the University Building. From a toe hung a sign reading "Prex" [slang for a college president]. For a few minutes, while the band played, the bones jiggled and danced over the heads of the audience. Campus tradition had it that after a measure of order was restored, Mrs. Fraser [the president's wife] innocently asked her husband what "Prex" meant.
> "The faculty," Fraser allegedly replied.

The other Kansas prank created an even bigger stir. In December 1879, a pair of students, William M. Thacher and Edward C. Meservey, struck by the solemn pomp of the memorial

LIFE AMONG THE UNFRIENDLY DAKOTANS

The most famous person ever to trod the halls of the University of North Dakota got the boot, not for any one particular incident, but on general principals. Vilhjalmur Stefansson, who in a few years would be living among Eskimos and writing bestselling books on exploration, was in 1902 a popular troublemaker at Grand Forks. Once he hopped into the president's carriage and ordered the driver to take him to Budge Hall; another time, he took a professor's distinctive buggy and parked it at the door of the town's most notorious brothel. Caught drinking beer on the front steps of Budge by President Merrifield himself, Stefansson forgot to cringe, but blandly offered the president a sip.

Such confident behavior cannot go unpunished, and the faculty voted to suspend Stefansson in March 1902. Merrifield visited Stefansson in his room, and explained that while the technical reason for the suspension was absence from class, the real reason was the suspicion that Stefansson was behind the general deterioration in discipline at the school. The understanding was that Stefansson's suspension would be permanent.

Instead of slinking out of town, he was paraded to the train station in a wheelbarrow, trailed by a crowd of student supporters.

After books such as *My Life with the Eskimo* and *The Friendly Arctic* made him famous, the school took a kinder look at Stefansson. In 1930, it realized, by gosh, it had never really expelled Stefansson after all, but simply suspended him. He was granted an honorary LL.D. degree.

services held for a deceased faculty geology lecturer, decided to see if they could provoke similar hoopla without the usual formality of someone dying. They picked a regent, Rev. Frank T. Ingalls, of Atchison, and arranged for a telegram from that town to reach campus, reporting Ingalls's demise.

On January 16, 1880, the faculty held an impressive memorial service for Ingalls. Inevitably, it was learned that Ingalls was alive. The prank was traced to Thacher and Meservey, who were suspended for a year pending expected expulsion. But in the spring, soothed by the balm of time and by the fact that the duo "had led exemplary lives both before and after the incident" (and perhaps considering that a good number of their fellow students marched through downtown Lawrence to the beat of a drum to show support for the pair) the faculty readmitted the two miscreants.

With the century running out, college presidents were not quite as apt to jump into the thick of discipline, though it may have been expected. Cornell's famed Andrew D. White stood by in 1882 while underclassmen destroyed a wooden bridge at the junction of Campus Road and Central Avenue, and was blamed by at least one trustee, Henry W. Sage, for his inaction. "His view was that I—in feeble health—ought at 2 in the morning to have thrown myself into a mob of nearly 100 men, many disguised and all bent on mischief," White wrote, resentfully, in his diary on November 8.

Perhaps the capstone prank of the era was the "Cannon War" between Rutgers and Princeton. There was a certain modernity to it, both in the planning needed to steal a massive Revolutionary War cannon buried muzzle down in the heart of a rival campus and in the moxie of, having been found out, acknowledging the wrongdoing, taking pride in it, and struggling to keep the stolen icon.

The most amazing thing about the prank is the hearty way it was embraced by everyone at Rutgers, including the administration, then and in years to come. The most complete version of the story is recounted in the 1924 *History of Rutgers College,* written with gusto by then-president William H.S. Demarest. He begins:

> For many years a tradition had flourished that a cannon planted on the campus at Princeton had been taken from New Brunswick and from Rutgers by the students of Princeton. The story was constantly active in the taunts of the men of Princeton, holders of the cannon, and in the hopes of the men of Rutgers that it might some day be recovered.

On April 26, 1875, nine sophomores hired a farmer's wagon and "invaded the Princeton campus," digging up the cannon and carting it back to Rutgers.

"It was a bold and exciting adventure," Demarest writes, re-
calling their glorious return to campus:

> It was half past ten in the morning when the cannon reached the
> Rutgers campus. The men, triumphant, but a sorry-looking lot,
> without sleep or breakfast and with the marks of their toil upon
> them . . . At once, of course, the college was alive with the joy of
> the achievement, and the city shared in the high feeling that pre-
> vailed. There was no more college that day.
>
> The heroes of the occasion were borne about the streets on the
> shoulders of their fellows. The cannon itself was taken from the
> campus and hid in a cellar downtown. Men of the city, firemen
> and factory men, held themselves ready to join the students in
> protecting their trophy if a counter attack should come.

Counterattack did come, with bands of Princeton students
roving around the Princeton campus, searching for their cannon.
At this point the college authorities stepped in and worsened
the situation. The college presidents—McCosh of Princeton and
Campbell of Rutgers—"both doughty Scotchmen," Demarest
writes, who "were not men to avoid a fray or to be unaware of the
joy of conflict" exchanged salty, threatening letters before a typi-
cally-academic solution to the problem was found—a joint committee was established to study the history of the cannons at both
schools and arbitrate the matter.
Much to Rutgers's dismay, the committee determined that the
stolen cannon had resided at Princeton since the Revolutionary
War and had never belonged to Rutgers.
Demarest finishes the tale with the mournful image of the
purloined cannon, heading out of town:

> The verdict that the cannon should be returned was, of course,
> most unwelcome. There was no little disposition to evade it and
> to keep the place of the cannon's concealing a secret. But the place
> became known, the cannon came into the keeping of the chief of
> police, and by his men it was returned, one sitting on the cannon
> with a revolver facing the indignant mob that followed from the
> city for some distance.

ANOTHER CANNON BANG

Stunned Tennesseans gradually absorb the fact that something has happened to their cannon.

*B*oth Princeton and Rutgers seemed to get into the competitive spirit underlying the cannon war (the two schools had, just six years earlier, politely inaugurated intercollegiate football, as will be seen in the next chapter). Much less amused were the good citizens of Nashville, Tennessee, upon discovering in March 1900 that their adored cannon had been defiled by Vanderbilt students. The cannon, captured during the jin-gomaniacal Spanish–American War and bestowed on the state by demigod Admiral George Dewey, was an object of great veneration. Citizens were incensed when students painted rings of black and gold up and down its length, and "Vanderbilt" and "V.U." along the base. President Kirkland, in the midst of a campaign to draw local dollars into Vanderbilt, was certainly not amused. Three students were dismissed for a year, though Admiral Dewey himself showed up on campus in May to display there were no hard feelings. 🐄

Sadly, most colleges could not count on being led by doughty Scotsmen—dour Presbyterians were more the model. In 1879, Middlebury College hosted a perfect example of mindless discipline's capacity for self-defeat. The tiniest infraction—almost too minor and harmless to even be considered a prank—was allowed to metastasize into a major crisis that came within inches of destroying Middlebury as an institution.

Students weren't supposed to play football between the college buildings. President Hulbert had been clear about that. But it was such a petty, pointless edict that students largely ignored it. Where else were they supposed to play? Well, if you couldn't play between the buildings, some reasoned, then perhaps you could play *in* them, and a group took to passing the pigskin inside the chapel building.

The prolate spheroid in question somehow got out of control, and found its way into the Latin recitation room of Professor Albee, who shared President Hulbert's addiction to control at all costs.

Through a chain of disciplinary proceedings too complicated to be worth recounting, involving draconian application of demerits and a poorly-timed cane rush (fighting over a cane, one of the many forms that interclass battle took at the time), a popular sophomore involved in the football incident, Clarence G. Leavenworth, '82, was suspended.

"Leavenworth's classmates were furious that a student could be suspended after committing such trivial offenses," wrote David Stameshkin, whose *The Town's College* presents a comprehensive description of the episode.

His classmates elected to join Leavenworth, and boycotted class. President Hulbert, still a fool, fanned the flames with threats, demands for apologies, suspensions, and letters to parents, none of which worked. When students failed to attend classes on Monday, November 17, the faculty took a step unique in the annals of excessive academic discipline: It suspended every student in the college, down to the last freshman, sophomore, junior, and senior.

By this time a distinct sniggering was heard from the national press. The *New York Sun* called Hulbert's original football ban "foolish" and the *Boston Journal* suggested that perhaps the stu-

BIG BOOTS

*W*hile Middlebury College's grand suspension is unrivaled in history, colleges did, with surprising frequency, display their devotion to order by kicking out a good percentage of the students they were supposedly trying to teach:

1.Three popular Princeton students, accused of insulting a college officer, were expelled in 1807. This inflamed the campus, and students organized a committee to appeal for the trio's reinstatement. The faculty held firm. President Smith called a meeting of the college where he proposed to take a roll call, asking each student to declare whether he would follow the rules of the school. The students rioted instead, howling and rushing from the building. When the dust settled, 68 of Princeton's 200 students were expelled and not permitted to return.

2. The Harvard class of 1823 was known for wildness, and during its senior year its rowdyism only intensified, with explosions in Harvard Yard and tutors being drenched in water and ink. As summer drew near, dissatisfaction at the faculty appointments for commencement exercises further agitated the seniors. When a member of the class was expelled, a group met under the Rebellion Tree and swore they would leave college until the senior was reinstated. He wasn't, and 43 of his supporters were dismissed on the eve of commencement.

3. The quality of food is always a problem at college. It was particularly bad, apparently, at the University of South Carolina, where students first officially complained to the president in November 1806, and the matter was not settled until the "Biscuit Rebellion" of 1853. During this half century of protest, students in the class of 1827 were accused of entering into "a combination"—an administration taboo word signifying conspiracies by students to break school laws—not to eat at Steward's Hall after March 1, 1827. As a result, almost the entire senior class was expelled.

4. As the spring of 1904 grew warm, the law students at the University of Colorado grew increasingly uncomfortable

on the hard wooden benches in Hale Hall. The wood must have seemed even harder considering that new chairs were stored in the basement of Main, chairs that President James Hutchins Baker, according to the May 5 law notes, considered "a little too good to use." That same month, both sophomore and junior law students took to dragging the "instruments of torture" out of the building and depositing them at various spots around campus. Not the most creative prank, but one that brought about noteworthy reaction. After the third episode, Baker, a man "not blessed with an abundant sense of humor" expelled the entire junior class. They might have stayed expelled, had not representatives of the class cleverly sent a letter to the budding Denver University law school, offering to enroll en masse. A copy was tactfully sent to Baker, and after hasty negotiations, the class was allowed to return—provided they brought all the benches back—and Baker promised to have the new chairs dragged up from the basement of Main.

dent strike would lead to an overdue shake-up of the Middlebury faculty.

Ordered to apologize and return to class, just one student—C.D. Pillsbury, '82—heeded the call.

Within a week the matter dissipated and the students returned to class (strangely, with Leavenworth's suspension still in place). The damage to Hulbert was done, however. By that spring he, Albee, and another professor involved had resigned.

The modern age shows university officials better prepared, occasionally, to deal with college pranks. At the University of Kentucky, the administration employed the clever device of *not* staging some grand inquiry into a student prank. According to a school history:

> In 1900 pranksters dismantled the old cart used for hauling various objects about the grounds, and the joke backfired when the authorities made no effort to recover it. At the end of the year, the boys, who had always used the cart for hauling their trunks,

were forced to patronize the city transfer companies with a resulting expenditure of money.

The coming of the 20th century did not, as will be seen, bring
benevolent reason to college administrations. Nor did it bring the
age of window breakers and horse shavers to a screeching close.

Rather, as is usually the case in history, one period melted
gently into the next. The new age, beginning in the years between
the Cannon War and the end of the Great War, eventually
brought a new brand of student—even more free, more independent, with money to spend, time on his hands, and a propensity
to cook up truly great pranks. Colleges became less insulated.
And because—at long last—college administrators were less able
or less willing to repress their students, those students didn't need
to rebel against them quite so much. Instead they could afford the
luxury of letting loose their pranks, more and more frequently,
not just on campusmates, but on the world at large.

SPORTS PRANKS
The Great Rose Bowl Hoax

> It was another college prank and
> we have learned not to be disturbed.
> —J. Gordon Gose
> University of Washington
> Faculty Athletic Rep.

*F*ewer great college pranks would exist were it not for college sports. Heck, fewer colleges would exist. But that's another matter.

Actually, "sports" is too vague a term. Substitute "intercollegiate varsity football." There's something about college football. Maybe it's the spirited marching songs. Maybe it's the lack of effective passing quarterbacks. Maybe it's those hydrocephalic costumed characters roaming the sidelines. Football makes people crazy.

It is the animating factor that can turn the dullest frat lout into a diabolical genius. At least temporarily.

Football games must be won or lost on the field, usually by the players themselves. But pranks allow any interested party to enter the fray, at almost any time, although the week preceding a big game is when many sports pranks are found.

The basic concept behind the pregame prank is to undermine the morale of the opposing team and cause it to lose the game. How can players feel like superhumans, like Thors and Apollos, with a galaxy of stars on their helmets and fire in their bellies, knowing that their beloved old mascot Butch is tied up in a barn somewhere, painted the enemy's purple-and-brown and wearing women's panties? They can't.

Not only does football drive students crazy but, apparently, it always has. From the very beginning, nobody could simply play the game. Football took the gentle sporting rivalries that had developed between neighboring schools and stoked them into intense, ritual hatreds.

When Rutgers challenged Princeton to the very first intercollegiate football game in autumn of 1869, the contest was to have been a best of three series. The first game took place placidly enough: "the Princeton players arrived at ten o'clock that morning, strolled around the town, were entertained at dinner, and met their foe on the field at three in the afternoon," a school history records.

The calm was not to last for long. To their everlasting glee, Rutgers won that historic first contest (which, truth be told, was a game much closer to soccer than modern football, with a few rugby-like touches thrown in). They lost the second at Princeton. The rubber game was never played. It was cancelled by a joint agreement of the two schools' faculties, nervous over the "great zest and rivalry aroused" by the game.

It was the same wherever football was played.

"Although college football had only been in the Deep South four years, Tech was already a hated rival," says an Auburn University history, describing the atmosphere on the Auburn campus when the first football game was played there, against Georgia Tech, in 1896.

The visiting Georgia Tech team was greeted before this first contest by a prank that had such a deep impact on the collective Auburn psyche that it was reenacted each year for nearly a century.

In that pre-bus era, teams traveled by train on the day of the game. The night before that first big game, Auburn students slipped out of their dorms and greased the rails—a common 19th-century prank—from before the station platform to well east and out of the town.

When the Tech team train arrived from Atlanta the next morning, it applied the brakes but could not stop. The train, with amazed Tech players and fans aboard, slid by the station and, if accounts of the time can be believed, halfway to Loachapoka, 10 miles away.

The team had to walk into town, with its fans trailing behind, and lost the game 45 to zip. Perhaps the lopsided loss was due to the humiliating effects of the prank, or perhaps the victory was due to Auburn being coached by John Heisman, the man for whom the Heisman Trophy was later named. Who can say?

Burning as much from the prank as from the loss, Georgia Tech refused to play Auburn the following year, and would only agree to a rematch in 1898 if the administration promised their team would not be traipsing along the Loachapoka road again.

Auburn administrators, with typical subtlety, announced that anyone caught trying to grease the tracks would be expelled.

This of course was the moral equivalent of an embossed invitation to track greasing, hand delivered to the students.

The faculty must have been aware of this because, the Friday night before the game, educators camped out trackside, hoping to apprehend students sneaking out of their rooms with pails of grease. At first the threat appeared successful, but as the evening wore on, more and more students poured out of their dorms, in their pajamas, and assembled at the tracks. Suddenly expulsion seemed somewhat problematic.

"If they expelled everyone who participated, there would be no need to have classes Monday. There would be no students," an Auburn history reasoned.

This wouldn't have stopped some administrators, but at Auburn calmer heads prevailed, both among the faculty and students. The faculty did not expel the students gathering trackside and the students, perhaps daunted at the thought of being nudged out into the chill of the real world, did not grease the tracks. Instead they held a giant pep rally, lining both sides of the railway easement.

Auburn students liked this so much that they repeated it, yearly, before the Georgia Tech game, in what eventually was called the "Wreck Tech Pajama Parade." This went on from the twilight of the 19th century to 1987, when Georgia Tech, which was obviously getting the short end of the stick (although they won a respectable 39 games to Auburn's 43) announced it was no longer scheduling games with Auburn.

And a good thing, too, in that it ended the Wreck Tech parade, which by then had been coopted by the university into a fluffy display of school pride backed by rigid intimidation. "The parade rules will be stressed and anyone who violates any of the rules will have to go before the disciplinary committee," warned parade chairman Frank Chalfont in 1983, citing a list of regulations that included "no running."

The fate of this early Auburn prank illustrates the particular dilemma of sports-related pranking. On one hand, nowhere else in college life is excitement and enthusiasm at such a fevered pitch. This is good for pranks. Practically every pair of rival colleges is rich with tales of students sneaking over to abuse each others' campuses and statues, of kidnapped mascots, faked newspapers, and defiled fetish objects.

On the other hand, no area of college life is so filled with straight arrow, back-the-president sorts who shy away from the unbridled energies of pranks. So we see, time and time again, a prank form, fresh and original, only to be seized and ruined by alumni-booster types, hoping to disarm the prank by setting it in a glass case and making it into a *tradition*.

THE CELESTIAL COMET

There is no rule that a college prank has to be pulled by a college student. Morris Newburger certainly wasn't in college; he was a stockbroker with the firm Newburger, Loeb & Company. He was also fascinated with the obscure schools that were listed in the college football roundup in the *New York Herald Tribune*.

In the fall of 1941, he amused himself during America's last moments of global innocence by creating his own school— Plainfield Teachers College—and phoning the scores in every week to the *Herald Tribune*.

Newburger did his homework. When asked, he was ready with 22 names for the lineup roster—names of his friends, neighbors, business partners. There was also a certain Morris Newburger starting at right tackle.

Every team should have a star, and Plainfield's was Johnny Chung, the half-Chinese, half-Hawaiian tailback known as the Celestial Comet. Under his leadership, Plainfield went 6–0, and seemed a shoo-in for the prestigious Blackboard Bowl.

As can happen with these things, matters got a little out of control. Newburger found himself printing up letterheads for the Plainfield Teachers Athletic Assocation and took a post office box in Newark. Jerry Croyden, the imaginary director of sports information, sent out news releases and phoned tidbits to the papers. The Celestial Comet was tearing up the field.

Sadly, the Plainfield Teachers never made it to the Blackboard Bowl. Enjoying himself immensely, Newburger bragged to one pal too many, and word leaked into journalism circles. With *Time* magazine preparing to expose the hoax in their next edition, Newburger rushed out a release having the Celestial Comet flunk his exams and so many players become inelligible that the rest of the season was cancelled.

The *Herald Tribune* finally smelled something fishy, and checked with the Plainfield Chamber of Commerce, discovering the utter nonexistence of a Plainfield Teachers College about the same time the November 17, 1941 issue of *Time* hit the stands. 🐄

This constant back-and-forth tension between pranksters and sportsters is obvious in the fierce war between the University of California at Los Angeles and the University of Southern California, perhaps the most prank-laden sports matchup in the country.

It may be difficult for outsiders to comprehend the intensity of the rivalry. The schools are only eight miles apart. They've played each other since 1929, with 33 of those games sending one of the teams to the Rose Bowl. At gametime, "the animosity hangs so thick in the air that it is a wonder the TV camera high above in the Goodyear blimp can even get a picture of the field," writes L.A. sports columnist Joe Jares. Families with split loyalties to both UCLA and USC are treated as objects of wonder, like those clans with various sons enlisted in both the Union and Confederate armies during the Civil War.

Manly Tommy Trojan takes a public shower after a visit from UCLA friends.

The earliest recorded prank between the schools was in 1937, when three USC Trojans burned "USC" into the UCLA quad. They bungled the job, and were caught. The same year, UCLA students were apprehended painting "UCLA" on the USC statue of its mascot, Tommy Trojan. They were tarred, feathered, and pulled down University Avenue displayed in a cage.

The Tommy Trojan statue, installed in 1930, has been a continual magnet for UCLA hatred. Nobody has ever stolen the massive, bronze Tommy. But his sword has been taken so often over the years that USC started replacing it with a wooden sword after each theft, since the bronze was getting expensive. (One story, probably apocryphal, has the sword removed and welded so it stuck from the middle of Tommy's back).

He has been painted so often that, in recent years, officials have taken to draping Tommy in canvas and plastic—referred to as "the baggie"—the week of the USC–UCLA game. A security guard sometimes watches over Tommy, other times bands of volunteer students (one year, 100 students armed with clubs camped out around the statue).

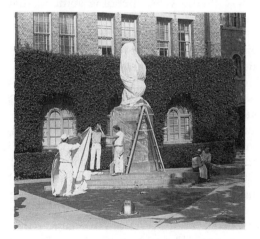

Tommy Trojan looks to his popular latex namesake for protection during UCLA game week in 1976.

Despite precautions, in 1979, a former *Daily Bruin* editor named Steve Hartman almost made off with Tommy's head after sneaking onto campus with a group of friends and an array of cutting tools, including a hacksaw.

"We made a pretty good incision in the Trojan's neck," said Hartman. "But then we saw these five squad cars pull up."

Now Tommy is under 24-hour surveillance by a video camera.

For a period of several years, the rivalry focused on what was known as the Victory Bell. The alumni association at UCLA bought a big train bell from the Southern Pacific Railroad in 1939 and presented it to the school. For two years, the bell rang out points during home games while the rooting section chanted along.

But in 1941, after the first game of the season with Washington State, six fraternity brothers from the Sigma Phi Epsilon chapter at USC secretly joined the UCLA rooters. At the end of the game, while they assisted the students loading the 295-pound bell into a waiting truck, one of the Trojans stole the keys. The UCLA students went to get another set, and the fratnicks drove the truck and bell back to USC.

To the growing rage of the UCLA campus, the bell remained missing for more than a year, spending some of that time in a Santa Ana haystack.

In retribution, UCLA initiated the tradition of drenching Tommy Trojan in blue-and-gold paint. USC retaliated by burning its initials onto UCLA lawns. After the campus raids escalated, including threats to kidnap USC student president Bob McCay (and threats by USC's comically named president, Dr. Rufus B. von KleinSmid, to cancel the game if the pranks continued) the two student governments decided to parlay.

On November 12, 1942, they agreed that the Victory Bell would no longer disrupt such an otherwise tranquil period in world affairs, but would forevermore be a trophy to be held by the winner of the yearly UCLA–USC game. It was never stolen again. (Concern over possible theft of the Victory Bell remains such, however, that it is removed from the stadium during the last quarter of the match. The victors display it for one day—the Monday after their triumph—then lock it away for another year).

Still, this accord did not stop the UCLA–USC rivalry from producing a number of extremely satisfying pranks.

In 1947, UCLA students kidnapped USC's beloved canine mascot, George Tirebiter, from a dog-and-cat hospital, returning him to the Trojans with "UCLA" shaved into his fur. USC sorority girls knitted George a little sweater so he could appear at the 1947 Rose Bowl without advertising his rivals.

In 1958, editors of the *Daily Trojan,* realizing that their newspaper was printed up at the same plant as the *Daily Bruin,* created the first of many game-paper pranks between the schools.

The Trojan editors used the printing plant connection to get their hands on plates for the *Bruin,* and went to work altering copy for their own, modified, game version of the *Bruin,* which they then printed up.

That done, they kidnapped the truck driver delivering the real *Bruin* to the UCLA campus and, while the driver was being given breakfast at USC's frat row, loaded the truck with the fake edition and drove to UCLA. They handed the guard a copy—as they had seen the real driver do during their stakeouts—and proceeded to the drop-off points, distributing the newspapers. The text of the fake *Bruin* shows how heightened school spirit is often at odds with a finely tuned sense of humor.

"I can't see any hope for our team," the UCLA head coach was quoted as saying in one article.

"I'd feel much better about our chances against those terrific Trojans if we had a couple of players who understood the game," an athlete said elsewhere.

They wisely saved a few copies of the fake *Bruin* to pass out in a meeting of the Trojan Club at a downtown hotel. The alums were so pleased with the prank they reimbursed the group the cost of printing up the fake edition (and, to mitigate their punishment should they be caught, they made sure to deliver the real *Bruin* around noontime, so it wouldn't be out the day's ad revenues. Sports. Fair play. All that.)

That same year, in 1958, UCLA tried a prank against USC that while accomplishing little, in fact, entered into joint college lore and illustrates the way myth often enhances the reality of a prank. This was the helicopter dumping of manure on the Tommy Trojan statue.

Various accounts have between 500 and 2,000 pounds of manure dumped on Tommy Trojan from a helicopter, used to thwart the phalanx of Trojan men guarding the statue round-the-clock the week before the game.

FE-FI-FAUX-FUM

*T*he replacement of the *Daily Bruin* with a fake was just one of many examples of faking an opponent's game-day newspaper. It was a cherished tradition at Harvard. In 1946, a copy of the *Dartmouth* was replaced with a *Crimson*-produced phony with the banner headline: SEVEN INDIAN STARTERS OVERCOME BY FOOD POISON ON EVE OF GAME. Duped fraternity members flocked to the field house in response to the coach's plea for emergency replacement athletes. In 1950, the *Crimson* struck Dartmouth again, this time the issue claiming the football coach had resigned that morning owing to ill health. At Princeton two years later, for two days in a row, Friday and Saturday November 7 and 8, 1952, "Crimson thugs" stole the entire press run of the *Daily Princetonian*, replacing it with their own version of the newspaper. The first was an obvious parody (though one junior reportedly missed an exam the fake said had been cancelled). The second was a more subtle one-page "extra" that sent hundreds of freshmen to the athletic office, wondering why their game tickets had been declared invalid.

"They hit the statue right on the nose," gloated an article in a UCLA booster magazine.

It's a nice image—cleverness and technology thwarting brute might. Tommy Trojan covered in all that horse flop.

Sadly, what happened is this. UCLA booster Irv Sepkowitz and his conspirators rented a helicopter. Initially they planned to loop a rope over the statue and tear it out of the ground. But they quailed at the thought of illegality, not to mention the very real risk of crashing the helicopter and killing themselves. Instead, they loaded the helicopter with four bags of fertilizer—perhaps a hundred pounds' worth. They flew to the USC campus, where they positioned themselves over Tommy Trojan. They overlooked, however, a basic property of helicopter aerodynamics.

"There is a wash of air that blows much of what you throw out of a helicopter back at you," said Sepkowitz. As the bags were torn open and dumped, the prop wash sucked the manure back into the helicopter.

"We were covered with the stuff. It looked like we were in a minstrel show when we were done. How much landed I do not know."

The rivalry continues to the present day, with UCLA generally getting the worst of it in recent years. In 1984, realizing it was being trounced in the symbolism department by Tommy Trojan, UCLA came up with "Bruin Bear." USC got to the oafish and redundantly-named mascot during its very first USC–UCLA game week, covering the bear in Trojan cardinal-and-gold. In the late eighties, someone spelled out "USC" in lime on the grass of UCLA's Royce Quad, and dumped hundreds of chirping crickets into their Powell Library.

There have also been a few UCLA–USC pranks that, while not substantiated, are claimed by some, and worth mentioning:

- USC supposedly, one year, tossed dynamite into UCLA's homecoming fire. The explosion was said to have shattered windows in Bel Air.
- USC students slipped onto the UCLA campus and sealed up the doors and windows of a sorority with bricks and mortar.
- UCLA students once rented a single-engine plane and strafed the USC campus with blue and gold paint.

Tommy Trojan is only the most famous of literally hundreds of mascots to be victimized by rivals. The whole purpose of school mascots is to drum up enthusiasm for the team; thus, one of the simplest and most common sports pranks is to grab your opponent's symbol and do something awful to it.

In the fall of 1971, Brutus Buckeye, the large papier-mâché mascot of the Ohio State University football team, travelled to Ann Arbor for the annual Armageddon against archenemy University of Michigan. The night before the match, the costume was kidnapped—presumably by a Michigan frat—from the custody of the block O cheering section.

Just before game time, he appeared at the stadium—mutilated, doused in Michigan colors of gold-and-blue.

The Occidental Tiger suffered a fate perhaps unique among mascots. Kidnapped by USC students in October 1919, it served as a focus of USC pep rallies until 1923, when the Trojans offered to return the Tiger "to foster friendly relations" between the schools. Oxy, for some reason, thought harmony could best be achieved by destroying the Tiger. Representatives from *both* schools hacked the statue apart with axes on December 1, 1923.

Occidental Tiger awaits vivisection.

The U.S. Air Force Academy, in Colorado Springs, makes a habit of kidnapping opponents' mascots without any attempt at stealth, but right during the game, on the field. The tradition started in 1956, during a game with the Colorado School of Mines. A freshman named Wayne Waterhouse was dressed as a miner—as obvious a school mascot as there can be. He was doing a skit where he pulled a cart around the field, picking up signs.

One of the signs was rigged to explode before Waterhouse got to it, but it malfunctioned and blew up in his face. The quickest way to get Waterhouse out of the stadium and to medical attention was for the cadets to pass him up through the stands, hand over hand.

Since then, it has become a home game tradition for the Air Force to grab whatever mascot they can lay hands on and pass him out of the stands.

There is a nice tale of theft of the Old Oaken Bucket, the prize in the Indiana–Purdue matchup. It has been kidnapped several times by both schools; one year officials were supposed to hand the bucket off to victorious Indiana on a railroad platform, but instead delivered it into the hands of a group of Purdue students wearing Indiana sweatshirts.

Perhaps the most sublime tale of a stolen school idol is the theft and eventual glorious recovery of the Stanford Axe. It is a story treasured at Stanford.

In 1896, a pair of undergraduates, Will Irwin and Chris Bradley, wrote a pep yell with the stirring if slightly morbid words: "Give 'em the axe, the axe, the axe, right in the neck, the neck, the neck . . ."

As a visual aid, Bradley bought a big, battered planing axe and painted a red "S" on the side. A history compiled by the *Stanford Observer* spots the Axe being ceremoniously sharpened at a bonfire rally in 1899 and lopping off the head of a blue-and-gold figure—the colors of rival University of California.

Shortly thereafter the Axe was used to rally Stanford fans at a baseball game against U of C in San Francisco. After the game, California students managed to grab the Axe, in what the *Observer* describes as "a chase complete with fistfights, flying tackles and other indelicacies." The Axe was spirited away to the University of California's Berkeley campus.

Later in 1899, Stanford students retaliated by stealing the Big C senior fence from Berkeley. There were no offers of ransoming the Axe for return of the fence, however, and disappointed Stanford students heaped it onto one of their famed Himalayan bonfires.

The Axe remained at the University of California for 31 years, despite occasional sorties by Stanford students trying to recover it. These were in vain, because when the Axe wasn't being used to drum up pep-rally fever against Stanford, it was resting securely in a vault at the America Trust Company Bank. Berkeley took no chances: The Axe was transferred from the vault to rallies and back in an armored car.

Attempts in 1928 and 1929 by undergraduates Don Kropp and Ed Soares and a half-dozen or so others to grab the Axe also failed, but led the two men—both members of the Sequoia Eating Club—to believe that a well planned, concerted effort could in theory succeed.

"It was important to get the right fellows," said Kropp, years later. "If some were not in place and ready to fight the whole thing would fizzle. . . . among the qualifications we sought were a happy indifference to one's personal well-being and a demonstrated aptitude for reasonable mayhem."

Kropp and Soares recruited 17 other Sequoia men, adding 2 more auto owners at the last minute to round out a gang of raiders that became known in Stanford lore as the "Immortal 21."

The "21" studied the circumstances when the Axe was removed from the vault, and decided that the best time to try to grab it was after the rally, on its return to the bank, when emotions were spent and guards dropped. A raid was scheduled for April 3, 1930.

The Stanford men were meticulous in their planning. Each man was instructed to leave behind his school ring, watch fob, or any other sign that could possibly tie him to Stanford. They had their own cars, but for the ruse itself rented a Buick roadster in Oakland so that no keen-eyed University of Californian would spy a car with Palo Alto registration plates and be tipped off. They also needed the rumble seat.

The 21 obtained the other materials they required—an old-fashioned camera on a tripod, a tear-gas bomb, handkerchiefs—and made their way to the University of California campus.

A sign of the cleverness and forethought of the Stanford men is that one of them, expecting trouble and knowing that the easily-breakable lens was the most costly part of the camera, for which they had placed a $50 security deposit, removed the lens and substituted a tube of Bakelite with an ink bottle jammed into it. (Lack of this sort of planning tripped up a similar plan at Oklahoma A & M 14 years later—see box).

THE WRONG WAY

The finesse and timing behind the Stanford Axe grab will be greater appreciated in light of the way Oklahoma A & M—now Oklahoma State University—bobbled a similar attempt in 1944. The Old Central Bell had been used to jubilate A & M Aggie victories over the University of Oklahoma Sooners since the 1920s. But in 1930 its clapper was stolen by a Sooner fraternity, and in the aftermath both schools decided to use the clapper as a trophy for the annual matchup. Shortly thereafter, A & M went into a severe losing streak. The clapper was gone for years, while the Sooners tortured them with tales of their beloved clapper laying neglected in various O.U. attics and trunks.

The Aggies began to despair they would never see it again. "If we don't hurry up and beat O.U. again, there will not be any object in trying. The clapper will have rusted away completely," an A & M student complained.

By 1944, with O.U. broadly hinting they would contribute the clapper to the national scrap metal drive, the Aggies decided not to pin their hopes upon gridiron victory to retrieve the clapper. The evening before the game, three A & M students went to the Tulsa home of L. Whitley Cox, Sr., president of the O.U. athletic booster club. He was said to possess the clapper.

Identifying themselves as being from the *Oklahoma Daily,* the University of Oklahoma student newspaper, they brandished a camera and asked to take a photo of Cox, his wife, and the Old Central Bell clapper. Cox fetched it from a trunk in his attic. The students asked to take a closer look and Cox handed them the clapper. They turned and fled.

Cox ran after them, leaping onto the running board of their

car as their drove away. "I could not get a hand on the clapper because it was under their feet, so I grabbed their expensive press camera belonging to the *Daily O'Collegian* (the risible name of the A & M newspaper) and returned to my house," Cox said.

He ransomed the camera for the clapper, which he promised to return if the Aggies won the next day. The trumped students returned the clapper, and the entire affair turned out to be moot, since the Aggies won anyway, and held the clapper for another two years, before the University of Oklahoma crushed them 73–12. For the next 19 years, the Sooners beat the Aggies, and by the time OSU won again, nobody much cared about the clapper anymore. In 1967 the tradition sputtered out and, surprisingly, the students left it that way.

Some deployed to the bank. Others to the Greek Theater, where the rally was held. There they watched the Axe waved before them, and their school ridiculed. But they kept quiet, did nothing, and waited.

Afterward, when the Axe was taken to the armored car—really a sedan converted with steel plate and bulletproof glass—members of the 21 tagged along with it, climbing atop the car with other zealous students.

It was 8 P.M., and dark, by the time the armored car pulled up alongside the bank. The Buick roadster, with Stanfordites manning a camera set up in the rumble seat, backed up to the truck, and the plotters began urging the Californians to pose for a picture "for the paper."

As the unsuspecting dupes grouped themselves, Norman Horner, captain of the California baseball team and official Axe custodian—exited the car, clutching the Axe to his chest.

Sixty years later, survivors of the 21 are still debating exactly what happened in the next five seconds. Lacking an Abraham Zapruder to document the event, the best we can do is piece together the event from eyewitnesses.

The accepted story goes like this:

At the moment Horner and the Axe left the car, an "enormous charge of magnesium flash powder" was ignited, blinding those posing. Sequoia man Howard Avery, who was on the roof of the armored car, dove onto Horner, grabbing the Axe as he fell.

Pandemonium broke out. Stanford and California men wrestled for the Axe, punching, shoving, falling to the ground.

The Axe ended up in the hands of Bob Loofbourow, a Sequoian. Realizing no one noticed where the Axe had gone in the general melee, Loofbourow had the presence of mind to turn his back on the scuffle, tuck the Axe under his sweater, and quietly walk away.

With the fight was still going on, Loofbourow stepped into the getaway car, which roared off, while yet another Sequoian detonated a tear gas grenade in the center of the fight—a sign the Axe was won and it was time to depart.

With the help of wet handkerchiefs they had brought along, the Stanford men who started the battle escaped and other Stanford men, still incognito, shouted for the students to head for the California bell tower—the opposite direction of the escape route—to "form a posse."

The Axe was borne triumphantly back to Stanford, where an impromptu pep rally formed at the Sequoia House. Hundreds of shouting, laughing students thundered the old Axe cheer.

Then, fearing a counterstrike, the Axe was hidden in a vault in the athletic department.

That evening an invading horde of several hundred California students arrived on campus, intent on recovering the Axe. Told the Axe was safely squirrelled away, they left campus, grumbling.

A headline on the next day's *Stanford Daily* blared AXE RE-GAINED in four-inch type. Morning classes were cancelled, and an even larger rally was held on the steps of the library.

Stanford was uniquely effusive in their gratitude to the 21. They were honored by alumni clubs. The university presented each with a gold-axe charm with the date of the theft engraved on it. The recovery of the Axe took its place in the official school histories, alongside the San Francisco Earthquake and big alumni donations.

Sadly, in 1933 the Axe was trophyized, as the administrations of the two schools, worried about potential retributions, decided the Axe should be presented yearly to the winner of the Big Game.

The Immortal 21 bask in olympian glory while posing in a bank lobby.

But did they put it on their resumes?

Neutralizing the Axe did not stop pranks between the two schools, however. Stanford produced a notable fake of its arch-rival's newspaper in the wake of the unbelievable finish to the November 20, 1982 Stanford–U of C football game. Down 20–19 with four seconds remaining, California took a Stanford kick and ran it back for a touchdown, making five laterals in the process and covering the final yards to the goal line across a field crowded with fans and the Stanford band, which had spilled out onto the field, thinking the game over. The final score was 25–20, with California winning one of the most exciting games ever.

A few days after the game, Stanford journalists replaced thousands of copies of *The Daily California* with a revenge-inspired fake headlined NCAA AWARDS BIG GAME TO STANFORD.

The story detailed how an NCAA panel, drawing on a "rarely-used amendment to its bylaws" determined that the California run had been stopped at the 45 when the ball carrier's knee touched the ground.

"Frankly I'm shocked and dismayed," athletic director Dave Maggard was quoted to say. "I know this has got to be a terrible blow both to the team and the fans who have supported the squad all season."

The fake struck just the right note of veracity, and caused a pleasing pulse of anxiety on the California campus.

But if Stanford is more closely associated with pranks than most schools—and it is—credit is due not to any famous past prank, but to the continuing efforts of the Stanford Marching Band.

Many marching bands are known for their close-to-the-edge performances. But Stanford has definitely leaped over the edge and into the abyss, mounting no less than a continual prank assault on rival teams in the mid-eighties.

In 1986, they formed a four-letter word with their bodies during the San Diego State game. They mooned the stands during a University of Washington game (during which time at least a half-dozen band members urinated on the field), and formed "obscene four-letter word scrambles" at the Washington State game.

Later in the year, the band was banned from the field during football games by the school's athletics director, Andy Geiger, dryly describing the situation as "an accumulation of problems." They're still at it. In 1991, during curiosity-of-nature David Duke's bid for the governorship of Louisiana, the Stanford band performed a halftime show at their game with UCLA that asked the musical question: "What would happen if Duke became president of Stanford?" The program began with a rendition of the Doors' "Light My Fire" while an announcer explained that the only fraternity permitted on campus would be Kappa Kappa Kappa and the Stanford colors would change from cardinal-and-white to "white-and-white."

Stanford is certainly not the only marching band to cook up a good prank. At the opening of the 1946 Army–Navy game fans were shocked when the routine of a group of Army cheerleaders began to take on a decidedly Navy slant, complete with appearance of the Navy's mascot, the goat Billy X. Puzzlement turned to shock when the Army cheerleaders tore off their Army outfits, to reveal Navy uniforms.

As Stanford knows, forming words on the field is a classic sports prank. Usually it is not the band, but some other medium used to convey a certain message.

Tiny Whittier College once burned a large "W" on Occidental's Patterson field. Branding letters is a prank best left to real grass fields. On September 24, 1989, three students attempted to use lighter fluid to burn the joke syllable "foo" into the field at the University of Illinois' Memorial Stadium. Rather than neatly forming the letters, however, the lighter fluid ignited the artificial turf, destroying a swath 15 yards wide and 40 yards long.

The University of Alabama planted turnip greens to form a giant "BAMA" in the center of the field in Birmingham where it met its rival, Auburn.

Auburn retaliated by spelling out its slogan, "War Eagle" in grass seed in the middle of Alabama's Quad.

(Speaking of Alabama, fans of the gardens in front of Alabama's Rose Administration Building can thank the persistence of pranksters inspired by Alabama's nickname, "the Crimson Tide." Those gardens were originally fountains when the building was built in the 1960s. After each football game the waters would run red with dye, or turn foamy with boxes of Tide de-

---

A REF SAYS HE'S WRONG

*W*ith Dartmouth leading Cornell 3 to zip and time almost gone in their 1940 matchup, referee William "Red" Friesell mistakenly gave Cornell a fifth down, which they capitalized on, making a touchdown and winning the game.

In the resulting postgame furor, Friesell reviewed the film and realized that, by gosh, he had made a mistake. The Cornell team took a vote, and sportingly agreed to concede the game to Dartmouth, voiding the final touchdown and returning the score to 3–0.

It's hard to resist kicking a ref when he's down, however. Friesell received a flurry of tweaking telegrams. Francis Schmidt, of Ohio State, wired "Wish you had worked our game Saturday. We needed something." Yale, which had lost to Harvard in a game Friesell officiated, sent the following urgent communication: "Entire Yale student body breathlessly awaiting word from you regarding Harvard game. Did we really lose? Can't you do something for us?"

---

tergent. This required constant refilling of the fountain and replacing of the ruined filters, and in 1982, Alabama's president, Dr. Joab Rose, grew tired of the bother, and installed the gardens).

A ritual that used to be an essential part of any big football game, but that now has gone the way of the snake dance, is the pregame bonfire. Once the centerpiece of any pep rally, students would spend days gathering a massive pile of combustables, scavanging the countryside for outhouses, fenceposts, doors, buildings, anything that would burn and could be carted away.

Sneaking in and setting off an opponent's bonfire, prematurely, and thus ruining the rally became a simple, yet intensely satisfying prank.

During the 1940s, homecoming day bonfires at Occidental were burned early by raiders more frequently than at their scheduled time.

Confused Stanford men, hoping to get a good view of that night's bonfire, position themselves unwisely.

Schools took great efforts to guarantee that this did not happen, as recounted in this description of the steps Texas A & M took to protect its bonfires against archrival University of Texas:

At bonfire time A. and M. is actually an armed camp. All persons entering or leaving are screened at the edge of the campus by jeep-borne sentries. The campus itself is patrolled by walkie-talkie-bearing infantry, while mobile fire-fighting equipment is on hand to extinguish any premature blaze. Yet in 1948 despite all these precautions, some University students armed with incendiaries piled into a plane, made an air attack on the A. and M. bonfire pile, and dropped their missiles. While this imaginative approach to the problem failed, the rumor was soon current that at least one Aggie had maintained steady rifle fire on the plane from the roof of his dormitory throughout the attack.

At Caltech, the entire freshman class would stand guard through the night over the bonfire preparations, which in the early 1940s consisted of three telephone poles lashed together to form a tripod, then filled with wooden crates, outhouses, and anything else flammable.

Their principal worry was rival Occidental College, whose bonfire was once touched off by Caltechers using a radio-controlled firebomb disguised as a log. In later years, the Pasadena fire department became a concern. They had the habit of racing to the giant bonfires and putting them out. Caltech students responded by lighting minor bonfires, as a diversion, to draw the fire department away from the main bonfire. One year a crate of calcium carbide was used as a foundation for the woodpile, so when the fire department threw water on the fire, it got bigger, burning the insulation off telephone wires overhead.

The fact that even brainy Caltech was reduced by the spell of football to scrabbling in the streets with fire departments should not lead to the conclusion that all sports pranks are brawny endeavors.

A famous 1926 football rift between Harvard and Princeton was due, in great part, to the brainy impishness of the *Harvard Lampoon*.

At the time, Harvard and Princeton were two-thirds of a triumvirate which, along with Yale, was referred to as the "Big Three." Their football games were sacred events anticipated with relish by nostalgic alums who liked nothing better than to head back to the old sod to cheer for the boys.

Harvard and Princeton had been playing each other in football since 1877. But relations had become strained over the past few

Scary pagan ritual at Stanford.

years. In early autumn 1926 Harvard announced its intention to drop Princeton from its football schedule and substitute the University of Michigan.

The exact motive behind Harvard's desire for change is unclear. There was vague talk of curing an "overemphasis" on football engendered by the Big Three. The *Harvard Crimson* saw the switch as a bald effort to "befriend a large group of wavering graduates in the Middle West." Cynics suggested that Princeton's slaughter of Harvard in their two previous matches, running up a total of 70 points to Harvard's zip, might have also been a factor.

Delicate negotiations between Harvard and Princeton, mediated by a nervous Yale, were minutely reported in the newspapers during the first week of October 1926.

After several days of talks, the Harvard–Princeton game was salvaged in a New Haven meeting that the *New York Times* described as ending "in a love feast."

Rift mended, the Harvard–Princeton game was set for November 6. The afternoon of the game, the *Lampoon* weighed in with their "Princeton Game" issue. While not a prank per se, since the *Lampoon* is in the business of producing satirical magazines, the prank aspect comes from the magazine's perverse sense of timing, its total disregard to the sanctity others attached to the subject, and the utter viciousness of the assault on Princeton.

The issue portrayed Princeton alumni as pigs, nuzzling the filth and commenting "Come, brother, let us root for dear old Princeton!" The ideal Princetonian was lauded in this bit of classic 1920s doggerel, perhaps best read aloud:

From that nursery of heroes
Known as Princeton where the beer flows
Round the campus like a most exclusive moat,
Comes the saga of a rounder
Who is worshipped with the founder
As the first to sound the truly Princeton note . . .

No, he was no good at writing,
Nor at acting, but at lighting
He was unexcelled. Perpetually lit,

He would cut such shocking capers
That they filled the daily papers
And the small-town journals always copied it.

"Princeton Student Jilts a Chorine,"
"Student Drunk on Hydro-fluorine,"
"Princeton Student in Some Other Awful Fix!"
Do not censor him. This gay gent
Was Old Nassau's best press-agent
For he brought the name of Princeton to the sticks.

The *Lampoon* also produced a fake *Crimson* "Football Extra," headlined, BILL ROPER PRINCETON COACH DIES ON FIELD. The coach was portrayed expiring in the arms of his assistants after holding his breath too long during the last quarter of the game.

This time it was Princeton's turn to talk of rupture. They were unmollified by their third straight shutout victory over Harvard, 12–0, after which Princeton fans tossed aside a contingent of Cambridge policemen and tore down the goalposts at Harvard stadium, dragging the shattered lumber before the Harvard cheering section to sing "Old Nassau" before cutting up the posts for vest-pocket souvenirs.

SLURS IN LAMPOON STIR PRINCETON MEN read a headline two days later in the *New York Times*, describing how the *Lampoon* was sold on the roads leading to the stadium and was passed, hand-to-hand, by spectators at the game.

The *Daily Princetonian*, somewhat pathetically, inquired whether the view of the *Lampoon* was the view of the Harvard student body. If so, it said, the Harvard–Princeton game should be cancelled. If not, it called for a "redeclaration of feeling" from Harvard.

Harvard officialdom responded with a yawn. The administration pointed out that it did not censor student expression. The athletic committee noted it was not to be held accountable for student publications.

The *Crimson*, on the other hand, despite once boosting the resumption of ties with Princeton, took the opportunity to indulge in a bit of the psychoanalysis so popular at the time. "Even colleges must retain prestige," it mused, suggesting that Princeton's ire was an outgrowth of its pathological sense of inferiority. "Irritated by its own complex, which is accentuated by the superciliousness of certain Harvard gaucheries, it wants to knock this 'superior' person, John Harvard, into the middle of next week." The battle was on. The *Yale News* denounced both parties as "the forces of evil" and divided blame between them. Both the president and the dean of Harvard fired off apologetic telegrams. But they were too late. The Thursday after the game, Princeton severed relations with Harvard. The *Times* ran the story on page one, directly under the masthead.

Reverberations continued for some time. The Harvard alumni clamored for the game to be reinstated. Yale wrung its hands and tried to patch things up. Someone sawed down an elm tree planted in front of the *Lampoon* building by one of the magazine's founders.

All was for naught. It took almost a decade for tempers to cool, and Harvard did not play Princeton again until 1934.

Several years after Harvard and Princeton kissed and made up, the *Lampoon* again leapt into national headlines via a sporting event, albeit one vastly different from a college football game.

Each May Day, the women of Wellesley College greet the spring with a race of hoop rolling—the ancient children's game where metal hoops are pushed along with a stick.

On May 1, 1939, Edward Cameron Kirk Read, president of the *Lampoon,* donned a red wig, blue skirt, white blouse, and saddle shoes, and hid himself in a clump of bushes around a curve along the race route.

As the girls raced by—some 400 of them—Read easily joined in, unnoticed. He kept pace for most of the race (earlier that week, Read had spent several mornings practicing hoop rolling, joined by his dog, along the Harvard track).

Toward the end, he raced ahead in a burst of speed and beat the nearest contender by three blocks.

At the finish line, he was mobbed by Wellesley girls. Class president Miss Nancy Reynolds presented him with a bridal bouquet of sweet peas (the winner, according to Wellesley lore, would be the first of her class to marry. Today, in a dreary mix of political correctness and greed, she is said to be the first of her class to become CEO of a *Fortune* 500 company).

Read named a Harvard man as his fiancé. At that moment, Read's wig skewed slightly (some accounts say he was given away by a deep, manly blurt of "Thank you very much") and the Wellesley women realized something was afoot. Acting as one, they stripped the academic robes from Read, dragged him to Lake Waban and tossed him in. Read's only concern was the wig, which cost him a $50 deposit, and he flung it to safety as he was hurled into the waters.

400 enraged Wellesley coeds propel Edward C. K. Read into the chill waters of Lake Waban.

EDITORS ON THE MEAT HOOK

*R*ead's hoop victory at Wellesley touched off one of the fiercest wars ever between the *Crimson* and the *Lampoon*. Barely dry from his plunge in Lake Waban, Read was kidnapped by *Crimson* photographers, reportedly out of jealousy for not having cooked up the prank themselves. The next day, a picture of a very unhappy Read—bound and gagged—was printed on the front page of the *Boston Globe*. The *Lampoon* responded by kidnapping three *Crimson* editors and—if accounts of time can be believed—hanging them from meat hooks in a refrigerator.

That night, a battle in the grand tradition broke out at Harvard Yard. Fifty windows were shattered in a free-for-all. FUN AT HARVARD; NOSES ARE BROKEN, the *New York Sun* headlined the next day. The *Crimson* planned to take Read to the New York World's Fair and display him in an open coffin. But overnight he escaped, running in his stocking feet the two miles back to the *Lampoon* offices. The *Crimson* editors were taken off their hooks and released.

Meanwhile, not to be insulted lightly, five Wellesley students infiltrated Harvard Yard about 5:30 A.M. on May 2 and dressed the statue of John Harvard in a Wellesley cap and gown, a blue scarf, a large "W" and, for good measure, a hoop encircling his shoulders.

The Welleslians were apprehended in the act by Harvard police, and escorted off the campus.

(A *Boston Evening American* article describing the adventure is a gem of sexism. Beginning with "Doughty Dianas of Wellesley struck back at Harvard today," it offers up a string of colorful labels including "Amazons," "lassies," "gals," "Rosalinds", and "delectables").

The Wellesley prank ignited the Harvard campus for the next 24 hours (see box on page 59). But the sports prank that achieved the greatest notoriety, and is considered in some quarters to be the single best college prank of all time, (even 30 years after the fact), is Caltech's Great Rose Bowl Hoax. Few college pranks can be said to be more grandly conceived, carefully planned, flawlessly executed, and publicly dramatic.

Pull up a chair, if you will, as we go back to the waning days of December 1960, during a sunny Christmas break at the California Institute of Technology. A group of 14 students were idling away their vacation stranded at Caltech's Lloyd House. Everyone else had gone home for the holidays, and those unfortunate Lloyd-bound students had a chance to let their minds wander.

The papers were ballyhooing the pending Rose Bowl, pitting the Washington Huskies against the Minnesota Golden Gophers. Now, the Rose Bowl was, technically, Caltech's home field. They played at the Rose Bowl all the time. Except on New Year's Day, when two other teams always played there.

To the Lloyd House group, soon to be known as the "Fiendish Fourteen," it seemed eminently unfair that Caltech, a fine school in many regards other than football, had never played in the Rose Bowl on the one day of the year that it really mattered. Never had and never would. The fact that the school even fields a team is a testament to the human spirit.

The Fourteen decided that this year, the team would be avenged. Caltech would be represented at the Bowl. The question then became: How? Pregame publicity trumpeted that NBC would broadcast the contest in "living color," a recent technological marvel put to good use in an elaborate and colorful halftime flip-card display. Like good scientists, the Caltech students thought: "Eureka! The flip cards!"

(For those who have never been to a college football game, or, for that matter, May Day in Beijing, flip-card displays are giant mosaic pictures formed by huge numbers of people holding up colored cards).

The victim of choice had been Minnesota, since their team and marching band would be staying at nearby, hated Occidental

College. But investigation determined that Minnesota, designated the "visitors," would not be having card stunts.

That left Washington. They were set to show up at Long Beach State shortly after Christmas, and when they did, a member of Lloyd House was waiting for them. Passing himself off as a reporter for the Dorsey High School student paper, the *Dorseygram*, the youngish-looking student located Washington's head cheerleader and, under the ruse of conducting an interview, quizzed him on how the card stunts were executed. The cheerleader, flattered by the attention, took great pains in explaining exactly how everything worked.

It was a complex system. Each student in the card section—2,232 in Washington's case—had a stack of large square colored cards. Tacked to the back of each seat in the cheering section was an instruction sheet. Each stunt was numbered and the instruction sheet indicated which card each student was to lift for a particular display. For example, if the instruction sheet said "3-Red," that student held up a red card when the leader called for stunt three, thus adding a Seuratian square of color to a huge, team-inspiring picture.

Each stunt was constructed on a "master plan"—nothing more than the picture worked out on a sheet of graph paper with numbered squares.

The fake *Dorseygram*ite noticed the master plan was kept in a satchel under the cheerleader's bed, along with the instruction sheets to be given to each member of the section.

The beauty of the Caltech plan was this: There was no way that any of the 2,232 members of the Washington card section could know ahead of time how their one card fit into the entire mosaic. Similarly, because of the size of the section, there could be no practices. The head cheerleader wouldn't see the actual picture until the section flipped up its 2,232 cards. At the Rose Bowl. On national television.

The day of the interview, Lloyd House collaborators staked out the head cheerleader's room. While he was at dinner, they picked the room lock (a required skill for Caltech undergraduates, as will be seen in chapter six), snuck in, and removed a single instruction sheet, which was taken to a printer, who was asked to duplicate the typesetting on the sheet.

Two-thousand, two hundred and thirty-two exact copies were made, at a cost of $30. But there was a hitch. The original instruction sheets were worn and grimy with use, and the new sheets looked new. A day was wasted baking the sheets in ovens, rubbing them with dirt, and soaking them in solutions to try to make them look like the old ones. But nothing worked and, with time running out, the young scientists decided to risk just substituting the new instruction sheets, hoping that since the old ones would be replaced, en masse, there would be no basis of comparison should suspicions arise.

It had been learned, during the interview, that the band would be at Disneyland on New Year's Eve. As soon as the buses left, the Lloyders were back inside the room, making off with the master instructions.

Time was of the essence. New Year's Day fell on a Sunday, which meant the Rose Bowl would be played on Monday, January 2. As the Lloyd House's New Year's Eve party unfolded in its lounge, the plans were spread out in the dining room, and the changes begun.

There were 15 separate Washington card stunts. Ironically, several of the stunts saluted science, the theme of the upcoming World's Fair in Seattle. Because of the time factor, it was decided to let the early stunts unfold, unmolested. (The group couldn't resist a few technical improvements, however. A picture of a sharp-cornered Erlenmeyer flask was rounded off so as to better mirror the beaker's blunt-edged reality).

The last 12th, 13th, and 14th stunts, however, were totally changed.

The redesign took hours, with partygoers wandering in to lend a hand with the changes.

Finished, the group rushed back to Long Beach. Lights were on in several of the dorm rooms, and with discovery possible at any second, a trio of Lloyd Housers labored for 10 agonizing minutes to pick the weary door lock. Finally, success was theirs; they filled the satchel with new sheets, replaced the old master plans and made their getaway.

The next day, halftime came with Washington ahead 17 to nothing. As the NBC cameras panned the Washington rooting section, Lloyd House picked up their subtle changes in the first 11 stunts. Not surprisingly, nobody else seemed to notice.

The 12th stunt was supposed to be a Washington Husky. But Lloyd House had rounded his ears and given him buck teeth— turning the dog into a beaver, the Caltech mascot.

Stunt 13 was supposed to spell out HUSKIES in script. This normally began with the "H" and proceeded to the final "S." But, because Lloyd House had reversed the numbers on the instruction cards, it spelled HUSKIES backwards—SEIKSUH.

Panic began to set in. The cheerleaders called stunt 14, which, to the horror of the Washington rooters, turned out to be a big, bold, block-lettered CALTECH, in black on a yellow background.

Viewers at home were treated to a few seconds of dead air.

"People were stunned," said Mel Allen, who along with Chick Hearn, broadcast the game for NBC. More than 30 years later, he still recalled the shock of looking across the immensity of the Rose Bowl and seeing CALTECH. "I was sort of stunned myself. Then I started laughing. It didn't last but a few seconds, but a few seconds on the air is a long time. It caused a lot of laughs. You wondered how they had managed to do it."

What a Caltech junior, watching at Lloyd House, remembers most are those few seconds of stunned silence from the broadcast booth, and the incredible luck that the prank worked.

"We had debated calling NBC and tipping them off, just to make sure they had a camera focused right," he said. "There was an element of luck. It happened and, boom-ba! The camera was right there. We could have done the whole thing and not been on national television."

The 100,000 spectators present, and millions watching across the country, didn't know what to think—some assumed it was part of the tribute to science; a nod to tiny, brainy Caltech. The band stopped playing and filtered off the field. The cheerleaders didn't have the nerve to call for the 15th stunt (an American flag that had been left unaltered). Caltech was victorious.

It should be pointed out, on the theme of pranks affecting onfield performance, that Washington didn't score again after its halftime show was infiltrated and ruined. It managed to hold onto the lead, however, and beat Minnesota 17–7.

In Beijing, it would have said "Increase Tractor Production."

GRAIN OF SALT

*T*he pride that Caltech takes in its Rose Bowl hoax should be tempered, somewhat, by the knowledge that the idea was borrowed from the University of Southern California, which did approximately the same prank four years earlier.

In 1957, a USC student joined the UCLA rally committee, beginning the first week in August and attending meetings until the game in the fall. Week after week, he rushed the eight miles between USC to the UCLA campus, parked, then sauntered to his committee meeting as if he were just another student. No one doubted him.

The USC student, using his position on the spirit committee, found it simple to borrow the instructions for the card stunts 12 hours before the game and alter them so that a small "SC," in contrasting colors, appeared in the upper left-hand corner of every card stunt.

The prank had a nice effect. Horrified UCLA cheerleaders,

thinking their card section had been infiltrated by USC fans, ran up into the stands, only to discover UCLA students, just doing what they were supposed to. No matter how quickly they flipped through the stunts, trying to get rid of that pesky "USC," there it was.

None of the voluminous Caltech material on the Rose Bowl hoax mentions the USC stunt, but the Southern California engineer who masterminded the hoax admits he was inspired by USC.

"I saw the fellow who did that on the 'Art Linkletter Show,' " said the engineer, who, like the other Lloyd House conspirators, prefers to keep his name out of print, even to this day. "The idea of doing it wasn't that innovative, even in 1960."

After the Great Rose Bowl Hoax, the Rose Bowl became the personal Mt. Everest of Caltech pranksters. After several efforts to do a repeat Rose Bowl prank ended in failure, success came again, in an even more technically sophisticated way, in 1984.

The prank was the handiwork of Mike Nolan, '85, and Art Fortini, '83, and it took months of preparation. They started by making several midnight expeditions into the Rose Bowl, to scope out the area, trace wires and fire up the scoreboard's decrepit PDP-8 computer.

To override the internal scoreboard controls, used by the scorer in the press box, Nolan and Fortini planted a microprocessor device on the cable between the computer and the scoreboard. The device was attached to a junction box, 20 feet off the floor.

They were confident that no one would notice the bypass, so high up the wall, but since they did the work several months before the Rose Bowl, they could not rely on battery power. They hooked their device into the stadium's electric circuit by installing an extra piece of conduit that both connected into the AC power and led their dipole wire antenna outside, where they concealed it in a tree.

Meanwhile, Dan Kegel, '86, and Ted Williams, '84, led the team designing the electronics for sending messages to the override device. They spent several nights in the Rose Bowl adjusting and debugging the override system, rappeling down a wall to the junction box and tinkering with it, aided by a miner's headlamp and tool belts.

By December, Kegel and Williams were hiding themselves in the stands in the late hours of the night, watching their messages flash across the Rose Bowl scoreboard in the otherwise blackened stadium.

As the case in 1961, New Year's fell on a Sunday, which meant the Rose Bowl was played Monday, January 2, 1984. By then all was in readiness. The scoreboard pictures were stored on a mini-cassette in the Epson laptop computer used to communicate with the override device via a radio modem. The gear was stored into backpacks. Kegel and Williams talked their way into the backyard of a home overlooking the stadium by claiming to be poor Caltech students who didnt' have the money to buy tickets to the game.

During the first quarter, they tested their system in a subtle way, changing U.C.L.A. to UCLA. Satisfied, in the second quarter they displayed D.E.I.—Caltech shorthand for "Dabney Eats It," referring to a dorm—in the message strip along the bottom of the scoreboard. Caltech president Murph Goldenberger, in the stands watching the game, saw the message, sunk his head and cringed, aware that his kids had something in the works.

The halftime show the pranksters planned—including an elaborate animated segment with a "Pac-Man" creature—was scuttled by radio interference. Their plan to play Wagner's "Ride of the Valkyries," the unofficial fight song of Caltech, also ran into trouble. The pranksters had rigged a tape machine to override the PA system to play the Wagnerian opus, but there were problems with the volume adjustment, and only Caltechers, listening hard for the famous strains, reported hearing it above the crowd noise.

The third quester began with a block CAL TECH displayed on the message strip. That was up for five minutes, replaced by the slogan, GO CIT. From a mile away, the pair could hear the UCLA rooters begin roaring "Go . . . Cal . . . Tech . . . Go . . . Cal . . . Tech."

At this point, the two realized with horror that the batteries of their system were losing power from continuous operation. Showing the sort of split-second know-how Caltech is famous for (see chapter five), they dragged the computer, antenna, and transmitter to Williams's car and quickly hooked it up to the auto battery.

Kegel had planned to put CALTECH 2, ROSE BOWL 0 on the scoreboard, as a nod to the earlier Rose Bowl triumph. But with balky equipment and a lopsided score (UCLA trouncing Illinois by 38–9), they kept the score and just changed the team names to read caltech 38; MIT 9 and displayed a pair of cartoon beavers, the mascot of both schools. (At this point, one of the scoreboard operators was heard to exclaim, "How did they get lowercase characters?" The font used by the Rose Bowl computer wasn't capable of them, but the hack program created by the Techers was).

That was enough. With four minutes to go, Rose Bowl officials cut the power to the scoreboard. (An act which the coach of the battered Illini, Mike White, later gave thanks).

The '84 pranksters would have been well-advised to follow their '61 predecessors and avoid the limelight. Instead, they went on TV afterward and even held a seminar at Caltech, entitled "Packet RF Control of Remote Digital Displays," RF standing for "rat fuck," a Caltech term for pranks.

The city of Pasadena, which had successfully prosecuted Caltech students for trespassing in a failed '81 attempt, slapped William and Kegel with trespassing, loitering and malicious mischief charges. Suddenly, they were facing up to four years in jail.

The *Los Angeles Times* leapt to their defense, dismissing the police suggestion that the equipment installed by the students could have been mistaken for a bomb and caused a panic.

"We are not persuaded," lectured the *Times*. "We have a feeling that the genius behind this exercise in good-natured, harmless computer electronics skullduggery should be encouraged, not deterred. It was about the most exciting thing that happened in the stadium that afternoon."

Kegel and Williams did not go to jail. They did, however, get several job offers from companies impressed with their electronics skill—one of them the company that made the scoreboard.

3

POLITICAL
PRANKS
"Freedom in the Land of the Free"

We regret that what was intended as a campus prank
should have been given such wide publicity.
We intended no disrespect to you, your office,
or the Republican party.
—E.T. Horn and L.A. Blumner
Cornell *Daily Sun,* 1930

*C*ountless valedictorians have belabored their audiences with tributes to our Founding Fathers and George Washington. Ashbel Green was no different, grandly pronouncing that "some future bard . . . shall tell in all the majesty of epic song the man whose gallant sword taught the tyrants of the earth to fear oppression and opened an asylum for the virtuous and free."

But what distinguished Green's speech, at the College of New Jersey's commencement on September 24, 1783, was that its subject, George Washington, was right there, squirming on the dais, clearly embarrassed by all this fulsome praise.

There is no evidence that Green was being sarcastic—that he *meant* to annoy the Father of Our Country with sugary buckets of flattery. Frankly, that would be too much to hope for. Had George Washington, not to mention seven signers of the Declaration of Independence and the French minister, the Marquis de la Luzerne, been treated to some sophomoric senior trick, pranks as an art form might receive greater respect in our society today.

As it was, Washington bumped into Green on campus the next day, shook his hand, and passed his best regards on to his classmates. But the very presence of Washington, and all those dignitaries at the College of New Jersey (which eventually changed its name to Princeton) points to the strong link between politics and college education in this country.

Perhaps the only institution more puffed up and self-important than academia is government. Just as universities need a good deal of grandiloquence to mask the fact that a student can get practically the same education at any public library for free, so politicians need to disguise that any randomly selected group of greengrocers and junior clerks could do a superior job running the machinery of government.

Colleges embrace politicians to make themselves feel an important part of the march of world events. And politicians embrace colleges to advance their own careers by associating with all that is young and collegiate, providing themselves with a ready audience and a mantle of unearned academic grace.

This makes them ripe suckers for college pranksters, who find the zeppelin-like egos of political figures and the genuflecting solemnity of their institutions the perfect target for irreverent pranks.

WHERE PUBLISHERS COME FROM

William Randolph Hearst, a newspaper baron most undergraduates probably remember as the model for *Citizen Kane*, was a man destined to be expelled from college. A free spender and a dandy, it was reported that his father, a California lumber millionaire, sent him nuggets of gold for expenses at Harvard. He became treasurer of the *Lampoon* in great part because of his ability to underwrite the struggling periodical's shortfalls out of his own pocket.

In the fall of 1884—his senior year—Hearst financed a celebratory riot in honor of the election of Grover Cleveland, whom he greatly admired. The fete featured several bands, cisterns of beer, a tremendous fireworks display, and caused such a stir it nearly got Hearst booted out of college.

He wasn't expelled, just yet. But with the encouragement of the dean he went to study in Washington, D.C. for several months. Hearst returned in the spring of 1885, but did not graduate. After a night of carousing, he hired messengers to deliver packages to his professors, each containing a chamber pot with either the professor's name or, in some versions, his picture inscribed inside. That did it. It was back to San Francisco for Hearst, where he cajoled his daddy into giving him control of the *San Francisco Examiner*. Thus was a newspaper magnate born.

Washington may have escaped, but many U.S. presidents have been victims or perpetrators of college pranks at one point or another, either in office or afterward.

Harry Truman, the last president who did not go to college, was no doubt tickled pink when he received a letter from the *Harvard Crimson,* in December 1946, naming him as honorary editor.

The *Crimson* was not so pleased to receive Truman's letter, cordially thanking them for the honor, since the *Crimson* was viciously anti-Truman and had labelled him a "mediocre Democrat."

The honor, it later turned out, had been bestowed by the newspaper's longtime arch enemy, the editors of the *Harvard Lampoon,* using stolen *Crimson* stationery.

The chagrined *Crimson* editors had no choice but to inform Truman that the paper did not grant honorary editorships.

"There seems to have been a minor species of fraud afoot," *Crimson* president Robert Sturgis gingerly wrote to Truman's personal secretary, leaving it up to him whether Truman need be informed of the deception. Truman was informed, and to his credit shot back with a blast of his own.

"I am greatly relieved . . ." the president wrote from the White House on December 14, 1946. ". . . for I was very certain it would not be possible for me to acquire a Harvard accent at this late date and, if I am not Lampooned by the Boston Irish, they will be the only ones who have not made an attempt to do it. My skin is elephant thick and my experience is great—if mean things are to be said they certainly have to be in a class by themselves to be new."

PRESIDENTS, PRANKING AND PRANKED UPON

1. Class president of Whittier College, fraternity founder, and runtish mascot member of the football team, Richard Nixon had a "colossal sense of humor," according to one biographer. When someone painted "OXY"—the letters of hated rival Occidental College—on the Whittier College Building, supposedly to fire up team passion before a big game, Nixon was the prime suspect. He escaped the blame for that, but was caught in the clutches of the law when, along with the entire Whittier football team, Nixon marched into the Roxy movie theater without paying, as a sort of undergraduate show of strength. The Roxy manager was not amused and called police. The team, including towel boy Nixon, was hauled off to jail, where they cooled their heels for several hours before being set free.

2. While attending tiny Southwest Texas State Teachers College in San Marcos, Texas, Lyndon Johnson nurtured the ruthlessness that would later serve him so well in his long political career. An example of this is recounted in the first volume of Robert Caro's monumental biography of the glad-handy Johnson, who is seen convincing a gullible fellow student that the best cure for his bad acne was to apply fresh cow manure to his face and keep it there. The student was skeptical, at first, but Johnson applied his considerable persuasive powers, and the student was convinced to wear the manure to class, wrapped in a towel with eyeholes cut out.

3. It was not exactly Benjamin Harrison, the man and 23rd president, who caused an uproar at Stanford in 1894. Rather it was his cigars, along with a collection of booze. Harrison had been invited to come to Stanford as a guest lecturer on constitutional law—the first ex-president to teach at a college.

Should anyone think that Ronald Reagan invented the practice of harvesting the presidential seal, Harrison was paid the stupendous salary of $10,000 for the one course.

He was to have been put up at the Stanford home, but the recent death of Leland Stanford required that he stay in the guest suite in Encina Hall, a residential dorm. To make him feel at home, Mrs. Stanford stocked his quarters with fine wines, whiskey, and cigars.

Harrison's stint as a professor was uneventful, but just after he left, a pair of students living in Encina (dubbed "the Madhouse" for its scholarly atmosphere) broke into Harrison's suite and made off with the liquor and cigars, which they shared with other residents of the hall.

The school proposed holding the Encina students responsible, but the students balked, pointing out that liquor and tobacco were forbidden in Encina and the administration had been breaking its own rules by bringing them in, even for a former president. Finally, Encina passed the hat and raised $28.55. The matter was then dropped, except by the newspapers, which bandied the story "the length and breadth of the land," says a school history, causing "embarrassment to all concerned."

(The San Francisco Examiner, stung by Stanford's earlier refusal to allow it to print Harrison's lectures, verbatim, was particularly ruthless, labelling Harrison a "slave of Demon Rum" who scattered "platoons of empty bottles" around his rooms. The ironic thing was that Harrison, inclined toward temperance, had never even touched the liquor so thoughtfully left for him).

4. Campaigning through Indiana in search of the presidency in 1980, Ronald Reagan came face to face with Dow Jones, a.k.a. Chris Clark, the physics major/bass player who at the time was leading Purdue's absurdist student government (for more on Dow, see chapter seven).

Clark had seen to it that Reagan's podium was draped with "Vegetable Awareness Week" banners (some less conspicuously-placed material declared "Vote Ronald Reagan Vegetable of the Week").

Clark shook the future president's hand, and presented him with a button that said I'M VEGETABLY AWARE.

Reagan pocketed the button and said, "So, that's what this is all about."

An earlier, minor version of "dupe-the-leader" was executed by future newspaper magnate William Randolph Hearst in 1883. Hearst, showing the verve that would get him booted out of Harvard two years later for his notorious chamber pot prank (see box on page 69) wrote a letter to Germany's Kaiser Wilhelm, describing himself as president of the "Medical Faculty Society" (in reality, the bland name given to a notorious Harvard club dedicated to devilry and drink). Hearst informed the German leader that he had been elected an honorary member. Later, Hearst was delighted with the "beautiful set of surgical instruments" the Kaiser sent in gratitude.

In 1930, a pair of Cornell University students used a clever ruse to exploit politicians' irrepressible desire to sound off about almost anything.

Lester Blumner and Edward Horn were in Martin Sampson's English class one spring day when the professor made a digression to tell them about a hoax that had taken place 16 years earlier in France.

Paul Birault, a reporter from the Parisian newspaper *L'Eclair*, had invited members of the Chamber of Deputies to the unveiling of a monument to the non-existent patriot Hegesippe Simon, coiner of the immortal phrase: "When the sun arises the darkness vanishes away." Those attending the unveiling were cruelly ridiculed in the newspaper. Eight deputies were forced to resign.

"He mentioned that this would be difficult to do in this country today because of all the checks and balances all over the place," recounted Horn, who along with Blumner was an editor of the *Cornell Daily Sun*'s "Berry Patch" column.

They knew a challenge when they saw one. Borrowing technique from the French, they created the "Hugo Norris Frye Sesquicentennial Committee," thinking it could be used to liven up their annual banquet.

Printing up letterhead, the editors Horn and Blumner wrote to a variety of prominent Republican leaders, requesting that they issue statements to honor the 150th birthday of Hugo N. Frye, "the father of the Republican party."

They identified Frye—in reality Blumner's pen name in the column—as a little-known patriot from Elmira, New York, whose slogans such as "Freedom in the land of the free" and "Protection for our prosperity" helped form the GOP.

Several Republican leaders took the bait, despite the pun of the patriot's name (You-Go-N'-Fry). Vice President Charles Curtis wired his deep regret at being unable to attend the dinner, adding, "I congratulate the Republicans on paying this respect to the memory of Hugo N. Frye and wish you a most successful occasion." Secretary of Labor James J. Davis lauded the stature of Frye: "If he were living today he would be the first to rejoice in evidence everywhere present that our government is still safe in the hands of the people."

Among the other respondents were a senator, a congresswoman, and the chairman of the Republican National Committee.

The tributes were mockingly read at the May 26 dinner, which "oozed with honeyed praise for Hugo." Six faculty members were in attendance, including Will Strunk, Jr., originator of the classic *Elements of Style,* who read a bombastic poem he had written in honor of Frye.

The hoax would have ended there but, unknown to the plotters, another of the faculty members present, Charles "Bull" Durham, the head of the classics department, had tipped off *New York World* reporter Frank Sullivan, who hid in the lobby of Willard Straight Hall, where the dinner was held.

"We noted that Prof. Durham had to go to the john frequently," said Horn. "He was slipping the word to the *New York World* reporter."

The *World's* front page story, tweaking the politicians involved, was read on the floor of the Senate by Senator Pat Harrison, a Democrat from Mississippi.

American lawmakers must be better able to withstand ridicule than the French. No one felt inclined to resign his seat of power. Rather, the senators had a hearty laugh, even Curtis, who "rubbing his hand over a grinning face, finally joined in the outburst as he rapped for order."

But the *Sun's* Cornell overlords were a bit more Gallic in their reaction to ridicule. Even though the politicians took the joke well, and even though several professors were among those in attendance at the Frye dinner, Cornell president Livingston Farrand prodded Horn and Blumner to write grovelling telegrams of apology to all concerned, just to be safe. Which they did, firing off copies of the following: "We regret that what was intended as a campus prank should have been given such wide publicity. We intended no disrespect to you, your office, or the Republican party, and sincerely apologize for any annoyance we may have caused. We appreciate your good sportsmanship."

The Hearst newspapers offered $500 to the pair for the originals of the letters, but preferring graduation to quick cash, Horn and Blumner decided to destroy them instead of inciting further publicity.

"We had a burning session in the living room fireplace of Martin Sampson," said Horn. "We read the letters to all present, then consigned them to the flames."

A level of difficulty above presenting yourself as something you are not is to present someone else as something they are not, then stand back and watch the developments. This was done with delightful effect to a social club early this century at Yale University.

Like most collegians, then and now, Yale students at the turn of the last century liked to drink and have a good time. In fact, students at Yale had a special reputation for living the high life. "I would sooner send my son to hell," a minister's wife said at the time, "than send him to Yale."

In 1901, a group of eight party-happy friends got together, secured four rooms at Fayerweather Hall—three for study and sleeping and the fourth as a sort of clubhouse—and dubbed themselves the "Jolly Eight."

A fellow student, a junior not in the Jolly Eight but feeling "a real or fanciful grievance" against one of its members, sat down on February 20, 1902 and typed out a letter to hatchet-wielding saloon-busting, temperance crusader Carry A. Nation, describing the club as a "party of Yale men who have banded together to promote the cause of total abstinence," calling itself the Jolly Eight "to show that men may lead consistent and yet cheerful lives." He asked for words of counsel and encouragement from Nation.

''THE BHOYS AT YALE''

*T*he Jolly Eight were just one of the countless informal drinking clubs that sprang up at colleges at the end of the 19th century. Another Yale club that distinguished itself through its letter writing was the Kipling Club, formed in 1896 for the benefit of all those "who thirst for Kipling or tippling." The club's president, Gouverneur Morris, Jr., hit upon the idea of inviting their namesake to the club's first annual banquet, and dashed off an inquiry to Rudyard Kipling. The master declined with a poem, still famous in New Haven:

Attind ye lasses av Swate Parnasses
An' wipe my burnin' tears away
For I'm declinin' a chanst av dinin'
Wid the bhoys at Yale on the foorteenth May.

A short time later, the group received a letter and several autographed photographs of Nation, shown standing with an open Bible in one hand and an upraised hatchet in the other. The author of the letter was found out and confronted. He confessed his guilt, the Jolly Eight let him off with stern threats. It was assumed the prank had run its course.

They had seriously underestimated Nation, who was capitalizing on her career breaking apart saloons by lecturing on the carnival circuit and even at burlesque houses, taking donations and hawking her little souvenir hatchets. Her zeal had made her something of a national joke.

On September 29, 1902, the letter-writing Yalie, whose name has been shielded from posterity, was walking on the campus when a fellow student ran up and informed him that Carry Nation was waiting to see him in the rooms of the Jolly Eight. He assumed that the club was getting its revenge for his letter—"It was preposterous," explained an eyewitness narrative of the event, published in 1931 in the *Yale Daily News*. "Carry Nation had only occasionally been even read of, demolishing some saloon in distant states." But his smugness dissolved into terror when he discovered the somber Nation seated in the center of the Jolly Eight's Fayerweather suite.

Nation, who was not known for her savvy, suspected nothing. She had spoken several times on campus, years before, and soon was lecturing a hasty gathering of the Jolly Eight and their guests on the vices of drinking and smoking, not to mention short skirts and foreign foods. Her audience was respectful, though many had to bite their lips to force back a smile.

"Occasionally, a man would as decorously as possible bolt out of the room to explode in laughter in the entry and then return, composed," the *Daily News* said.

Those in attendance reported that Nation's smiling face clouded into an angry frown when she noticed a well-filled pipe rack hanging over the fireplace. But some quick-thinking "Eight" explained that the pipes were trophies given up by smokers persuaded to abandon the vice by their organization.

"It was a reply worthy of a degree in itself," noted the history, and Nation bought it.

Nation then announced she would speak from the steps of Osborn Hall at 5 P.M. In the meantime, she went to visit friends in New Haven and to harangue a dean for serving champagne sauce at Yale commons.

If it may seem odd that Nation was not informed by *someone* that her host on campus was a drinking club, remember that Nation was known for her attacks on saloons. The driving force behind keeping her deluded was a general desire to get her out of town before she could turn on Yale's beloved tap houses.

"The deception must be continued, for should Mrs. Nation learn the truth a hatchet crusade would be inevitable and would probably be directed upon Mory's where near-innocent tobies of ale attended upon surpassing rarebits and English mutton chops," reasoned the narrative. "The newspapers, always eager to distort with sensationalism any unfortunate meeting of Yale men, would revel in the story of such an attack, and to the unknowing, make Yale appear to be an inebriate's asylum."

At 5 P.M., Nation mounted the steps of Osborn Hall, a grandiose structure with soaring archways. She was robustly cheered, and members of the glee club, scattered throughout the audience, led the crowd in singing "Good Mornin' Carry."

It was a wild, stormy encounter, with Nation trying to deliver her temperance message amidst the constant interruption of cheers and increasingly double-entendre songs from the crowd (such as "Down with King Alcohol," which pleased Nation, until the part of the drinking melody where the singers make the down-the-hatch gesture).

Finally, after about an hour, during which Nation managed to have some respectful silence by brandishing her Bible aloft, the songs grew more blatantly inebriate, the catcalls more unabashed, and she beat a hasty retreat.

The prank would have just been an amusing episode had it ended there. But it didn't. Invigorated by the day's events, eight students—it is unclear whether these were the Jolly Eight, or another group from the *Yale Record*—grabbed a camera and flash apparatus and headed for Nation's room at the New Haven House.

Waiting until Nation had finished selling her little hatchets (with DEATH TO RUM emblazoned on the handles) to a crowd in the hall, the men interviewed Nation about her views on prohibition and requested she pose for a photograph.

In 1902, taking a photograph after nightfall was a complicated process. It involved extinguishing all the lights, exposing a photographic plate in darkness, igniting flash powder, then covering the plate before turning the lights back on.

Nation was handed a glass of water. It was explained to her that she would be photographed toasting to temperance with life's essential liquid. The eight students took their places around her. One held another glass of water, to toast with, but the others were empty-handed.

Empty-handed, that is, until the lights went out. In the momentary darkness, the Yalie to Nation's right produced a large beer stein, and the others reached for concealed props and arranged themselves around the temperance leader in a tableau the *Daily News* compared to a "Bacchanalian orgy."

"The Vices of Colleges, Especially Yale"

There were actually two photos taken. In the first, Nation is standing, wearing a dark travelling cloak and headpiece. As soon as the lights went out, the students quickly produced a beer bottle, cigarettes, pipes, and a noose, which was held over the unsuspecting Nation's head. The props were put away, the lights came up, and they prepared for a second photo. This time they moved to her bed—the only seat in the room—and took the time to compose a better shot.

The photographer, Harry Arnold, '00, a graduate enrolled in the medical school, made the exposures, posing in the pictures and tripping the shutter with a string. The props were hidden, and the lights turned back on. Later Arnold doctored the second photograph to add a cigarette in Nation's hand and a foamy head on the beer stein. It looks as if Nation has just blown a trio of perfect smoke rings, to the delight of her drinking buddies.

This second picture makes for a classic prank photograph.

"I've been to all the principal Universities of the United States . . .
also Yale, the latter being the worst I have ever seen."

Nation, in pristine white, surrounded by the dark-suited imbibers
with their high starched collars and pomaded hair. Notice the
expression of unrestrained glee on the face of the prankster just
to Nation's left.

To rub in the insult, the real *Yale Record* published the photo
on October 1, 1902, adding the caption: " 'I have always taken
mine straight,' she said, laughing."

One can't help but wonder if Nation ever caught on to how
much she had been ridiculed during her day at Yale. It appears
likely she did. In her 1908 autobiography, Nation displays herself
as a woman quite aware that she was taken for a fool in New
Haven. Her chapter on college life is titled "The Vices of Colleges, Especially Yale" and begins "I have been to all the principal Universities of the United States . . . also Yale, the latter being

the worst I have ever seen." She then spends the bulk of the section teeing off on Yale, in splendid sentences such as: "The distillers and brewers dominate the republican party and they are the controlling party at Yale and will desolate and enslave our darling boys."

Nation's brush with the Jolly Eight, while souring her on the charms of New Haven, did nothing to damage her captivating naïveté. In documenting the excesses of Yale, she includes two anonymous letters received, on the same day, after her visit. Both complain bitterly of the practice of using intoxicating liquors in sauces at Yale dining halls:

"Yale is supposed to be a Christian College, but to give these poisons by consent of the college authorities is nothing more or less than starting them on the road to hell!" reads the first letter.

"I feel it is my duty to inform you that even after your soul-stirring address of warning and reproof, the Devil still grins at Yale Dining Hall," reads the second. "Assist us, Mrs. Nation; aid us; pray for us . . . Let the world know that Yale is being made a training school for Drunkards."

While Nation accepted these letters as whole cloth, it is difficult not to look at them as perhaps less than sincere, especially when remembering that it was a joke letter that brought Nation to Yale in the first place.

As gullible as Nation may have been, she was not the ripest dupe ever skewered by collegians. That honor must rest with a buffoonish, possibly unbalanced political candidate, Andrew Townsend Heisey, who in early November 1904 stumbled upon the campus of Drake University in his quixotic quest for the Iowa governorship.

A score of law students at Cole Hall, recognizing the humor value of encouraging Heisey, immediately formed themselves into a campaign committee. Promising a sure path to the state house, they carried Heisey on their shoulders to the 10 o'clock chapel, where they presented him to Dean Haggard of the Bible College, who was conducting the service.

Haggard greeted the candidate, and tried to seat him with the deans. But students called loudly for a speech, and Heisey obliged them, endlessly. Most of the faculty slipped away during the speech, and Heisey was still going on when Haggard dismissed the students, some of whom appropriated one of Dean

Cole's wagons and, placing Heisey in the seat, bore him to the Capitol.

The wagon, pulled by the boisterous students, went up the Capitol steps, into the center of the rotunda, and to the office of Albert G. Cummins, the governor, who departed "with all possible dignity before the invading army and left his rival temporarily in charge," according to an eyewitness. Having kept their promise and installed Heisey in the governor's chair, the students slipped away.

While Cornell, Yale, and Drake can assault such Humpty Dumptyesque targets as the Republicans, Carry Nation or Andrew Townsend Heisey, it takes the utter smugness of a Harvard to level its sights on the most cherished American emblems. In the 1930s, the *Harvard Lampoon* had a brilliant string of pranks involving important and beloved icons, beginning with what is perhaps their most notorious prank of all—theft of the Sacred Cod of the State of Massachusetts.

The Sacred Cod is a large wooden fish that normally hangs above the Massachusetts State Legislature's center public gallery and serves as some sort of funky piscine god of the marriage between commerce and government. Those outside of Massachusetts might have difficulty understanding the importance Bay Staters attach to the 4 foot, 11½ inch piece of painted wood. Think of it as a fish-shaped version of the Liberty Bell.

There was a bit of a smokescreen thrown up the morning of the theft, Wednesday, April 26, 1933. About 9 A.M. a group of *Lampoon* editors burst into the *Crimson* offices and kidnapped J.M. Boyd, '35, driving him to Wellesley Hills. The kidnapping achieved its goal—occupying the attention of the often tattletale staff of the *Crimson*.

While the *Crimson* newsmen were focused on the welfare of their purloined coworker, a trio of *Lampoon* writers entered the State House public gallery late in the afternoon. One, who police later labeled the "curly-headed youth," carried a huge flower box of lilies. Easter was just over, and no one paid much attention to the students.

As soon as the legislature adjourned and the observers left, the students snipped the Cod from its wires, stashed it in the florist's box, and fled.

The theft was discovered that evening. It was big, front page

April 26, 1933: Loyal Crimson staffers storm the Lampoon Castle hoping to rescue their leader, foolishly falling for their enemy's ploy and thereby dooming a wooden fish.

news—the Cod had hung in Massachusetts legislative halls since 1799, and had not been touched by human hands since it was moved to the new State House in 1895. The multideck screamer in the next day's *Boston Herald* is a classic of 1930s tabloid cliché, beginning SACRED COD OF STATE STOLEN, and including, among its 11 headline tiers, OFFICIALS MYSTIFIED, CALL IN STATE POLICE and THOROUGH SEARCH OF BUILDING AND GROUNDS—POWERFUL SEARCHLIGHTS USED.

The newspapers fanned the flames with poorly written, over-wrought prose. The *Post* gushed the following sentence in one hot breath:

> The cold finger of fear and amazement that touched the hearts of those five guards [who discovered the theft] was quickly changed to pulses that raced and before five minutes were up the State House contained more excitement per square foot than at

any time since its walls were raised block upon block of good old
New England Workmanship.

Guards and State House workers remembered that four young
men, one carrying a flower box, had been to the gallery late in the
day. Two wore white saddle sport shoes "of the type that are
presently in vogue in the vicinity of Harvard" and one appeared
drunk. Suspicion immediately fell to the *Lampoon.*

All day Thursday the search intensified. Every flower store in
the Cambridge area was visited by police. The state police were
brought in to help (BAY STATE TROOPERS IN GRIM HUNT FOR COD
bellowed one headline). The Charles River basin was dragged.
The *Crimson* accused the *Lampoon* of the theft and promised a
complete exposé on the crime. The *Lampoon* denied it took the
Cod, but congratulated whoever was responsible. Police examined photos of the *Lampoon* editorial staff.

Rumors flew, and were believed. At a hint that the Cod would
be left at the Beacon Street home of former Governor Alvan T.
Fuller, a squad of police, with newspaper reporters in close pursuit, raced to the scene. All was quiet. Someone called the
mayor's office and said the Cod would be returned, wrapped in
the city flag that was to be stolen from in front of City Hall. The
newspapers printed a photo of the flag. Tipped off that the Cod
could be found in the basement of a building at MIT, police
rushed there, tore open a large oblong box, and found a sardine.

Meeting for the first time in over a century without their
aquatic chum, state representatives poured over lawbooks, "seeking all possible court action against the culprits."

There is some indication the *Lampoon* intended to fly the Cod
out of Boston Friday evening, but this might have been a ruse to
cover its real return. Anyway, two *Lampoon* men were cut off at
the airport by four *Crimson* reporters and two autos filled with
reporters from metropolitan newspapers. They sped away in a
roadster just as the state police, called in by the city newsmen,
arrived, and the two cars passed each other at the airport gate.

The Cod was returned late Friday night. Charles R. Apted,
superintendent of Harvard Yard, received a phone call telling
him that if he parked his car on the West Roxbury parkway, then
followed a roadster without license plates that would pass him by,
he would be given the Cod.

The roadster appeared. Apted followed it for 20 minutes, until the car abruptly stopped. Two men jumped out, thrust the Cod into Apted's hands, then jumped back in their car and sped away.

Of course, by the time this measured handoff got into the papers, it had become a "wild chase." Recovering the Cod made Apted's career, and he was soon promoted to head of Harvard security.

The moment the Cod was in state possession, the matter melted away. Talk of finding the culprits and prosecuting them was dropped. State House carpenters made three new fins, to replace the ones that had been damaged in transit and the Cod was rehung—six inches higher than before.

Three years later, the *Lampoon* scored another coup, hitting more than just a cherished icon, but the very definition of respect and authority—the Supreme Court of the United States.

The incident began before sunrise on May 7, 1936, when a trio of juniors, Donald B. Armstrong, Jr., James C. Stone, Jr., and John G. Underhill, Jr., eluded Court guards and, sometime before 4:20 A.M., hoisted the bright-red flag of the Soviet Union up one of the 80-foot flagpoles in front of the Court's Greek-collonaded edifice.

The flag was noticed by a passing streetcar motorman. He phoned police, who gathered and tried to stare the flag down. Quickly realizing that just looking up at the flag was getting them nowhere, as was tugging on the knotted and cut ropes leading to the banner, the police called in the fire department.

Phone calls had already been placed to the newspapers, presumably by the guilty parties themselves. Representatives from half-a-dozen newspapers and wire services watched the frenzied efforts to get the flag down. Officials feared the flag would still be there when Court opened, forcing the justices to ascend the steps of law under the flapping red banner of godless communism.

But even the fire department's tallest extension ladder fell 20 feet short of the scarlet emblem at the top of the pole. Police, firemen, Supreme Court guards, and bemused passersby debated what should be done.

Finally a fireman, borrowing a blowtorch from a worker repairing the street nearby, attached the torch to the end of a pole, and used the device to burn the flag away.

Police collected bits of the charred flag as they fluttered to the ground, for evidence, and dusted the flagpole for fingerprints, acts that were unnecessary, if not idiotic, considering that a copy of the *Lampoon*'s new *Saturday Evening Post* parody was found resting on the base of the flagpole. Inside, an article entitled "Down With Capitalism" was heavily marked in blue pencil.

At least the police were more savvy than Representative Thomas L. Blanton (D-Texas) who rushed to the rostrum of the House of Representatives "suspecting that the flag might mean the signal for social revolution," according to the *New York Herald Tribune.*

"Visibly agitated, he described the outrage at some length and blamed communist plotters for it," the *Herald* continued. "Stern measures, he declared, were required."

It is worth noting that the *Herald* and most other newspapers of the day cast their stories of the flag raising in an approving tone, gently ridiculing people like Blanton, who didn't get the joke. Even the stoical *New York Times* was tinged with admiration.

"The flag-raising was conducted with considerable skill," the *Times* said. "Supreme Court attachés concluded that the raiser had familiarized himself with the movements of the guard . . . and also the mechanism for raising and lowering the national emblems ordinarily streaming from the pole in question."

Still, federal officials complained to Harvard, which announced it would consider disciplinary action, then let the matter drop. The diligent Associated Press tracked down *Lampoon* treasurer Woods McCahill in Cambridge. He admitted, as if it were necessary, that *Lampoon* editors were behind the prank.

"It was only in a spirit of fun," McCahill explained. "There was nothing malicious in it. Certainly we have no disrespect for the Supreme Court. That is one thing we are behind."

But despite its prowess, Harvard can't lay claim to pulling the most controversial political prank of the prank-laden 1930s. That honor has to go to Princeton which, in March 1936, offered up to the world "the Veterans of Future Wars."

The VFW was organized as a put-down of the Bonus Bill (thousands of World War I veterans, caught in the grip of the Depression, were demanding their pensions). Reasoning that

---

RAW!

No moment of historical extremity is so serious that collegians can't have some fun with it. On the night of April 5, 1917, after a long vigil, word came into the *Harvard Crimson's* editorial offices that the House of Representatives had voted to declare war on Germany. The young journalists, responding to the biggest story of their careers, set up a dramatic two-column, three-inch headline of the single word: WAR. But levity could not be suppressed, as a 1923 *Crimson* history notes, and "serious as the occasion was, it was impossible to resist the temptation to run off a few copies with the letters transposed to read RAW, for private distribution to the President and the Managing Editor."

---

they would certainly someday be sacrificed in a future war, they argued that it was only natural, when prematurely doling out pension money, that the future vet be remembered as well. The most deserving, the group noted, would be killed or severely wounded in the pending war, and thus would not enjoy the full benefit of their country's gratitude unless it was bestowed before the fact.

Coming from an enclave of privilege such as Princeton, the Future Veterans perhaps can be seen as a mean-spirited effort, which may explain why it was quickly embraced by more than 50 campuses across the country. Many professors joined the organization, and women's colleges formed Gold Star Mothers of Veterans of Future Wars, demanding to be sent to France at government expense (as actual Gold Star Mothers had been) to see the future graves of their as-yet-unconceived sons. The City College of New York formed Foreign Correspondents of Future Wars, to "establish training courses for members of the association in the writing of atrocity stories and garbled war dispatches for patriotic purposes."

Before long, the Veterans of Future Wars had over 6,000 members, drawing the livid, sputtering rage of real veterans' organizations, particularly incensed at the lampoon of Gold Star Mothers, whose sacrifice in what was still being referred to as the "recent world war" made them objects of deep veneration.

The future veterans, fumed James E. Van Zandt, national commander of the Veterans of Foreign Wars, "are too yellow to go to war. Therefore they'll never be veterans of a future war."

It was inevitable that some boob should rise in Congress and condemn the matter, and that role was snapped up by a Representative Fuller of Arkansas.

"Shame to citizens who would ridicule these real patriotic mothers who were granted the privilege by an American Congress to visit the graves of their beloved sons buried in the poppy fields of France," he said. "Such organizations are unworthy of public notice and should be denounced by every true American." He added that the group was a "disgrace" and carried the threat of communism.

A rally at Princeton drew 1,000 people, who gave the Future Veterans salute, described as "right arm held out, palm up, expectant."

The effort continued through April and May, culminating in a convention in New York City in June. But by October, its treasury empty and its message overshadowed by the presidential campaign, the Princeton headquarters revoked the charters of the 500 posts scattered throughout the United States.

Inspired by the hubbub created at Princeton, other colleges over the next few years launched their own movements, from Reed College's campaign to make Wallis Simpson the Queen of England to a Roosevelt For King Club at Yale. None, however, caught the national interest in the way the Future Veterans did.

Despite the great success of the Future Veterans, the most consistent source of political prankery in the years that followed was still Harvard, particularly the *Lampoon*. Not all of their pranks, however, were on the Olympic scale of the Cod and the Court. A small, yet pleasing *Lampoon* prank was pulled on Mayor James Curley of Boston. Approaching the mayor in 1949 as the "Boston College for Curley Club," the *Lampoon* held a brief ceremony and presented him with the *Crimson*'s punch bowl. It held a place of honor in his office for a day, until the *Crimson* came and asked for it back.

Rallies have been a specialty in recent decades, such as the fall 1971 "Thieu for President" gathering in the Yard to show support for Nguyen Van Thieu, the South Vietnamese leader who was running unopposed in that country's theoretically democratic elections. The rally was complete with a baby elephant and supporters wearing coolie hats and carrying signs that read THIEU'S THE ONE—THE ONLY ONE and IN YOUR HUT YOU KNOW HE'S RIGHT.

In keeping with its deep yearnings toward sovereignty, the *Lampoon* has, over the years, taken to declaring itself either an independent city, state, or country, usually in reaction to larger events on the world stage. A rally or demonstration typically accompanies the pronouncement.

The first time was in October 1938. The Cambridge city council, in that sort of bruised-ego meanness that afflicts college towns, floated a plan to sever Harvard from Cambridge, as a way to avoid providing the university with public services.

Following Cambridge's lead, on October 20, nine *Lampoon* members marched out of Harvard Yard and demanded their own "City of Lampoon" to secede from the de-annexed Harvard University. (In an attempt to tie their move in with the recent

---

FUN WITH RAGING LUNATICS

On February 21, 1987, the guest on the odious "Morton Downey, Jr. Show" was Christopher Coon, a member of the notorious North American Man-Boy Love Association and student at Harvard. It was a typically acrimonious show, with members of the audience shrieking insults and death threats at Coon, who cooly defended the tenets of NAMBLA to a clearly horrified Downey. It was all a hoax. Coon was a false name assumed by an engineering junior at MIT and an aspiring actor, who had wanted to test his dramatic abilities and, at the same time, prove his hypothesis that it was easy for anybody to go on those talk shows and claim anything. 🐄

de-annexation of the Sudetenland from Czechoslovakia, the nine dressed as storm troopers, certainly not a memory that Elliot Richardson, future Nixon attorney general and one of the nine brownshirts, liked to trot out at his Harvard reunions).

The students were met at the Harvard Gate by city council member Michael Sullivan, where a shoving match ensued after Sullivan grabbed for the "City of Lampoon" banner one of the freshmen was carrying.

In 1949, the "State of Lampoon" was declared, delineated by Linden, Bow, and Mount Auburn streets, the roads surrounding the *Lampoon*'s castle. The minute-by-minute independence program followed a theme common to such *Lampoon* announcements. It began at 2 P.M., offered "refreshments" at 2:01, "buffet" at 2:03, "*vin d'honneur*" at 2:05, "ale" at 2:07, and "free beer" throughout.

The most ambitious liberation was announced December 22, 1975, when "the Free Nation-State of Lampoon" was declared at a press conference at the United Nations Plaza, replete with a belly dancer and open bar. The move quickly received the endorsement of retiring US representative to the UN, Daniel Patrick Moynihan. "Go right ahead," he wrote. "We need all the votes we can get."

Surprisingly, the newspapers gave the effort a modicum of serious attention. LAMPOON TO QUIT U.S. read one headline.

The *Lampoon* struggle for independence continued into 1976, melding into the publicity for the magazine's centennial. For a while the *Lampoon* castle was surrounded with sandbags, klieg lights, and chicken wire, and nearby residents complained of the loud drumbeats and sounds of barking dogs blaring from loudspeakers.

The centennial celebration itself was a wild, sodden affair of massive extravagance, reflecting the great influx of capital brought about by licensing the "Lampoon" name to the successful *National Lampoon*, begun in 1970.

The *Lampoon*'s flush state led to a deft centennial honor that was among the most subtle of college pranks. Certainly it was the most expensive. The magazine named noted economist John Kenneth Galbraith as "Harvard's Funniest Professor in 100 Years" and gave him an award of $10,000 and a purple-and-gold

Cadillac convertible with a custom-built Ibis hood ornament (the Ibis, a sort of Egyptian stork, is the magazine's mascot). Galbraith, critiquer of the culture of conspicuous consumption and himself a wealthy man, got into the spirit of the honor, delivering a wry acceptance speech at the February 8 banquet. He later gave the money to the Fogg Museum, but kept the car, calling it a representation of "incredible vulgarity and decadence."

Esteemed economist John Kenneth Galbraith demonstrates how to pick up girls—the Harvard way.

GREAT MOMENTS IN APOCRYPHA

H. Allen Smith tells the wonderful story of Horace Norton, founder of Norton College, visiting president Ulysses S. Grant in Washington. As a token, Grant bestowed on Norton one of his trademark cigars. Norton did not smoke the cigar, but kept it as a memento of the visit, passing the stogie on to his son, Winstead Norton. At a Norton College reunion in Chicago in 1932, Norton displayed the cigar, made a short speech lauding Grant, then lit the cigar up. It exploded.

Or so Smith says. There are several problems with the story. First, it comes from H. Allen Smith, master of the "a man in a large midwestern college once did something . . ." school of reportage. Second, a fairly exhaustive search turns up no evidence of either Horace or Winstead Norton (actually, there are several Horace Nortons sprinkled through U.S. history, but none of them founded a college). Third, there is no record of a Norton reunion being held in Chicago in 1932 and, to top it off, there is no trace of a Norton College.

On the odd chance that there still is a Norton College out there, somewhere, or that somebody knows about this tale and can fill me in, please direct your attention to the address at the end of the book.

4

TECHNOPRANKS
The Great Breast of Knowledge

All Tech men carry batteries for emergencies.
—MIT student arrested
at Harvard Stadium, 1948.

*H*arvard has a history of great pranks, but their archive doesn't keep a file on them. Amherst students have practiced a prank cult around a naked statue for more than a century. Yet the school's administration doesn't want any part of it.

And Brandeis doesn't have any pranks and wouldn't tell us if they did.

In fact, only two schools in the nation really recognize their students' pranks as having value, in and of themselves, as episodes to take pride in and treasure. Not coincidentally, both of these schools—the California Institute of Technology and the Massachusetts Institute of Technology—are science schools. (Their English and history departments will howl. But so what? No matter how good the food is served aboard airplanes, they never become restaurants. Caltech and MIT are science schools.)

The clear-sightedness of Caltech and MIT in regards to

pranks should not be a surprise. Valuing pranks is in keeping with the nature of science. The great scientists have been, by and large, a group of nonconformists and oddballs, anemic dreamers sitting at the back of the room, gazing into the distance and mulling thoughts soon to outdate the very pieties their classmates are at that moment chanting.

A new scientific idea and a good prank require the same creative spark, the same formulation of a hypothesis and the same courage to carry it to its conclusion.

One can just see some bleary-eyed MIT student, exhausted from hours spent memorizing periodic tables and titrating urine, looking up at the 148-foot Great Dome, the same one he has been gazing at for years, and suddenly thinking: "You know . . . that would look so much better . . . as a giant . . . tit."

It may not be Archimedes in the bathtub, or Crick and the double helix, but it's something.

If Caltech and MIT were separated by a short bridge, or even in adjoining states, they no doubt would have become fierce rivals in their quest for science, knowledge, and good pranks. Three thousand miles is very far, however, even in this age of Skyfones, and the two schools just do not interact much.

They did lock wits once in what was called the Great Transcontinental Electric Car Race. At noon, August 26, 1968, after several technical delays at both schools, student-built electric cars set off from their respective schools, at the same moment, bound for their rival's campus. Two hundred and ten hours later, Caltech's modified two-tone 1958 VW bus, having stopped to recharge more than 50 times, roared into Cambridge. A half hour later, MIT's modified white 1968 Corvair arrived in Pasadena.

Score one for Caltech.

Almost 20 years later, the schools met again, in the decidedly-less cerebral "Beaver Cup"—so-called because both schools have the same bridge-building mascot—a meeting between MIT's experienced ice hockey team and a band of Caltech amateurs. Despite some pregame bluster by the Californians (their press release referred to MIT as "the Caltech of the East") they were slaughtered by the MIT squad, 11–3. The press expected the game to be fraught with pranks, considering the reputations of the two schools, but the only prank was a disappointing one—someone spray painted "UCLA Bruins" on the ice before the game. The *L.A. Times* said the prank was "considered extremely lame" and noted that the Zamboni scraped it away in a single pass.

Score one for MIT.

In the absence of significant activity against each other, it is fitting to compare the schools' pranks, individually. Which school is the more creative? Which student body has shown itself best able to hypothesize a prank, then do the research and expend the lab hours necessary to prove their prank in the harsh beaker of reality?

MIT had a head start. It was founded in 1861, and traces its first pranks to the 1870s. John Ripley Freeman, a civil engineer who graduated MIT in 1876, recalls in his memoirs "episodes when iodine of nitrogen [a mild contact explosive] was sprinklered on the drill room floor just before the assembly."

Caltech is newer and smaller. Founded in 1891 as the Throop Institute, it has just 800 undergraduates, less than a fifth of MIT's

---

MIT TALE # 1

*I*n the early 1940s, MIT students perfected the rare prank of celebrity kidnappings, where they would swoop down upon stars on their way to entertain at Harvard parties and, pretending to be Harvard students, escort them to MIT functions. In April 1940, they nabbed Eddie Anderson—"Rochester" on "The Jack Benny Show"—and took him to a smoker at an MIT frat. A year later, the same fate awaited stripper Sally Rand (who was also honored with the designation "Associate Professor of Entertainment Engineering") and Yvette, the French singer. All were eventually delivered to their Harvard appointments.

horde of 4,400. The early Throop pranks (the Caltech name dates to 1920), it must be said, were of a strictly plebian nature— relocating a suite of dorm room furniture in a courtyard, moving a cement mixer to a student's room, where a load of cement was mixed and allowed to harden so it had to be jackhammered out of the drum, assembling a Model T inside a dorm room (though the Model T was rigged to be working and at full throttle when the student came home).

One of the earliest recorded "scientific" pranks at Caltech was a noble failure. J.B. Stevens, '40, recalled a weekend when women from Clark Hall at nearby Scripps College of Claremont agreed to spend the night after a dance at Caltech's Fleming House— provided the men of Fleming House found somewhere else to sleep. The men agreed but, as junior radio buffs (at the time, most young scientists were) they realized they could bug their rooms by rigging up the speakers of their radios to act as microphones.

Radios in several rooms were wired to a central amplifier, and the reception where the Techmen were bunking out was great— the Fleming boys, waiting to hear their dates' steamy midnight confessions, could pick up ticking clocks and traffic going by on California Street.

But, as is so often the case, they had underestimated the

CALTECH TALE # 1

*C*altech students are known for their affinity for disrupting traffic. In 1964, a team of Tech students acquired a quantity of flashing traffic barricades, which they used to divert cars off Colorado Blvd., down a long expanse of Michigan Avenue, through the Caltech parking lot by Beckman Auditorium, then north on Chester Avenue and back to Colorado. Motorists placidly wormed through the "net" the students had created, until a police squad found itself diverted through the Beckman parking lot and ended the fun.

women. The most they heard were phrases like: "What's wrong with this radio, it doesn't work" followed by a click, or "Hey, there is something funny going on here. I heard they were going to wire these rooms" followed by yet another click.

Both have had their share of notorious pranks. Caltech's famous Rose Bowl Hoax was detailed in chapter three. MIT has an almost equally-famous sports prank to its credit—inflation of a giant weather baloon, which burst through the turf in the middle of the 1982 Harvard–Yale match.

The Yale eleven pull the old inflate-the-weather-balloon-and-distract-the-opposition play.

The prank required a good bit of skill. The black weather balloon, along with a complex inflation device, was housed in a plastic tube and had to be smuggled into Harvard Stadium (which MIT claims is heavily guarded. Harvardites, perhaps trying to pooh-pooh the prank, claim that it was an easy thing to saunter in anytime and plant a mechanical device under the sod).

Either way, the balloon exploded from the 46-yard line in a puff of talcum powder (used to lubricate the pipe) and inflated to full size. Written all over it were numerous MITs.

It was not the only prank to dog the game. Between halftime shows, the MIT marching band, which had snuck in disguised as the Yale band, ran onto the field and formed the letters "MIT" with their bodies. They also handed out 1,134 cards to a block of Harvard fans and told them that, when flipped, they would spell BEAT YALE. The cards, of course, spelled MIT.

Afterward, MIT's president used a bit of clout to get the balloon device back, sending the following plea to Harvard president Derek Bok:

Dear Derek:

Word has come to me that your campus police are holding some property which rightfully should be located in the MIT museum. Can this be true? Surely you have little use for a makeshift device constructed from vacuum cleaner parts, points from a 1967 Mustang and a handful of marbles. We, however, being the sentimental sort, would take great care of—indeed, we would enshrine—this symbolic highlight of the 1982 football season. Please give it back.

Sincerely yours,

Paul E. Gray

Harvard returned the device, and MIT, true to its word, put it on display. MIT took great pride in the prank. "I had several of the boys [who did the prank] in my class," beamed an MIT professor, a decade later. "If they needed a few points to go from a B to an A, or a C to a B, they got 'em."

OTHER COOL PRESIDENTS

*W*hile Caltech and MIT presidents are known for going to bat for their student pranksters, they are not alone. Over the years, other college presidents have shown surprising good humor when pranksters were on the hot seat. A few examples:

1. After Cornell students rioted at the Lyceum Theater in February 1911, disrupting a performance of *Three Weeks* by throwing coins, potatoes, and eggs at the stage, several were arrested and sent to jail for a week. Cornell's President White sent one of the unfortunate students, Ralph Perkins, '14, a copy of the Victor Hugo classic of misapplied justice, *Les Misérables*, along with a note consoling him that the week of solitude should provide a welcome respite to reread the book.

2. In all honesty, the junior class at the University of Pittsburgh deserved to be suspended in the spring of 1898, what with fixing Professor Herman Schmitz's record book to an iron bar and sinking it in the Allegheny River, then smearing glue on the walls of his classroom and scattering turkey feathers. They were given the boot, and told not to come back until they paid a $15 fine. The other three classes walked in sympathy.

Dr. Holland, the president, had been away during all this chaos. He returned at the apex of the crisis; called the classes into the chapel, where he also gathered the entire faculty. A prayer was offered. Dr. Holland turned to the dean and said "What's all this about?" The dean explained.

"How much did you say that fine is, Dean?" Holland is recorded to have asked, fishing a roll of money out of his pocket. He peeled off $15, handed it to the dean, then turned to the boys and said: "Now, gentlemen, go back to your classes, and let us hear no more about this."

In gratitude, the class slogan of 1898 became: "Holland, he pays the freight!"

3. Despite a general clenching of the collective jaw in recent times, some college presidents still manage to cling to their senses of humor. In May, 1991 a group calling it self RAISE—

Replace All Institutional Symbols with Elvis—kidnapped the American flag from atop Willis Hall at Carleton College in Minnesota and replaced it with a large Elvis flag. They then delivered a ransom note decrying "a general lack of sensitivity toward Elvis on campus" and demanding "the leader of our community perform an Elvis impersonation."

At a College Council meeting that week, Carleton president Stephen R. Lewis, Jr., performed a heartfelt rendition of "You Ain't Nothin' but a Hound Dog." The flag was returned.

Just as the Great Rose Bowl Hoax must be weighed in light of a similar prank by the University of Southern California four years earlier, so MIT's masterful Harvard–Yale prank came hard on the heels of some well-publicized Caltech failures. In the first wee hours of 1980, four Caltech students were arrested trying to plant a balloon-inflation device at the Rose Bowl. The next year, Bowl officials discovered an elaborate helium-hydraulic gizmo that would have sent a balloon trailing a Caltech banner bursting out of the path the teams take from their dressing rooms.

MIT may have taken inspiration from these West Coast attempts. But on the other hand, *theirs* worked.

But we are getting ahead of ourselves. Before the details of MIT's and Caltech's pranks can be examined, the greater question of exactly what is a technoprank must be addressed.

Pranks involving scientific knowledge (such as MIT's iodine of nitrogen or Shelley's galvanic-battery-to-the-doorknob) could be considered technopranks. But then Cornell's infamous Chlorine Banquet involved a similar fascination with chemistry, and dragging stuff atop MIT's dome is no more an engineering feat than dragging stuff atop the University of Virginia's dome or any of the scores of other buildings decorated, nationwide.

Intent has a lot to do with it. Activities that otherwise would be considered merely stupid are elevated to the level of "science" by the application of vigorous analytic technique. If I crawl around the forest, picking up frogs and peering at their butts, I'm a lunatic. But if I record how many spots are on the butts and try to derive some sort of meaning from it, I'm a scientist.

This is not to say that a prank becomes a technoprank merely because it is done by science students. Rather, in doing a particular prank, science students, by their very nature, tend to skew an otherwise ordinary prank into the realm of science.

Take the standard hazing task of measuring a large expanse in a ridiculous fashion—the old rolling an egg across the quad with your nose routine. Now normally, such a stunt would fall into the category of frat sadomasochism and thus more of interest to anthropologists than to readers of this book.

But measurement is an important scientific characteristic. When the old measuring haze is put into the hands of budding scientists it becomes more interesting and noteworthy. Both schools have several good measurement stories.

At Caltech, in 1937, a group of pledges at Throop Hall were assigned the task of measuring the distance from Throop to the Pasadena City Hall in mackerels.

Now, any bunch of freshmen could grab a bucket of fish and start applying mackerel to pavement. But being scientists, at least aspiring ones, the Techmen used a certain procedure. According to Frank Casserly, '41, they did library research and determined there are perhaps 16 species of mackerel. Armed with rulers, they headed to the waterfront and made a number of measurements of the different types of mackerel available. Finally, they developed a Gaussian distribution of mackerel lengths to determine the modal length of an average mackerel.

Selecting six mackerel of exactly average length, the group set out for City Hall one Saturday morning in October 1937. They selected a point precisely under the center of the Throop dome, and began laying down fish. The Pasadena cops, bemused by this Herculean task, held traffic while the students mackereled their way across the street and toward City Hall.

A formal technical report of the experiment was drawn up for inspection by the Throop hierarchy. Sadly, it has been lost. But the distance between Pasadena City Hall and Throop Hall has been preserved—5,678 standard mackerel units, measured along pedestrian routes.

While the mackerel has gone the way of the rood or the cubit as a popular form of measurement, a similar case at MIT has resulted in a somewhat better-known unit: the Smoot.

The Smoot grew out of the torment MIT students feel cross-

M I T   T A L E   # 2

*T*he 199 seats in lecture room 2-190 are bolted to the floor with two bolts under each armrest and connected together in long rows. One morning in November 1982, students came to class to find someone had unbolted the seats and turned them around, so all 199 now faced toward the back of the room.

---

ing the Harvard Bridge over the Charles River during cold weather. In the mist and sleet it isn't always possible to see the other side and, with your head down against the wind, the walk can seem endless.

In the fall of 1958, the pledge masters at MIT's Lambda Chi Alpha house, dreading the approaching freeze, charged their pledges with remedying the bridge situation. They gave them the task of marking off the bridge so that a person crossing could know how far it was to the other side without looking up. The unit of measurement selected by the frat elders was the body length of one of the pledges. That role, and immortality of a sort, fell to the shortest member of the pledge class, Oliver Reed Smoot, Jr.

One October night, Smoot, several fellow pledges and an upperclass overseer, armed themselves with white paint and headed for the bridge. There they laid Smoot end over end, painting a Smoot mark at every 5'7 interval delineated by Smoot's body. The Harvard Bridge is long, and by the end they were picking up Smoot and moving him along.

The bridge measured precisely 364.4 Smoots, plus one ear.

Here is where the important role of routine maintenance in the formation of history can be observed in action. The Smoot would have gone the route of the mackerel, no doubt, as a forgotten unit of measurement, had the Lambda Chis not seen fit—with the regularity of monks performing a holy rite—to maintain the Smoot marks, repainting them twice a year as the decades rolled by.

In the beginning, the Lambda Chis had to dodge police to paint the Smoots, but eventually the police came to embrace the markings, too, using them to indicate location when filling out reports on traffic accidents taking place on the bridge.

So when it became time to renovate the decaying Harvard Bridge in 1989, the Smoot marks were still fresh, and too much of a cherished Cambridge tradition to be allowed to slip into obscurity. There was some talk of re-Smooting the new bridge with a New Smoot—Stephen R. Smoot, the son of Oliver, who happened to be an MIT junior at the time of the bridge repair.

But the 5'11 younger Smoot would throw off the calibration of the bridge and, more important, change the tradition. After enduring considerable public outcry, the Metropolitan District Commission, the government agency responsible for the bridge, decided to transfer the Smoot markings to the new bridge.

"We don't normally encourage writing on public property," said an MDC spokeswoman. "But the Smoots have become part of the legend of the bridge and local college lore, and they're so popular with the public at large that we thought they should be preserved."

Yet another instance of using scientific method to enhance an otherwise average prank was MIT's calculation of the Bruno. Students at any school with buildings taller than two stories can be expected to occasionally throw things off roofs—cigarette machines, cinder blocks, bed frames, dressers—anything that will make a satisfying crash on impact.

At MIT this practice led to a new unit of measure—the Bruno—defined as the volume of a dent in an asphalt street, in cubic centimeters, caused by an upright piano being hurled from the top of six-story Baker Hall.

Like many famous experiments, the one defining the Bruno was the result of serendipity. Baker Hall had a worn-out piano that needed to be disposed of, and a student whose first name was Bruno suggested the initial experiment. It was conducted on October 24, 1972, filmed by high-speed movie cameras and recorded with audio equipment. Close data analysis by the MIT students revealed the piano to be travelling at 43 miles per hour at point of impact, resulting in a Bruno reading of 1158 cubic centimeters.

CALTECH TALE # 2

$\mathcal{F}$reshman Tony C. was returning from glee club practice to his Page House dorm in October 1962. He happened upon a group of upperclassmen pushing a bed down the corridor. Tony asked them what was going on, and they said they were playing a prank on a freshman who lived down the hall. "What a fantastic idea," Tony said, and he volunteered to help. They dragged the bed to the Beckman Auditorium, which at that time was under construction, and used a block and tackle to hoist the bed—steel frame, box spring, mattress, sheets, blankets, and pillows—to the roof of the structure, 40 feet off the ground. Working into the evening, they reassembled the bed on a tiny platform on the center of the scaffolding on the roof. Tony delighted in the prank, taking great care to neatly make up the bed and gently fluff the pillows. It was dark by the time they returned to Page. The rest of the pranksters bid a hearty good night to Tony, who walked into his room, turned on the light, and discovered that his bed was gone.

The experiment was performed at least six more times—every year an old piano was available—until 1984, when new construction eliminated the alley alongside Baker Hall.

In terms of excellence in scientific measurement, MIT's Smoot and Bruno have to be considered more significant than Caltech's mackerel. But measurement is only one of many criteria.

For instance, there is publication. Scientists know that all the ground-breaking research in the world doesn't mean a thing unless it is gotten into print, so one's colleagues can steal the data and base their own work upon it.

Caltech is the winner here, at least in the sense of being first. Ten years ago, in the early eighties, they collected their pranks into a smart little 80-page booklet called *Legends of Caltech,* published by the university alumni office.

Highlights of the Baker Hall Piano Recital through the years.

Filled with photographs and detailed descriptions of famous Caltech pranks, *Legends* was followed up a few years later by a companion publication, *More Legends of Caltech*.

No other university has anything matching the brio and verve of this handy pair of volumes. "We salute those Techers who have unintentionally become legendary by their acts of ingenuity and humor, both spontaneous and planned, using the technology of their time to solve an injustice, bring fame to Caltech, or simply relieve boredom," the second volume trumpets in its forward. "We acknowledge with thanks a *very* patient Caltech administration that time and again displayed remarkable restraint as it bailed out of jail, alibied to an enraged public, and then forgave many of these legend-makers."

Compared to the mean-spirited denial, grudging nod, or halting, baffled shrug that most universities grant their pranks, the Caltech attitude is revolutionary, and they back it up with painstaking, microscopic examinations of their famous pranks, complete with maps, diagrams, and first-person testimony, whenever possible.

MIT weighed in late, but mightily, in the publications department with *The Journal of the Institute for Hacks, Tom-Foolery & Pranks*. Published in 1990, it is a beautiful volume that documents the history of MIT pranks—mostly through photographs. The title itself is a joke: "Institute for Hacks, Tom-Foolery & Pranks" shares the acronym for "I hate this fucking place," apparently a common MIT undergraduate sentiment.

As a guide to MIT's pranks, however, the book is hampered somewhat by its big-picture format and lack of the first-person accounts that makes Caltech's volumes so helpful.

The book—a publication of the MIT Museum—leaves little question of MIT's official position on the subject, however, as evidenced by this statement by President Gray:

"The spirit of MIT, its inventiveness and thoroughness, finds expression in the lighthearted project as well as the scholarly. Humor at MIT might be considered an anomaly by some, but is, in fact, the warp of the fabric of this unique community."

Caltech has to win in the publications department, but both schools' prank books are important because they allow an overview of the type of prank each prefers. The bulk of MIT pranks—with noteworthy exceptions—involve decoration. Funny signs and banners, placing things atop buildings, marking up stuff like the bridge.

Caltech's pranks are more poetic and offbeat. Avoiding traditions, the standard Caltech prank is one involving some uniquely perverse application of technology. The approach has given Caltech more "great" pranks, but also blessed them with minor pranks of simplicity and beauty.

Here are two examples, at the same time typical and outstanding.

The first made use of a small electrical device and an astute observation about a mathematics professor, Tom Apostol, who perhaps had fallen into a rut in his presentation.

Bob Durst, '74, the perpetrator, describes the setup of the prank in *Legends:*

> In the spring of 1972, Dr. Apostol, the Math 2c lecturer, had the material very well memorized and rehearsed. He was lecturing straight from the text he had written and had been using for a number of years. He almost always used the alloted 50 minutes for class. He also did not wear a watch, but relied on the clock in the back of the lecture hall to pace himself.

Durst and his coconspirator, Fred Sigworth, '74, decided to test Apostol's "mechanical approach to teaching" using a device that altered an electrical line's normal 60 Hz frequency, effectively speeding up or slowing down any electrical appliance—in this case a clock—attached to it.

Sneaking into lecture hall before class, Durst plugged the clock into the frequency changer and jacked it up 10 percent. Spurred by the racing clock, Apostol hurried through the last part of his lecture, and was forced to finish without quite covering it all.

After rushing Apostol through several more lectures, Durst increased the speed of the clock by 12.5 percent. The speed, plus a problem adjusting the clock, led Apostol to conduct a particularly brief lecture, dismissing the puzzled class long before the period was over.

Durst lay low for a while, then reintroduced the device, speeding up the clock 10 percent. Apostol also sped up by 10 percent, and was able to finish most of his material though he was "obviously flustered."

For a final test, Durst decided to really challenge his professor, and jacked the device up 15 percent:

> With about 30 minutes (by the clock) left to go in the period he noticed that he was once again behind and noticeably sped up. With 15 minutes remaining (by the clock) he realized that, in spite of having sped up, he was still falling behind. With real determination to complete all of the planned material he sped up even more. With five minutes left to go and maybe ten minutes of material remaining he let out all the stops, and in a very atypical manner began being sloppy. He started writing down the side of the blackboard instead of starting a new line, and talking so fast that we couldn't understand what he was saying. He may have finished all of the material, but we couldn't tell. He dismissed class and left. People with watches were left scratching their heads wondering why he had hurried so much at the end of class when there was plenty of time left. Those of us who knew what was going on realized that he had been pushed beyond his limit.

Apostol says he had no idea of what was going on at the time, and only learned of the prank when Caltech published its first *Legends* booklet. He has since purchased a wristwatch.

The second Caltech gem involves a freshman's introduction to the security system at the local Ralph's supermarket. In the fall of 1986, Dwight Berg, '90, became interested in how the store's antishoplifting system worked. A helpful cashier pointed out the security decals which, upon inspection, Berg realized were a form of antenna that affected the radio signal emitted from the posts flanking the exit doors.

Intrigued, Berg wondered whether the stickers would trigger alarms at other stores. To test this hypothesis, he peeled off a security sticker from Ralph's, and stuck it on the back of the blood donor card in the wallet of his friend, Earl Taylor.

Soon, Taylor was exiting stores holding his wallet over his

M I T   T A L E   # 3

*I*t makes sense that in such an atmosphere of brilliant pranking, sometimes the professors themselves will catch the bug. Dr. Kenneth Russell, professor of metallurgy and nuclear engineering at MIT, uses a neat ploy to drive home the fact that chemical reactions can take place in a solid (and, in his own way, encourage honesty among MIT freshmen).

While delivering "innocuous patter" about some benign aspect of metal casting, Dr. Russell distributes small zinc-aluminum medallions, purportedly as an example of the casting method. He asks that they be passed around, then returned to the front of the room. The medallions have some image on them—the school seal, a smiley face, something—and inevitably, when they are passed back up, one or two are missing.

"In a class of 300, I know darn well somebody's going to pocket it," says Russell. "A freshman will put anything in his pocket."

Then all Dr. Russell has to do is wait until time and the student's body heat sets off a "phase transformation" in the medallion, shooting its temperature into the discomfort zone.

"Somebody gives out a yelp and tries to jerk the thing out of his pocket, and I get to the point of the demonstration," said Dr. Russell, who calls the prank an old "metallurgist's trick."

---

head—he had decided his automatic teller card must be setting off store alarms.

Ready to take the gag further, Berg snuck into Taylor's room and sewed security stickers into a pair of Taylor's Levis and a pair of green khaki shorts.

But Taylor transferred to another school before he entered any stores in his "shoplifting pants" and Berg, frustrated, sought other victims. A gregarious freshman, Tod Schamberger, '91, unknowingly presented himself as a prime victim. Berg arranged it so that he handled Schamberger's ID card at preregistration, affixing two different security stickers to the back of the card before it was laminated.

Here Berg found success. At a trip to Pasadena Plaza, a nearby mall, Schamberger was stopped at every store after setting off security alarms both on his way in and on his way out. Sadly, Berg's interest in security alarms had become public by then, and Schamberger, complaining of his ruined shopping day, was soon directed back to Berg, who he put in a "hearty choke hold."

Not to slight MIT, whose fondness for tradition shouldn't be considered a criticism. Unlike Caltech, its campus is distinguished by a single outstanding architectural landmark—the Great Dome atop the Barker Engineering Library. The dome is 148 feet tall, and it is natural that MIT students over the years would express their engineering skill by hoisting unusual objects up to the dome, and draping the dome in a variety of disguises.

Boo!

MIT also has a second, smaller dome that gets its share of adornment.

The earliest dome festoonery was a nine-foot tall cardboard candle, and a banner reading HAPPY BIRTHDAY, marking the MIT centennial in 1961. The next year, the dome was transformed into a giant pumpkin for Halloween—students not only affixed a grinning jack-o'-lantern face, but placed red-and-yellow gels over the floodlamps to create an orange glow.

Exactly a decade later, Halloween was marked again—this time by a technically clever "Kilroy was here" face constructed out of 6,000 square feet of black plastic draped over MIT's smaller dome. Dubbed "George", the face lasted only a few hours before MIT grounds keepers removed it, prompting complaints from the students. "What harm would there have been to let poor George exist for one full day?" asked a letter to *The Tech*. A week later, George was back. Chastened, the school let him stay up for a full day.

By the end of the seventies, dome decorating was a Halloween tradition. A giant screw—the unofficial MIT mascot—dominated the dome for Halloween 1977.

Perhaps in an unconscious comment on the level of sexual activity at MIT, a group living in the Burton One dorm in 1979 was struck by the similarity between the Great Dome and a breast. Determined to enhance this resemblance, they constructed a giant pink nipple and aureole to scale. Bad luck and bad timing thwarted their first three attempts to haul the nipple atop the dome, but on the fourth try, using a special collapsible nipple that could be carried in backpacks, the group found success, dubbing their work the Great Breast of Knowledge with the banner MAMMA MAXIMA SCIENTIAE.

Later that year, the dome was topped by a fiberglass cow borrowed from the nearby Hilltop Steak House (to mark their mascot's journey and celebrate her safe return, Hilltop's management placed a mortarboard on her head and a diploma in her mouth. The cow returned to MIT several years later to appear in an exhibit by the MIT Museum dedicated to pranks and humor at the school).

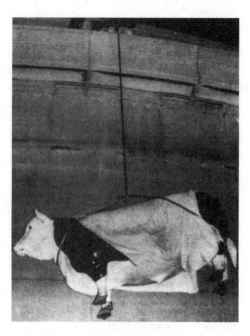

Future guardians of American technological prowess hoist big plastic cow to top of dome.

One of the more daring and technically sophisticated dome toppings was an antique wooden phone booth—stolen, naturally, from outside the president's office. The intrepid pranksters rigged it so the lights and telephone both worked. Campus security officers, puzzling what to do about the booth, were even more surprised when the phone began ringing.

An officer radioing headquarters led to the following exchange, perhaps a little too pat to be true.

"The phone's ringing; what should I do?" the policeman asked.

"Well, why don't you answer it?" was the reply.

A prefabricated house graced the dome in September 1986. The house was complete with a mailbox and welcome mat, but without a roof, since campus security interrupted the students before that finishing touch could be put in place.

CALTECH TALE # 3

$\mathcal{P}$asadena residents are understandably frightened of the technical interlopers in their midst, and Caltech students occasionally take advantage of that fear by staging mock disasters of one sort or another. John South, '60, had been experimenting creating colored smoke with titanium tetrachloride when he struck upon the idea of pouring a line of it across California Avenue near Caltech's fabled synchrotron. South and some friends dressed in white lab coats and, waving impressive 260 volt-ohmmeters, stopped traffic, telling drivers the synchrotron beam "had gone wild" and was eating up the street. For about half an hour, until the titanium tetrachloride stopped smoking, no one would drive across the line. 🐄

Without the constant challenge of a dome, Caltechers must cast their gaze farther afield to find targets for their pranks. This led to another truly great Caltech prank, certainly at the level of the Great Rose Bowl Hoax—the alteration of the famous HOLLYWOOD sign.

The venerable HOLLYWOOD sign had long been an object of interest to Caltech students. In May 1987, with the Hollywood centennial approaching, students from Page House thought they would tap into the festivities by changing the sign to say something more appropriate. Something more cerebral. Something such as CALTECH.

This was no small task. Each of the 9 letters in the sign is 5 stories tall and 33 feet across. They are also surrounded by razor-sharp concertina wire, and patrolled by the park service.

The Page House team was in the process of precisely measuring the letters when they chanced upon a coincidence that can only happen at Caltech. Another dorm, Ricketts House, was independently planning the same prank. The two houses joined forces and conducted a nighttime reconnaissance of the sign.

Once the letters had been closely measured, the group figured it would need 1000 square yards of burlap, at a cost of some $600, to do the appropriate masking.

The question of how to raise the money was addressed in a typically brazen way. The students formed a group, calling themselves the Prank Club, and secured initial funding of $200 from the Caltech student government association.

Problems with delivery of the burlap caused the Prank Club to switch to plastic, which was cheaper and easier to handle anyway. Giant templates were constructed to alter the letters (the "H" in the sign was completely blacked out, for instance, and the middle section of the right half of the first "O" was masked, turning it into the "C" in "CALTECH").

At 1 A.M., May 18, a team of 35 Caltech students, carrying plastic sheeting, nylon ropes, duct tape, and climbing equipment, made the 25-minute hike from the roadway up to the sign.

By 3:45 A.M., the plastic sections had been hoisted into place and unfurled, and the long process of firmly securing them to resist the strong California winds began. The students finished the job by 5 A.M., and descended the mountain, relieved that the police they had been expecting to show up at any moment had failed to arrive.

Come morning, and with the inevitable calls to the media, reporters and TV crews swarmed to the campus and to the altered sign. One TV report featured a pair of German tourists asking how old the CALTECH sign was and trying to get directions to the HOLLYWOOD sign.

Another great Caltech prank, this one in the mid-1970s, resulted in more negative publicity for the school than any other Caltech prank. It also had more impact on everyday life than the average prank, occupying the attention of Southern California for a number of days and, to some degree, changing the way contests are held across the country—next time you squint at the block of small type that accompanies most promotions and giveaways, thank the creators of this highly-controversial episode, known at Caltech as "The McDonald's Affair."

It was 1975, a bleak period for life in America, with unemployment and inflation and all manner of banality raging in the land.

Confused starlets rush to audition for parts in "The Union Carbide Story."

McDonald's of Southern California, wishing to ease the burden of its loyal, burger-gobbling customers, announced a sweepstakes, "A Year of Groceries and a Datsun Z," giving away $50,000 worth of foreign cars, groceries and, of course, lots of McDonald's gift certificates. All patrons had to do was fill out an entry form, or a facsimile of an entry form. "Enter as often as you wish," the rules chirped.

That sentence—"Enter as often as you wish"—infected the minds of three Page House seniors—Steve Klein, Dave Novikoff, and Barry Megdal. How many times in life are you given the opportunity to do anything "as often as you wish"? It was a chance they could not let slip away. Even though it was the beginning of finals week, they decided to take up the gauntlet.

The trio decided they wished to enter the contest a million times.

They enlisted 26 Page House students to loan their names as contestants, and had a friend, Glenn Hightower, write a computer program to create contest entries. The program he designed, called ARCHES, simply instructed the computer to print out roughly 40,000 entries for each of the 26 students.

Off and on for three days, the program was run on Caltech's IBM System 370 mainframe computer. It generated 140,000 pages of computer paper, and cost the students $320.

They raced to the Occidental print shop, where the boxes of paper were sliced into 1.2 million coupons, each measuring 3 × 5 inches, as stated in the rules.

The entries were divided among 8 groups, who visited 98 different McDonald's in Southern California, delivering cardboard boxes, each jammed with tens of thousands of slips of paper.

The press was tipped off, but this time the publicity brought not praise, but carping protest. Computers were not the drab household appliance they are today, and Caltech's use of a mainframe to stuff the ballot boxes (Caltech's entries constituted one-third of all the entries in the entire contest) touched a populist, anti-intellectual nerve, well-developed in those who spend their lives entering sweepstakes.

"If that is the height of your intellectual scheming you have succeeded in arousing nothing but contempt for craftiness—certainly nowhere near admiration," read a typical letter to the *Los Angeles Times*.

The situation was not helped by Page House conspirator Steve Klein who, asked by the press what they planned to do with the winnings, responded: "Parties. Lots of parties."

Meanwhile, Burger King, showing a certain institutional flair, donated $3,000 to Caltech for establishing the "John Denker Memorial Scholarship," named for one of the Page House conspirators. It also publicized a "John Denker Memorial Offer," promising free french fries or onion rings to anyone bringing in a computer card.

There was no flair in McDonaldland, however. In a state of McAgony over the complaints from outraged hamburger consumers who were not about to let their sense of justice and order in life be shattered by a bunch of pampered college boys, McDonald's announced on April 11 that even though "the students acted in complete contradiction to the American standards of fairplay and sportsmanship," they would honor their entries to avoid "a drawn-out legal contest."

However, McDonald's said, to prevent any whiff of unfairness to the great burger-absorbing lay public, it would award a duplicate prize among the non-Caltech entrants for each prize won by a Caltech student. It would cost them more money, McDonald's pointed out, but that's the sort of open and generous people they are.

The drawing was held on April 23. Caltech won 300 5-dollar McDonald's gift certificates, a Datsun 710 station wagon, and a check for $3,000. In an effort to dispel their image as partyhound technofiends abusing the public, Page House decided to immediately donate the station wagon to the United Way. The check was used to pay back-taxes at Page House, minus the $320 computer expenses.

All this back and forth comparison of Caltech and MIT doesn't really answer the question of which school has the better pranks. Perhaps, like pi, it is something that can be calculated, but never arrived at, probably because what it really boils down to is a matter of taste.

MIT's pranks are on the more traditional side; Caltech's more free-form.

Even the campuses vary wildly. Caltech is a warm Biblical garden. MIT, chillier and Bostonian, is right next to Harvard, for good and ill.

Caltech has Bob's Big Boy and direct highway access to Fatburger. MIT is right next to the New England Confectionary Company, and MIT students doubtlessly benefit by being forced to ponder how such an immense, looming factory, billowing clouds of caramelized sugar vapor, can be dedicated to the creation of as quaintly marginal a product as Necco wafers.

Caltech students display a sunny affection for their school. MIT students are given to self-deprecation, if not self-loathing.

For pranks to work, you need both license and tradition, both the clubby and the weird. Just as MIT is a little too regimented for its own good (its pranksters even belong to a group, the Technology Hackers Association) Caltech sometimes threatens to blow apart at the seams into some state of Californian blissophication.

So rather than raising the gloved hand of either Caltech or MIT, the pranks in this chapter point out the important dynamic tension between rigidity and disorder necessary for good pranks.

Without tradition—the single-file line of honorees, resplendent in their gowns and floppy hats, putting one foot in front and then the other—there is no need for pranks. Remember the Middle Ages. Tradition provides the framework that makes lifting of the academic robes to flash a healthy, mind-clearing expanse of ass so splendid an experience.

But too much tradition and there is nobody of a mind to commit pranks. The creepy, "Twilight Zone" feeling that certain religious colleges put off, with their clean-cut, cookie-cut Brads and Lindas in their loafers and their blue Oxford shirts, comes not from the religion, itself, but from the utter lack of that spice of opposition, that dissenting grace note of prankery.

MITIGATING HUSKY
GLORY—PART II

*A*nother place to search for the sort of pranking gusto found at MIT and Caltech is, oddly enough, in Canada, where several schools carry on the European tradition of engineering students viewing themselves as deranged agents of merry chaos.

At the University of Toronto, the engineers have their own shadow organization, the Brute Force Committee, and its initials can be found near acts of engineering mayhem, the best of which in recent years was a massive ceremonial arch, six feet tall and utilizing four tons of concrete, constructed in the middle of King's College Circle, a major thoroughfare.

The University of British Columbia engineers are famous for their pranks, a yearly tradition during winter engineering week. Some of their pranks are wonderfully subtle, such as wiring the lights on the Lions Gate Bridge to blink "UBC Engineers" in Morse code. They once changed the the the chimes of the UBC clock to sound out the engineers' theme song. The engineers have a ritual involving the shell of a red Volkswagen beetle, which is deposited at some challenging spot around Vancouver, such as atop the 15-story Buchanan Tower, at the summit of a downtown clock tower, or suspended under a bridge (in a tour de force, one year the bug was suspended *between* the Granville and Burrand bridges). In 1992, it was floated on empty beer kegs to the middle of Stanley Park's Lost Lagoon, and the fountain—which had been activated for the occasion—was redirected so it shot out the car's sunroof.

Like their brother scientists down the coast, the UBC engineers have developed a fascination with the Rose Bowl. On February 3, 1992, they slipped over the border and, smashing a glass case, liberated the Rose Bowl trophy from the University of Washington (the same school, you may recall, which suffered at the hands of Caltech in 1961. You have to almost feel sorry for them at this point).

The trophy hadn't been in Canada for a day, however, before the Royal Canadian Mounted Police, acting on a tip,

came to reclaim it. The engineers paid $450 for the dam-
aged display case, wrote a letter of apology, and had to
defend their actions to a campus that frowned on such unso-
phistication.

"Most people admire a well-executed stunt," the campus
newspaper lectured. "But this year's smash and grab just makes
us wonder whether the engineers of tomorrow have as much to
offer society as they like to think."

A similar sort of creepiness is felt from the touchy-feely, no
walls, no grades, call-me-Professor-Steve colleges where there is
no need for pranks because everything is OK and there are no
traditions to tweak.

So the ideal college has enough discipline and tradition to
make the hunt worthwhile, but not so much that you'll end up in
the stockade for chewing gum on the sabbath.

5

STATUARY PRANKS

Giving the Commies the Bird

It is deplorable that they've carried college jokes
into the arena of international relations.
—John Updike
April 1953

$\mathcal{U}$niversities, like most small places with unelected forms of government, are simply chock-a-block with statues. Honoring themselves; honoring generous alumni; honoring quaint Victorian virtues such as "forthrightness." Honoring almost anything at all. Statues and monuments add to the ivy-strewn, tradition-bound, changeless atmosphere cultivated—apparently without irony—by organizations that otherwise claim to be outposts on the cutting edge of progressive thought.

Tweaking these symbols of tradition make for some of the most common, yet most complex and satisfying, college pranks.

Take the case of Vanishing Joe Medill. On an average day, the bust of school founder and Civil War newspaper baron Medill could be seen on a pedestal at the center of a compass formed by yellowed, worn tiles in the lobby of Fisk Hall. There, Joe would keep watch over the ugly, decaying four-story brick building that houses his namesake school of journalism at Northwestern University, just north of Chicago.

Most students surging past on their way to class hardly noticed Joe, with his neatly cropped beard and face set in the grim fury that at one time passed for dignity. But a few did notice, and had pity on him. They thought Joe, like themselves, would perk up if only he could get away from the airless chambers of Fisk. Away from the clunking, outdated Royal manual typewriters and the solemn, droning professors who still mourned the passing of hot-lead typography and the *New York Herald Tribune.*

Thus Joe Medill would be periodically dragged out of Fisk, over to swarming student hives such as the seven-story Northwestern Apartments. There, dandied up in a purple Wildcat baseball cap or a handful of colorful leis, he presided over frenzied beer parties, freed at last from all those fusty memories of Mary Todd Lincoln and Free Silver.

It didn't take a lot of equipment to steal Joe—maybe a few burly guys and a shopping cart ripped off from the local supermarket.

Nor did it take a particularly great amount of planning. Nobody guarded the guy. Fisk Hall was largely abandoned after 4 o'clock. Just walk in and take him, keeping an eye out for the occasional security guard blundering by to stock up on Moon Pies out of the food machines in the basement.

Borrowing Joe—and the scores of similar statues regularly snatched across the country—is a way to turn the university's symbolism against itself. Students would prefer, ideally, to drag the entire university, en masse, away from its schedules and fees and tired curricula, pinch its nose, pour a few beers down its throat, and force it out on the dance floor.

But since that is not possible, a surrogate has to do.

Wherever they are, pranksters take the same two-pronged approach to ridiculing university statues. If, like Joe Medill, monuments are light enough to move, students steal them and take them to some more, ah, *appropriate* setting. If not, then the monuments must be defiled where they are.

While stealing is definitely the prank of choice, creativity can be applied to decorating a big immobile statue. John Harvard, trapped in his chair in Harvard Square, routinely suffers a range of interesting humiliations, from being painted a Dartmouth green or a Yale blue to having metal rats welded to his neck.

We've seen the revenge Wellesley students have taken on John—dressing him in a cap and gown and jamming a hoop over his shoulders. MIT students have also done their share. In May 1979, they epoxied a custom-made, jumbo-sized bronze 1980 MIT class ring on the statue's finger. Another time, MIT editorialized on Harvard's poor shape by slapping plaster casts on John's head, leg, and neck.

THE STATUE OF THE THREE LIES

The John Harvard statue is referred to by Cambridge wags as "The Statue of the Three Lies." First, the legend "Founded in 1638" is plain wrong. Harvard was founded in 1636. Second, the statue identifies Harvard as the "Founder," which of course he was not. ("Funder" would be more like it). And third, the person depicted in the statue is not John Harvard, but a friend of the sculptor, Daniel Chester French, a graduate of MIT (in that light, perhaps the work should be called "The Statue of the Three Pranks").

Of course, a statue can be mocked without the obvious routes of a paintbrush or derisory trappings. One of the many water fountains the Women's Christian Temperance Union donated to colleges at the turn of the century (no doubt under the impression that students drank liquor because they lacked convenient access to tap water) was given to Cornell University. It featured the statue of a young girl labelled "Purity." A standard freshman task of the time assigned by upperclassmen was to climb the statue and plant a big kiss on Purity's virginal lips.

Some statues are both stolen *and* defiled where they stand, such as the Oz-like head of Russell Conwell, founder of Temple University in Philadelphia. Conwell is usually planted, along with a companion head of his wife Sarah, in the "Founders Garden" on the Philadelphia campus.

The head is such a massive bronze globe, it's easy to see why most students blanch at the thought of trying to cart it away. They satisfy themselves with painting the nose an appropriately clownish shade of pink, purple, or blue.

But some students, upset enough over the offensive, Orwellian cast of this giant, hovering head, muster the manpower to drag it over to the cemetery, or the athletic fields, or in front of its namesake, Conwell Hall.

Huge hovering head intimidates Temple students.

Ridicule is not always the goal. About 50 years ago at Cornell, someone painted a trail of footprints to suggest that the statues of Ezra Cornell and Andrew D. White had hopped off their pedestals, engaged in a midnight conference, then returned. The footprints have been preserved, more out of whimsy than anything else.

Even better than stealing your own university's statue, is to steal someone else's—as was the case in perhaps the earliest statue-napping on record.

In 1865, President Oren Cheney of the then-budding Bates College in Lewiston, Maine had a bust of himself that he reportedly "idolized." Hoping to inject a bit of humility into the situation, members of Phi Chi, a secret society "formed with a purpose of violating college rules" at nearby Bowdoin College, infiltrated the Bates campus and located the building where the bust was displayed.

"By cutting out a pane of glass, an entrance was effected and . . . the bust, carefully wrapped to keep it from injury, was on its way to the carriage," an anonymous conspirator in the prank reminisced 35 years later.

The bust was prominently displayed at the Phi Chi rooms, known as "Sodom" for their moral tone, where it became a target of ridicule. Meanwhile, Cheney took great pains to find his bust. Suspecting his own sophomore class, he threatened to expel them all. He also made tearful inquiries at colleges up and down New England, including Bowdoin. But to no avail.

With the school year drawing to a close, the Phi Chis were becoming uncomfortable at the thought of leaving the bust in their quarters over summer break, where it might be discovered, and nobody wanted to cart the heavy piece of stonework home.

In desperation, they hit upon the idea of shipping the bust, anonymously, to showman P.T. Barnum, who was setting up his second American Museum in New York City after the first one burned down. From here, the unnamed Phi Chi who told the tale in 1901 finishes the story:

It came about a few years later that a son of President Cheney found himself in New York with a little leisure on his hands, and decided to "take in Barnum's." As he strayed, from ward to ward, looking at the various curios and phenomona, behold the lost bust of his father, marked "Sophocles," and claiming to have been made from a death mask of that worthy by an eminent artist, and obtained by the "Great Showman" at a cost of $25,000.

Young Cheney, as you may surmise, lost no time in reporting the discovery to his father, and also in bringing the matter to the attention of Barnum. As the bust was neither a freak nor a fraud, Barnum was willing to part with it, and thus at length the lost found its way back into the possession of its owner.

The veracity of this story is impossible to confirm, but indications are that it is for the most part true. Bates College did have a President Cheney and he did have a son, Horace. Bowdoin did have a notorious group called the Phi Chis, and Barnum had a museum that did burn down and was rebuilt—although not until July of that year, two months after Bowdoin's commencement. Perhaps most telling is an official 1927 school history that treats the episode as fact and apologizes for it, something completely unnecessary if it never occurred.

There must be something about tiny liberal arts colleges conducive to swiping statues, because three of the most consistently-

---

DISPOSING OF THE GOODS

*W*hat to do with a stolen statue is sometimes a problem. When *Lampoon* editors stole the bust of John Keats out of the Houghton Library, they had the presence of mind to leave in its place a decoy—a "large Mr. Potato Head." But they were afraid to hold on to the hot property for long, so they delivered it, wrapped in swaddling clothes, to the doorstep of Walter Jackson Bate, Harvard's Pulitzer Prize–winning Keatsian scholar.

stolen university monuments in the nation are found at welter-
weight Oberlin College in Ohio, petite Amherst College in Massachusetts, and Oregon's microscopic Reed College.

Oberlin is an intriguing case, simply because its monument—a
hulking statue of benefactor Charles Martin Hall—was made so
enticingly portable through a chance union of corporate puffery
and the particular physical qualities of the metal aluminum.

Hall graduated from Oberlin College in 1885. Eight months
later, while still working in an Oberlin lab, he discovered the
electrolytic process for extracting pure aluminum from a solution
of sodium aluminum fluoride. Having thus paved the way for
both zeppelins and cheese sandwiches wrapped in foil, Hall
founded the Pittsburgh Reduction Company, later named Alcoa,
and became a multimillionaire.

Upon his death in 1914, Hall willed the bulk of his fortune, $16
million, to Oberlin, and soon Hall's name was popping up on
plaques and over doorways sprinkled across campus.

But Oberlin apparently did not express its gratitude in a sufficiently pharaonic way because, in 1929, Alcoa commissioned a
statue of Hall to give to Oberlin, as a gentle reminder of who was
buttering its bread, still, from beyond the grave.

To underscore the subtlety of their point, Alcoa had the statue
cast not of the usual bronze, but of Hall's meal ticket, aluminum.

Oberlin placed the life-size, hollow, aluminum statue in a niche
in the foyer of its Severance Chemical Laboratory. The race was
on. For the next 50 years students busied themselves snatching
the easily-transportable Hall, and trying to outdo each other in
finding outlandish places to deposit him.

Chemistry Emeritus Professor Werner Bromund remembered
one commencement morning, sometime in the 1940s, when he
was awakened at 6:30 A.M. and told: "Charlie's gone."

"I thought someone had died," Bromund said, "until the laboratory curator explained that the Hall statue was missing. We
found it on top of the campus Memorial Arch, waiting for the
commencement procession to file through underneath."

In his journeys, Hall has not only been to the summit of the
27-foot arch, but to the top of every other building on campus.
When, in 1953, the college tried to make a dent in the remaining
Hall swag by constructing a Hall Auditorium, Hall was instantly

dragged to the top of *that*. To mark the event, students composed a new, perhaps inevitable, song, "Who Hauled Hall on Top of Hall?"

Chemistry professor Norman Craig remembers when students in the 1950s took Hall, who is portrayed in a sitting position with a book in one hand and a lump of bauxite in the other, and placed him in an outhouse nabbed from the Ohio countryside. The tableaux was set up in the middle of campus, with the door propped open to reveal an aluminum-faced Hall apparently answering nature's call.

Not only did Hall visit spots on campus, but he roamed the countryside like a gypsy, travelling as far as the fortuitously abbreviatable College of Wooster, 45 miles away.

The peripatetic Hall seems as rooted as a tree, however, compared to Sabrina, the elusive nymph of Amherst College. Without doubt the most fought over, most celebrated statue in academe, Sabrina (rolling off Amherst tongues, it rhymes with "Carolina," among other things) is a four-foot tall bronze statue donated to the college in 1857 by Joel Hayden, the lieutenant governor of Massachusetts. Legend has it that the donation came about because Hayden's wife was scandalized by the sprite's nudity, which also may have had something to do with the insane frenzy with which Sabrina was regarded by generations of men at Amherst, an all-male school until 1975.

For her first 20 years at Amherst, Sabrina was just another piece of decorative lawn sculpture, resting on a circular sandstone base on a terrace between Old North College and the Octagon. She was occasionally subject to the standard whitewashing and lewd adornment.

She first was stolen by members of the class of 1877. For a while, it became a tradition to sink Sabrina to the bottom of the school well after Amherst victories. Her status did not really change until the 1880s, however, as students began stealing Sabrina from her perch to make appearances at their class dinners.

Today graduating classes hardly distinguish between each other. But a century ago they dressed differently, spoke differently, obeyed codified rules of conduct, and tended to violently hate one another. College football, remember, got its beginnings not as a sluice for pouring unlimited revenue in university coffers, but as a sanctioned way for the sophomores to beat up incoming freshmen.

By 1890, Sabrina became a trophy in the elaborate, ritualized interclass rivalries that took up so much of college life at the time. As was often the case in such contests, each class did not pit itself against all the others, rather the even-year classes—say freshmen and juniors—were allies, as were the odd classes—say sophomores and seniors.

Those attending college within the past few decades may have difficulty in believing the great lengths that Amherst Odd and Even classes went to steal, hold, and display Sabrina. They hired private detectives and Pinkerton guards, burglarized freight companies and private homes. They sent fake telegrams, rented cars, trucks, and railroad carriages. Parents and families became involved in Pynchonesque conspiracies. Students armed themselves with clubs and firearms, and drove hundreds of miles away from campus. People were shot at, beaten, bound, and held captive. Roads were blocked. A class holding Sabrina, and wishing to taunt the Sabrinaless classes, thought nothing of locking the student body in chapel and disabling all the cars parked outside to thwart any possible pursuit.

A rare 1921 volume of her exploits, *Sabrina, Being a Chronicle of the Life of the Goddess of Amherst College* goes on for more than 150 pages of exacting detail about student efforts over almost half a century to get, or keep, Sabrina.

A few highlights from those early years:

- Ben Hyde, class of 1894, discovered how the Odd classes were shipping Sabrina home from their banquet. Presenting himself at the proper American Express office (at the time, AmEx was a shipping firm), he redirected Sabrina to his home in Boston. Later, the *Chronicle* records, "Hyde had returned to Amherst, where he was confronted with arrest on the charge of forgery by the American Express Company. He lost no time in getting to New York, and with a promptitude which was characteristic of his splendid daring and quick judgment throughout this entire escapade, took a steamer for Europe, and remained abroad for a few months while the disturbance he had kicked up died down."

- Odd classmen, having managed, after great effort, to seize what they thought was the crate containing Sabrina, opened it to find a load of scrap iron.
- In her journeys, Sabrina has resided in warehouses, barns and factories from Maine to New York, and as far from Amherst as West Virginia. She has been buried in fields and submerged in the Connecticut River.
- In 1917, the Odd classmen, frustrated after years of being unable to wrest Sabrina from the Even classes, located a duplicate Sabrina from the original cast in a garden in North Caro-

Companionship-starved Amherst students with their date for the evening.

lina. They stole her, brought her to campus and claimed she was the real Sabrina, hoping to confound the Evens. The ensuing uproar was only settled by a joint committee of the classes of '18 and '19, which set down codified rules of Sabrina theft. The rules said, basically, that the class with Sabrina must display her before the college at least once a year, that Sabrina couldn't be placed into the custody of banks or railway companies, and that burglary charges arising from theft of Sabrina would be null. They also banned the use of firearms in "any Sabrina or non-Sabrina activities."

- After holding Sabrina for 29 years, the Even class got careless, leading to a mad struggle in front of the Hotel Copely Plaza and a famous chase through the streets of Boston. After much reluctance, the Even class had been convinced by an alumni group to loan the nymph for the alumni dinner on March 3, 1920. The dinner was attended by graduates from nearly every year since 1857, and included a speech by alumnus Calvin Coolidge, then governor of Massachusetts.

The *Chronicle* describes the riotous scene of Sabrina's entrance into the hall:

> While President Meiklejohn was paying tribute to the lasting interest of college traditions, the folding doors at the side of the hall suddenly opened and a huge representation of a bottle of Gordon's Gin was brought into the room.
>
> When it had progressed well into the center of the group of Even Class tables, which were placed in a circle around the door, the effigy was torn aside and Sabrina in all her loveliness was revealed to the astonished gaze of the men there present.
>
> The cheering which broke loose, and the conflicting cries of Odd and Even Classes filled the hotel, while frantic scurrying about on the part of Odd Classmen, and the self-congratulatory back-slapping of Even Classmen heightened the excitement.

Unknown to the Evens, however, the Odds had guessed that Sabrina would appear at the gala, and laid an ambush for her. The street outside the hotel was crawling with private detectives and waiting motorcars hired by the Odds. No sooner was Sabrina removed from the celebration for her return to the factory, where she had been stored for several years then the Odds and their hirelings snapped into action.

As the truck bearing Sabrina tried to pull away, it was blocked by an Odd car. The driver of the truck, trying to maneuver around, became stuck in heavy snowdrifts. Odd and Even classmen scrambled and struggled outside the trapped vehicle, and in the confusion the Evens loaded Sabrina into a Ford driven by Odd Class-hired henchmen. With the help of several well-positioned roadblocks, and a private detective posing as a police officer, the Odds were able to shake their pursuers and spirit Sabrina away over the Harvard Bridge into Cambridge.

The back-and-forth battle continued for another 13 years, often involving high-speed car chases. In 1934, the possessors of Sabrina, members of the class of 1935, "concerned for human safety," turned the statue back to the university. She was then locked in the Hitchcock Memorabilia Room of Morgan Hall, where she rested for 15 years, surviving at least two attempts to grab her by students from nearby Williams College, along with a temporary decapitation (her head was recovered and reunited with her body within a few days of its disappearance.)

Sabrina was regained by the students a few hours before commencement in June 1951, in an elaborate heist engineered by more than a dozen members of the class of 1951. By secretly making clay impressions of all the curator's keys, and carefully timing the watchman's rounds, the conspirators were able to create the two keys needed to enter the memorabilia room. There, a student who had travelled to Springfield to learn how to use an acetylene torch cut the metal rods fastening Sabrina to her base. The goddess was spirited away to a temporary perch in Brattleboro, Vermont.

A year later, she made a dramatic appearance—projecting from a small airplane flown over the Amherst–Holy Cross commencement baseball game at Memorial Field on June 7, 1952.

Sabrina disappeared for another three years, until her abductors abruptly returned her to the school in 1955. For over 20 years, she was kept hidden behind a false partition in an administrator's attic. It was her longest period of quiescence since the 1870s. During this time, the university refurbished her, patching the various holes and dents and giving her a new patina of bronze.

As can happen with longstanding pranks, there was an attempt to slather a patina of alumni boosterism over Sabrina as well.

In the mid-1970s, the class of 1952—perhaps shamed by the memory of the class of 1951's theft of Sabrina and subsequent aerial display—requested that the university designate the class of 1952 "the Sabrina class" and agree to display Sabrina if they managed to raise a quarter million dollars for Amherst to mark the class's 25th reunion. The administration accepted the offer, and the class raised $300,508.

Sabrina was trundled out on June 4, 1977, for the alumni weekend, then forced to pose beside a giant check and lots of aging alumni in ridiculous plaid pants and comb-over hairdos. Special Gifts Chairman Gordon Hall declared that Sabrina's days as a theft object were over. She was about to "begin her third job at Amherst . . . as a fund raiser."

The class of '52 revealed it had made provisions so that should any other class top its donation by 10 percent, then that class would become the new "Sabrina class."

Sabrina was placed in a Plexiglas enclosure in Converse Hall where, in the Babbitty dreams of Amherst officialdom, she would serenly draw funds to the college, as alumni groups dug into their pockets for the empty honor of being designated "the Sabrina class."

As usual, the college administration neglected to consider just one factor: the students. On October 13, 1977, three students, their faces masked by nylon stockings, entered Converse shortly after 3 A.M., and bound the night switchboard operator (who was so situated as to be able to monitor Sabrina). They pried off one side of the Plexiglas case and dragged Sabrina out the basement door. Nearby students, awake pulling all-nighters, applauded.

This was no impromptu grab. For two weeks, they had staked out the Converse lobby, to learn the schedule of security checks. A rope was hidden in the hall beforehand, and tools were rented at an obscure rental center in Chicopee Falls.

See how much spooky symbolism you can find in this photo of Sabrina in the clutches of grinning Amherst alumni.

Sabrina must have thought she was back in 1919, for all the activity of the coming month. The statue, pried off its base and loaded into a Volvo station wagon, was driven to the house of a friend of the conspirators in Darien, Connecticut and hidden in the basement.

But in success the trio grew careless. Lauding their accomplishment at a victory lunch that afternoon, the conspirators tipped off another Sabrina-fixated group—the duo of Bill Hunter and Mike Callahan, who had been plotting their own heist of Sabrina.

The two immediately headed to Darien, to the house of Richard Borneman, one of the trio who stole Sabrina the day before.

They "told Rick's mother we were friends of Rick and that Rick was in lots of trouble; he'd been called in on the carpet in the dean's office and we had only about a 20-minute lead on Security. We told her that if Security found the statue it would further implicate Rick and that's why we had to get the statue out of there."

Borneman's mother directed the two to the friend who had Sabrina, where they repeated the story and were ushered into the basement. They found Sabrina and loaded her into a car. Speeding to Westport, they buried the goddess five feet deep in a remote section of Hunter's yard.

But just as the administration lost Sabrina through narrowness of vision, so the students lost her through grandiosity. Hunter and Callahan made plans to fly Sabrina over the Williams–Amherst game November 12, renting a plane and lettering SABRINA on a 30-foot banner to trail from the aircraft.

Amherst security, tipped off that a flyover was in the works, showed some ingenuity of their own. Calling area airports, they found that someone had made arrangements to fly a statue from the airport at Turner Falls.

They set up their own grab.

On the morning of November 12, Hunter and his father dug up Sabrina and drove her to the airport in the trunk of a white sedan—the trunk lid held down with ropes and Sabrina peeking out. While the two went inside the airport to see after the plane, the security men loaded Sabrina into a van and sped away.

This time, the school kept a white-knuckle grip on Sabrina, bringing her out for alumni functions, then returning her to hiding, where she remained until a band of alumni stole her in 1984. Fans at the Williams–Amherst lacrosse game later that year were treated to the sight of Sabrina flying overhead, suspended by a rope from a hovering helicopter.

From there, her path becomes hazy. In the fall of 1990, members of the class of 1991 used radio scanners, beepers, and five walkie-talkies in a chase after Sabrina, but supposedly they were after just a Fiberglas replica. Most recent reports put her in the hands of an alumnus, David Esty, '54, who, like the misguided class of 1952, plans to use it as an incentive for college fund-raising. Good luck, pal.

The school certainly doesn't provide much illumination on the matter. Drawing away from even appearing to remotely approve of "any activity which involves suspending a 350-pound piece of metal over crowded football stands," the college has officially washed its hands of Sabrina.

While perhaps not as hotly contested as Sabrina, the Doyle Owl of Oregon's Reed College is even better travelled—the 300-pound, three-foot tall concrete bird has been seen nearly everywhere: perched on the Eiffel Tower; taking in the sights of New York City; visiting the shark tank at Sea World in San Diego. The Owl even makes a cameo appearance in the video "Sowing in the Seeds of Love" by the rock group Tears for Fears. (But don't blink. The owl appears for about two seconds, peeking from the grass at the right bottom corner of the screen. Look for it just after the hovering couple floats away).

Campus lore has it that the Owl began as a pair of owls—twin lawn sculptures snatched in 1919 from a residence in suburban Eastmoreland and removed to Doyle dormitory on Reed's Southeast Portland campus.

This touched off a series of thefts and counter thefts between various dorms. During a brouhaha, one of the owls was pitched off the Ross Island Bridge and sank, unrecoverable, in deep waters.

Made of concrete, not the most transportable of substances, the remaining Owl eventually broke apart. But such was the desire of the students to have an Owl that pieces of the original were recast into a new Owl and the thefts continued.

The bird had been missing for years when, on May 4, 1975, it appeared chained to a grate at the bottom of the college sports-center swimming pool.

"A riot ensued," the *Portland Oregonian* reported, "as hundreds of students broke into the locked building, clamoring to touch the mystic creature."

A third type of theft, besides stealing your school's statues or stealing some other school's statues, is stealing non-college statues. This slender category includes the theft of beloved icons like the Sacred Cod (chronicled in chapter four, since the Cod's political ramifications overshadowed its mere statueness) and the kidnapping of one of Southern California's most beloved denizens.

In 1958, a group of Caltech students realized that despite their frequent visits to Bob's Big Boy to wolf down late-night cheeseburgers and fries, the coverall-clad burger deity had never returned the favor and visited them. So early one morning they spirited the giant Boy statue from outside the restaurant and trucked it to their dorm, leaving behind a ransom note demanding 10,000 hamburgers.

Big Boy apparatchiks didn't take long to figure out where the Boy had gone, and he was dutifully returned—not, however, before posing for the requisite documentary photograph, lofting his burger in the midst of Caltech's Fleming House courtyard.

While students busily nab the Medills and Sabrinas of their particular schools, taking breaks for extracurricular grabs such as the Cod and the Boy, there is an even rarer form of statue theft—students within a school stealing other students' statues. Most schools just never accumulate such massive quantities of pomp that it filters down to the students and they begin developing statues and regalia of their own.

KIDNAPPING THE PORCELAIN GOD

*O*f course, the icon stolen from a rival campus does not have to be necessarily an object of veneration. In the late 1970s several students at Concordia University in Montreal marked their winter carnival by slipping over to nearby McGill. Posing as plumbers, they presented themselves at the office of Robert E. Bell, McGill's principal (what Canadians call their college presidents) and announced that the toilet needed repairs. They proceeded to unhook the toilet and carry it away. The prosaic, yet intensely-personal ceramic object was displayed on the Concordia campus during the carnival.

Needless to say, Harvard is an exception. At Harvard, students have both the wherewithal and the desire to rival the most tradition-fixated college administration at creating odd rituals and symbols on a nearly Masonic scale.

Consider the *Harvard Lampoon*'s Ibis, a four-foot copper statue of an Egyptian bird which, more often than not, can be found serenely perched on the weirdly stunted Flemish castle occupied by the humor magazine at 44 Bow Street in Cambridge.

Dubious tradition has it that alumnus William Randolph Hearst donated the Ibis in 1909, the year the castle was constructed. It was only a matter of time before the Ibis would fall victim to the intense rivalry between the *Lampoon* and the *Crimson*.

The two publications were natural enemies, with the *Lampoon* continually turning out fake issues of the *Crimson* (the first time being on Memorial Day 1901, when it published a fake *Crimson* containing, among other things, an editorial offering to refund one dollar to each subscriber "from the huge surplus amassed." For more noteworthy fake *Crimson*s, see chapter nine).

The *Crimson* struck back in a variety of ways—through its editorial columns, kidnapping *Lampoon* editors and, later in the century, by nabbing the *Lampoon*'s bird.

The earliest recorded instance of Ibis-stealing took place in 1930. Suspicion first fell to the *Yale Record*, after a copy of the publication was found in the *Lampoon* castle and "reports" were circulated of a car with Connecticut plates seen driving away.

But the *Crimson* was so solicitous of the safety of the bird, sending a telegram to Yale beseeching for information about the "sacred symbol of the *Lampoon*" and offering to pay the expenses of the former police commissioner of New York City to come to Boston to investigate the theft, that soon the *Lampoon* began to suspect culprits a lot closer than New Haven.

The bird was eventually returned, but disappeared again in 1941. The *Lampoon*—which had no questions as to those responsible this time—responded by kidnapping five *Crimson* staff members and holding them in a barn, bound and covered in copies of the *Crimson*.

"The Ibis is worth $150, and those guys aren't worth $20 apiece," said the *Lampoon* president. "They'll get nothing but dried toast and an occasional drink of water until we get it back."

Intimidated, the *Crimson* returned the bird to ransom its writers.

In 1946 the Ibis was stolen again, this time ending up on the stage of the Colonial Theater with Blackstone the magician. But the bird's most amazing journey took place late in April 1953, in an odyssey which was to involve, in order of appearance, two future Pulitzer Prize winners, the Soviet Union, the United Nations, the national press, an infamous senator, and finally, the U.S. State Department.

First, a bit of background. The Ibis had blown down from atop the castle in a storm in 1951 and been unceremoniously dumped in the campus lost and found. It was claimed by *Crimson* editors, who used their news pages to tweak the *Lampoon* by running photographs of the Ibis in various locations—such as the observation deck of the Empire State Building and the dance floor of a New York club—and with various celebrities.

The *Lampoon* got the bird back, only to have it disappear again on April 16, 1953—plucked from the top of the castle by *Crimson* editor David Royce, a.k.a. "the human fly."

The morning the bird vanished an editorial in the *Crimson* mentioned the theft. The next day, the *Crimson* printed a photo on its front page of the Ibis being scrutinized by a reporter. Over the photo they ran a headline referring to the current *Lampoon* president, a future novelist of some fame—UPSET UPDIKE WANTS THE BIRD.

Chaffing at the torment, the *Lampoon* returned to the trick that had worked in 1941 and kidnapped *Crimson* editor Michael Maccoby ('54).

"No *Crimson* editor can rest safe in his bed," said the *Lampoon*'s John Updike, announcing the editor would not be freed until the bird was returned. "We will depopulate Cambridge totally of this unfortunate element. After that, we will publish a daily newspaper ourselves."

But the Ibis was not returned and, eventually, Maccoby was rescued. There was supposed to be a handoff—Maccoby for the bird. But the *Crimson* car was being driven by burly, menacing, future Pulitzer Prize–winning journalist David Halberstam ("I was sort of a bodyguard in those days," he remembers today), who grabbed Maccoby and kept the bird. (Updike claims they allowed Maccoby to escape: "Kidnappings were rather sad," he wrote in a reminiscence of his *Lampoon* days. "I helped kidnap Michael Maccoby, and after driving around for hours in the Somerville region there seemed little to do but let him escape.")

Maccoby and fellow editor George S. Abrams decided it was time to get the Ibis out of town.

Thirty-eight years later, Abrams fondly recalled the *Crimson*'s pièce de résistance.

"The Ibis had gone to various places, we had done enough of it and were nearing the end of the trail. What could we do with it? Just give it back to the *Lampoon*?"

Never. Abrams and Maccoby fled to New York City with the bird. The *Lampoon*, hot on their trail, followed them. Unsure what to do, they sought refuge at the Manhattan apartment of John Loengard, at the time a Harvard freshman and photographer for the *Crimson*.

"We were sitting there in Loengard's apartment," remembers Maccoby. "I opened up *Life* magazine, and there was a picture of the new University of Moscow. I said: 'This is it!' "

This was 1953, remember. The height of the Cold War. The article that Maccoby saw, "I Photographed Russia," portrayed the nation as the most inaccessible spot on earth. One of the photos, snapped by a U.S. housewife "breathless with wonder" over her glimpse of the forbidden nation, was of the massive new University of Moscow. Its spires, rearing 38 stories above the Kremlin, seemed the perfect perch for a bird.

"The concept of it being sent over to Russia to be placed on a spire of the new University of Moscow seemed a pretty good way to end the travels of the Ibis," Abrams says.

The *Crimson* sent a telegram to the Russian consul in New York, announcing that the editors of the *Lampoon* wished to make a gift of its sacred Ibis statue and requesting it be placed on a spire at Moscow University "as a symbol of friendship with the Soviet people and the universality of the search for truth."

The Soviets graciously accepted the offer.

There was something very illicit about contacting Soviet authorities, even as part of a prank. Just before Maccoby and Abrams went to see the Russians on Monday morning, one of them was so nervous, he threw up—though Abrams claims it was Maccoby, and Maccoby insists it was Abrams.

Either way, they collected themselves and presented the statue, still specked with pigeon guano, to Semyon K. Tsarapkin, the Soviet Union's deputy delegate to the United Nations, at his 680 Park Avenue office. "He was just an embassy guy being nice to us," remembers Loengard, enlisted to accompany Maccoby and Abrams.

They told Tsarapkin that the Ibis was a goodwill gift from the students of the United States to the students of the Soviet Union.

The photo documenting the event—snapped by Loengard, who later went on to become a noted photographer for *Life*— shows Abrams and Maccoby handing the bird to a somber Tsarapkin, under the watchful gaze of a giant portrait of Joseph Stalin.

Tsarapkin was reportedly puzzled by the gift—he thought it looked like a stork—but the pair assured him the Ibis was "sort of an American peace dove."

Their job done, they returned to campus to break the news.

"The *Lampoon*'s Sacred Ibis," the *Crimson* crowed on April 21, 1953, "now rests in Russian Territory."

With mock seriousness, a *Crimson* editorial compared the presentation of the Ibis to France's gift of the Statue of Liberty, terming both "an exchange of monuments" meant to further "international friendship and understanding."

"The recent gift of the *Lampoon* to the Soviet Government of one of its most treasured possessions is a firm step forward in the path to peace," it opined, thanking the *Lampoon* "for letting us do the official honors."

The *Lampoon*, for once, reacted with actual seriousness, if not outright horror.

"The *Crimson* pranksters seem to have forgotten the rights of property," complained Updike. "It is deplorable that they've carried college jokes into the arena of international relations."

The *Lampoon* did retain enough good humor—or perhaps, was grimly desperate enough—to fire off a telegram to Wisconsin's junior senator, the execrable Joseph McCarthy, suggesting that their rival's prank was more Red than *Crimson*, and demanding an investigation. Or at least it claimed to have done this. Perhaps the *Lampoon* was just trying to scare its rival with the spectre of Tailgunner Joe. Either way, McCarthy, busy ruining the nation, did not respond.

"Sort of an American peace dove"—Crimson *editors and Soviet official share a warm moment in the Cold War.*

The next day Maccoby and Abrams berated Updike for lacking the vision to see humor as "a strategic weapon in the present fight against communism." Noting that the *Lampoon* had appealed to the U.S. government to retrieve its bird, the *Crimson* chided: "It's sad indeed that such a petty piece of property has caused the *Lampoon* to crawl sniveling and whining to the State Department" and added that any government action on the *Lampoon*'s behalf "would be nothing short of appeasement."

The *Crimson* launched a campus-wide petition drive urging that the Soviets be allowed to keep the bird, and hundreds of Harvard students signed. Meanwhile, the *Lampoon* lit up phone lines to New York, succeeding only, according to the *Crimson,* "in completely confusing the hapless Russians."

But the *Lampoon* was adamant about not allowing its mascot to slip behind the Iron Curtain forever. That Friday, four days after the Ibis was given to the Soviets, the United Press International reported that John Goelet, "handsome heir to one of New York's greatest real estate fortunes" and treasurer of the *Lampoon,* spent a half hour explaining the subtleties of American college humor to the USSR representative in his Park Avenue headquarters. Asked by reporters to smile, Goelet replied: "I am unsmiling."

Looking back on the prank years later, Abrams has one regret—that they hadn't been more restrained, and let a few weeks go by before revealing that the Soviets had been given the bird.

"It would be over in Moscow right now," he says, a tad wistfully.

While the Ibis's brush with Red Communism was by far its most dramatic adventure, it was not the bird's last. The very next year, the *Crimson* got its hands on the bird again, this time photographing it in a variety of local circumstances—being examined by a doctor at the health center, attending a Museum of Science lecture, among whirling fellow avians at the Boston docks. Later it was stolen and presented to fellow Bostonian Caroline Kennedy, whose father returned it to the *Lampoon.*

Recovered temporarily, in 1961 the Ibis disappeared again, and not a peep was heard from it for two years, when a *Crimson* writer, Andrew T. Weil, announced the formation of a new company, "Find-a-Bird, Inc." Opening an office, printing stationery and hiring an answering service, Weil told the *Lampoon* he would search the world for their bird and return it, *if* the *Lampoon* promised to hold a huge public party on Harvard Square to welcome it back. At first, suspecting that Weil already had the Ibis in his possession, the *Lampoon* was hesitant, but when Weil hinted that Find-a-Bird could easily be corporately restructured into Melt-a-Bird, party plans were underway.

The day before the gala, however, two graduate students, unconnected to either publication, stole the bird, and turned it over to Alfred E. Vellucci, a Cambridge city councilman who had made a career of slamming Harvard. He gained television time for himself by announcing he had the Ibis and would return it to the *Lampoon*—on election eve.

Given the popularity of stealing campus statues, one might almost suspect that the statues are put up with the specific intent of providing students with something to absorb their extracurricular energies. Alas, frequent lead-thumbed reaction to statue nabbing on the part of university administrations deflates that theory.

Northwestern eventually locked Joe Medill in the Dean's office, then decided to remodel Fisk Hall after a century of neglect, perhaps to get rid of the yellowed tile compass with nothing at its center where Joe's pedestal once sat. Oberlin cracked down on the thefts of Charles Martin Hall with Soviet-like ruthlessness: They filled the statue with concrete and bolted Hall to a one-ton block of granite. Amherst, like St. Peter, finds it necessary to deny its deity.

"The school has made a decision not to express any interest in it anymore," sniffed an official.

Even the *Lampoon* has, from time to time, betrayed its own puckish precepts by lashing out at Ibis stealers. When *Crimson* editors were caught with the Ibis in April 1985, after using technical climbing equipment to scale the castle, the *Lampoon* had them arrested and threatened to press larceny charges in court.

But in that beautiful cycle of self-correction where increased repression only leads to more pranks, as soon as the *Lampoon* dropped charges against the *Crimson* for stealing its Ibis, a *Crimson* editor stopped by the Cambridge police station and, posing as a *Lampoon* executive, claimed the bird.

6

SPECIAL CASE #1
Blowing Up the Moon

Johnny and I have a plan to blow up the moon.
—Raif Majeed
Caltech senior

The C and H Sales Company is a large, cluttered empo-
rium on Colorado Boulevard in Pasadena, California. It has the
airy feel of an old hardware store, with the same cool dimness, the
same ancient glass counters and endless bins. But instead of
offering nails and hammers, C and H Sales deals in used, surplus,
discontinued, obsolete, and otherwise disfavored scientific, electrical, and electronic gear.

If NASA had an attic, it would look like this. The place is
jammed floor to ceiling with meters, transistors, relays, motors,
blowers, fans, gauges, oscilloscopes, O-rings, altimeters—the de-
tritus of the technical world.

Size seems out of proportion here. Rows of capacitors as large
as oil cans line up beside tiny motors the size of fingertips.
Nearby are light bulbs ranging in dimension from robin's eggs to
honeydews. A giant glass dome sits on a high shelf; a person
could curl up inside.

The place is a mecca for students from the nearby California

Institute of Technology. They come to browse the aisles and fill their lungs with the pleasing smell of machine oil, mixed with old cardboard, dust, and perhaps a whiff of sadness at all these relics of technical glory. These old companies—Motronics and Airpax and Honeywell and Bendix and General Radio and Indiana General Motor and U.S. Electrical Motor—which once represented the sort of shimmering science that draws young people to places like Caltech, are now reduced to dinosaur names, tagged to fossils lining the aisles at C and H Sales.

The students not only browse; they buy. All this exotic hardware is going for cheap. A Panametrics Model 2000 hygrometer sells for $15; a MTS 410 digital function generator for $50. The dome is $100. You can see how Caltech students go crazy here. They buy floor mat switches and motion detectors and Klixon air flow sensors and don't even know what they are going to do with them. They trust they'll think of something. It's impossible to look at the rows of heavy cutting wheels, their blades coated in a protective layer of ruby wax, or the aluminum heat sinks, with their splayed fins of geometric ridges, without being tempted to take one home, for no particular purpose. They're beautiful.

In the springtime, traffic from Caltech to C and H Sales increases to flood levels, flowing among the yellow plastic bins of transistors, microswitches, and rectifiers. "I stopped in today," said Tom Capellari, a Caltech senior, in the middle of May 1991. "I have no doubt there were 25 Techers in there within a fifteen-minute period, using those precious last moments when you can buy all the relays you need."

The students are searching for material for their "stacks"— contraptions assembled to challenge underclassmen in a half century old pranking phenomenon known as Ditch Day.

Every college in the country has a springtime day of boilerplate drollery. There are hundreds of May Fests and Spring Flings and Summer Sendoffs and Cut Days. Yet Caltech's Ditch Day stands out for its freshness, its continual ability to surprise and bite, the way the students have managed—in general—to keep it from being coopted and ruined. Despite the dead weight of 60 years of tradition, and the corrosiveness of administration approval, Ditch Day is still a viable way for students to tweak the icons of their lives—the endless demands of studies, the hip calm of seniors, the hubris of underclassmen, the momentary slavering attention of the media, and the bland Californian hamlet of Pasadena that eyes them, year in and year out, with dull unease.

Ditch Day began in the early 1930s, true to its name, with the seniors selecting a day to ditch classes and go to the beach. Simple enough. But quickly the underclassmen, sore at being left behind to actually attend class, took to breaking into the seniors' rooms and planting surprises for them—moving a roomful of furniture onto a lawn, say, or relocating a chugging Model T next to a bed.

The seniors tried to prevent this by stacking their furniture against the doors and exiting through their windows. Hence the word "stack," which soon came to mean, in Caltech lingo, any device for keeping people out of a room—including the owner. An early usage of "stack" also implies breaking into a room while the occupants are away and arranging the furniture in a tight stack so they can't get back in. Stack also can refer to the unique Caltech practice of stealing a room, in its entirety. The contents of the rooms are stripped, down to the wallpaper, switchplates, light bulbs, sinks and, in extreme cases, the floorboards, then removed and hidden, usually in Caltech's 6900 feet of underground steam tunnels.

The beautiful symmetry of this struggle—the underclassmen wanting in, the seniors wanting to keep them out—and the zeal brought to the challenge by Caltech students, has kept Ditch Day new and vital, evolving over the years.

By the 1950s furniture was an inadequate mode of defense and seniors took to constructing "bank vault" stacks—using massive steel beams, tons of concrete, time locks, and thick planking to barricade their rooms.

Underclassmen reacted in kind, bringing to bear all sorts of heavy equipment—chain saws, front end loaders, cranes, bolt cutters, jackhammers—on the senior stacks. If humans are separated from the animal kingdom by the ability to use tools, then Caltech students are separated from the rest of the species by their ability to quickly locate and utilize those tools, be they lock picks or backhoes or anything in between.

In the best tradition of "we had to destroy the village in order to save it," the rooms often got pretty torn up. To placate the administration, the informal rule evolved that anyone doing damage—say ripping out a wall or using a wet saw to cut through a concrete ceiling—had to pay to repair it.

Still, a half century of Ditch Days has left its mark on Caltech's architecture, particularly the residence halls, which are honeycombed with secret passageways and hiding places. It is not unusual for a student to duck into a kitchen cabinet, then emerge from a broom closet a floor below.

Traditionally Ditch Day begins at 8 A.M. and ends, promptly at 5 P.M. Under the increasingly sophisticated assault of the underclassmen, it soon became plain that one of the drawbacks of the brute force stack was that no conceivable combination of steel doors, wooden planks, concrete blocks, and booby traps could keep a group of determined Techers out of a room for nine hours. The underclassmen were always getting in and wreaking their vengeance—known as a "counterstack." These counterstacks became rather complicated themselves, ranging from nailing a senior's furniture to the ceiling to filling a room with several feet of water. In 1968, Ed Seguine returned to his room in Ruddock to find a small desert, complete with palm trees and two tons of sand. One year, a student found his doorway filled with a two-foot thick wall of solid ice.

The general success of the underclassmen led to the concept of the bribe. Not only would seniors stack their rooms, but they would leave behind caches of booze, beer, drugs, and food to placate the underclassmen once they busted in. The unspoken arrangement was, if you take the bribe, you can't counterstack the room.

The failure of the brute force stack ultimately led to the development of the finesse stack. The finesse stack challenges a student to get into a room, not by busting in, but by deciphering some sort of problem—a computer code, a puzzle, rebus, an elegant equation, a maze—something that has to be solved to gain entry. The door itself is left open.

One year, a finesse stack was simply a disassembled Dodge V-8 engine. To gain entry, underclassmen had to put the engine together and get it running. (They did).

To give an idea how the brute force stack compared to the finesse stack, in 1979, Werner Pyka's brute force stack utilized ⅜ inch steel plate, plywood backed with concrete slabs, and a protective layer of sand. It was defeated by sophomores wielding 35-pound sledgehammers, bolt cutters, and pry bars. But a finesse stack by Chris Lee, involving a musical synthesizer gently playing random notes, a musical scale drawn on a sheet of paper, and a push button at the end of a wire, was not solved. Students knew that pressing the button did something—every time they did, the synthesizer would shift to a new key—but they couldn't figure out the message in the musical scale, and the room was left untouched.

If readers at Michigan State are wondering why underclassmen don't just jackboot open the finesse stack door and gorge themselves on the bribe, they need to understand the concept of what students at Caltech call the Code. A single sentence in the school rules, the Code reads that no Caltech student will take "unfair advantage" of another. In some places it would be just so much chin music, but at Caltech the average student puts a great deal of faith in the Code. Most tests are unproctored, and profes-

---

B O O B Y T R A P S

*B*efore the rise of the honor stack, Caltech seniors tried to slow the assault of the underclassmen on their rooms by booby-trapping their brute force stacks. Among the more effective:

1. Shaving cream cans. Dangerous method used to slow down someone chipping through a concrete wall. A half-dozen cans of shaving cream are sprinkled into the concrete as it is being poured. One hit with a chisel or jackhammer results in a face full of foam.

2. Fiberglass insulation. The perfect backing for wooden planking—fouls drill bits and blades that try to cut through it.

3. Sand. Good to put behind steel plate. It not only fouls power tools, but pours dramatically out of any holes cut into the steel. 🐄

sors have been known to hand out exams, tell students to take them home and spend no more than two hours on them, then bring them back. And the students do.

The latest twist on the finesse stack is the honor stack. This stack involves the presentation of some sort of scenario that ties together a combination of the old brute force stack, the finesse stack, and a new permutation that probably should be more accurately described as a theme stack—sending underclassmen out to get things and humiliate themselves in a variety of creative ways, tied together under an underlying plot or scenario.

Some noteworthy honor stacks have forced undergraduates to buy a house (they did), or run nude through campus.

This newest form of stacking at times flirts with becoming a sort of big pajama party, losing the essential prankish nature of Ditch Day. But fortunately, seniors always find a way to give Ditch Day at least something of an edge.

For instance, nobody knows when Ditch Day is going to be held. The date is fixed between the senior class president and the dean of students and is a well-guarded secret. Professors don't know when Ditch Day is until they show up for class and no one is there; underclassmen don't know until the seniors suddenly disappear. They try hard to guess, and the seniors try equally hard to deceive them, contriving fake Ditch Days and diversionary tactics.

Besides keeping the underclassmen on edge, this system also has the benefit of keeping Ditch Day from becoming just another fluffy alumni magnet. Not knowing when the day is scheduled prevents hordes of misty-eyed alumni from drifting back to watch the colorful affair, and discourages the attentions of the media, which like to plan ahead.

The instructions of a particular stack can help maintain Ditch Day's raw quality. In 1986, students solving a stack were required to steal the athletic director's car. In 1991, various honor stacks ended up in two bonfires that brought out the Pasadena fire department, a disturbance inside a Ralph's Supermarket, and numerous acts of public humiliation and quasi-legality.

Caltech is a small place. The residential section consists of seven small dorms tucked on either side of the main campus drag—called the Olive Walk. The south dorms—Fleming, Dabney, Ricketts, and Blacker—are beautiful two-story Spanish-style villas with tiled courtyards and stuccoed balconies. The dorms on the north side of Olive Walk—Page, Lloyd, and Ruddock—are modern and hideous, but do have certain amenities. Lloyd has a hot tub. (Then again, so does the swankier Dabney). Being in California, the area is lush with tropical vegetation: giant, post-apocalyptic flowers, weird rubber plants, and man-sized pineap-ple-like trees jut out of the earth.

The weather in the last few hours before Ditch Day, 1991, is warm and still. Tuesday night the seniors are for the most part ensconced in their rooms, working on their stacks. It's easy to tell which are the seniors' rooms because the doors are covered by bedsheets scribbled with warnings—SENIORS ONLY ZONE and DON'T EVEN THINK ABOUT ENTERING. From behind the sheets come sounds of construction—hammering, the roar of power saws, hushed conversations, the clunk of heavy objects.

In the hallways, undergraduates drape themselves over thrift-shop sofas and debate when they think Ditch Day will be. They know something is up, but the senior activity is not a giveaway because it has been going on for some time. The sheets have been up over a month, and for the past several days the seniors have been using a variety of tricks to keep the underclass off guard. Many underclassmen thought Ditch Day would be Monday, owing to the flurry of activity—revving motorcycle engines, rush-ing seniors carrying bags of empty bottles, odd items set out in public spaces. All a ploy. Several undergraduates were so certain that Monday would be Ditch Day they made the mistake of not doing their homework.

Actually, the only thing underclassmen can agree on is that Ditch Day couldn't be tomorrow, because Wednesday is the last day of Drop-Add, and Ditch Day couldn't possibly be on such a life-or-death scheduling day. Unaware that senior class officials have arranged for Drop-Add to be extended an extra day, con-ventional wisdom settles on Thursday.

Most stacks are the result of collaboration. A group of three or four seniors will get together and work on a stack in one person's room. Come Ditch Day, notes on the doors of the participating seniors will direct underclassmen to their particular stack.

Lloyd House seniors Raif Majeed and his roommate, John

Gass, are laboring on the electronics of their stack. Like many stacks this year, theirs has an overlay of the weary Dungeons and Dragons fantasy that scientific types embrace when they no longer believe in a real future.

"Johnny and I have a plan to blow up the moon, and basically the people doing the stack have to find out where the detonator to blow up the moon is and have to deactivate that," says Majeed, explaining his theme. "It turns out Johnny and I have been taken hostage by aliens and as we were taken aboard the mother ship, we managed to launch a space probe. . . ."

"They'll use ciphers to find the detonator, clip the right wires that will give them an eight-bit code to use later in the stack," says Gass, dourly examining a small circuit board under a powerful light, testing it with a voltage meter. "We've been working on this stack for eight weeks."

On the table is a square metal device, which Majeed identifies as a "sensor pod."

"I got it because it looked cool," he says. "I don't know how it functions, but I kind of know how I will use it."

Keith Akama, a biology senior, walks in holding a jigsaw. He is wearing a painters cap, turned backward, and big shorts. His knees have paint smeared on them.

Akama's stack has an Arthurian tone.

"The whole thing is a quest—not for the Holy Grail, but for an Erlenmeyer flask," he says, referring to the squat, conical beaker found in any chemistry lab. "I have a reputation, I guess, as being a pyromaniac. You need to heat a plate to six hundred degrees, using a torch or thermite, to get in."

(Keith Akama also has the distinction of being part of the theme of another Lloyd House stack. The premise of the "Adobe Stack" is that a virus released by Akama will destroy life on the planet unless the stack is solved in time).

The construction of Akama's stack is detailed in a loose-leaf notebook, which he runs to get. The thick notebook looks like a thesis, with neat, Mac-quality labels, three-dimensional diagrams, schematics, and rough working notes. His stack involves a "u-trap"—basically a waist-high tank of water, fitted into his room's doorway and "filled with twenty-three goldfish, or ice cubes, or both." The tank has a partition halfway down the middle, forcing those trying to get through the trap and into the room to completely submerge themselves to pass under the partition.

Inside the room, there is a small motorized car. Solving the stack requires underclassmen to guide the car through a course, knocking over flags attached to mercury switches. The trick is that the person controlling the car cannot see it, and the person with a view of the car cannot control it. The task is complicated by the blaring of bad heavy metal music.

"I made everything into modules for convenience and storability," Akama says. At the back of the notebook are photocopied receipts, some from C and H Sales. Among his many purchases are a thermo switch, door handles, eye rings, C channels, and six mousetraps. Akama explains that the mousetraps can be used as relays to convert a tiny force—say somebody brushing against a trip wire—into a larger one.

Akama says he spent at least $500 on his stack.

"Half the trick is to build as cheaply as possible," he says. "You see a solenoid lying on the floor"—he snaps his fingers and ogles the imaginary wire coil at his feet—"Helloooooooooo!"

He has round glasses, and talks in a torrent of words, earnest and delighted. Many seniors speak nostalgically about being underclassmen and working on cracking stacks. They slightly resent the fact they will be off campus, away from the fun, come their last Ditch Day. But not Akama. He has been waiting for the chance to craft his stack. This is his moment.

"One of the only reasons I came to this school is because of Ditch Day," he says. A muffled scream is heard from the next room, accompanied by a thud on the wall.

The seniors have been working solving other people's stacks for three years. They are filled with tales of awe—the computer programed so that, if left alone for 20 minutes, it would open the door lock automatically. The stack that included a plane ticket to San Francisco (short-hop plane tickets are a common stack feature. In 1991 a student was sent to Las Vegas). The famous "Cornucopia" wall-of-food stack—you had to eat your way through several feet of things like sheet cake and Rice Krispies treats, hands behind your back. (There have been several Cornucopias. The 1986 version was abandoned, unbreached, when underclassmen bogged down in a layer of homemade baklava). Akama says his remote-control car module is based on a laser-control stack he saw several years ago involving communication between an operator who had the controls to a laser device but could not see it, and an observer who could see the device move but could not operate it.

The biggest misconception about Ditch Day is that the purpose of the stacks is to keep underclassmen out. Most agree that it would be simple to design a finesse stack that keeps underclassmen out—an unsolvable physics problem, or a list of extremely time-consuming tasks.

"That's not the point," says senior Scott Harris, whose stack involves color-coded locks, magnets, a topographical map, a motion detector, a phone, and an aluminum bar with a series of various sized holes which, if matched to the letters of their corresponding drill bits, form a message. "The point is to give somebody an adventure for eight hours. There is usually what they call the '4:50 P.M. clue,' which begins 'If you haven't got it by now . . .' "

Indeed, most stacks include a phone number, so if the youngsters hit a dead end, they can be nudged forward with hints by the creator of the stack, lounging at some senior pool party or beach house.

"You owe it to people to provide them a good time," said Chris Myers. "I think stacks are funnest if you can pretend what's going on is real."

Despite the evidence of considerable planning, everywhere, the stacks are still being pulled together at the last moment. Midnight comes and goes, with scant sign of any stack being ready anytime soon. Senior Pete Dussin, glassy eyed with exhaustion and despair, sits in the middle of his tiny room in Blacker House, trashed and cluttered with construction paper, wooden sticks, black yarn, balloons, nuts, a volt meter, black electrical tape, gray duct tape, copper coil, and a heavy-duty, orange extension cord. Dozens of empty plastic water bottles are shoved under the bed.

"One side works," he says, staring at a contraption of wires.

"Have you tried just running the relay out of the nine volt?" asks Mark Montague, who was a senior in 1989 and, apparently, still is. Montague is trying to be the Helpful Friend, lending encouragement while Dussin despairs.

"I've talked to two EEs [electrical engineers], and this is their plan," complains Dussin. "Of course, it's overengineered."

Before explaining his stack, Pete, without a trace of irony, checks the door and turns up the radio, loud. Even then, he speaks in a low voice.

The stack, called "The Pirates of Millikan," works like this: There is treasure hidden in Pete's locked room. To find the key, the searchers must become pirates. They will be given bandanas and wooden toy swords. They must find the 80 plastic water bottles Pete has collected, find the caps hidden around campus, lash the bottles to two air mattresses, then sail across the decorative pond in front of Millikan Library to the device Pete is now working on. It is basically an electromagnet surrounded by a crown of trip wires. The key to the room will be held by the electromagnet. The whole affair will be suspended above a pipe leading into a bucket of concrete. All the pirates will have to do is reach in and grab the key without touching the wires. If they touch a wire, the electromagnet will cut out and the key will fall down the pipe and into the center of the concrete, and fix itself there. It's an elegant contraption; if he can make it work.

"See, my mistake was buying FOURTEEN GAUGE WIRE!" Pete hisses.

The question is whether Pete can operate the electromagnet off a nine volt battery, or whether he must run 220 volt power out to the middle of the pond. Mark gingerly adds his counsel.

"Shorting across the nine volt current is not going to hurt anybody," he offers. "Shorting across the wall current is bad."

Dussin sits, grabbing his hair in both fists and pulling it, like in the cartoons. The next day, without mentioning any names, I will tell a student that before coming to Caltech I had never actually seen anyone pull at his hair in frustration. Her reply will be: "Pete Dussin!"

Caltech has only 800 undergraduates.

It seems like Pete will never get his stack done. "I spent a hundred and one dollars on my stupid bribe; I shouldn't have worried about a bribe because they're going to counterstack me anyway," he says.

Mark wants to show more stack preparations to who one Techer will refer to as "the book writer man," but is hesitant to leave Pete alone in his moment of extremity.

"Am I serving much purpose as moral support?" he asks.

Dussin, sitting on his haunches, looks up at him. His manic energy cranks down one notch. "Actually, it does help," he says. We stay a while longer, then move through the dimmed corridors.

Three levels of sheets protect a room down the hall. Ed Vail pops his head through a hatch in a black plywood partition. "It doesn't work yet, which is a problem," he says. Ed has glasses, a beard, and thinning, curly blond hair, combining for an impish look. He is making a transmogrifier, à la the comic strip "Calvin & Hobbes." A spinning black carousel will provide different outfits for the transmogrified to wear. They will dress as nerds, as members of the opposite sex, as 1970s-types, and then perform a variety of tasks. He is working on a device so that, when the person has dressed as a "nerd," a computer will instruct a secret port to spray a shot of water crotch high to complete the nerd image.

Providing visual effects are a small ruby laser, a Jacob's ladder, and a white smoke generator. "If you see any bright lights, look away," Ed says, matter-of-factly, activating the device. He and Mark get in a discussion of just how powerful a laser you can stare directly into without damaging yourself. Mark, apparently, has made a practice of gazing into lasers.

"It overloads the photoreceptors in your eyes," he says, launching into a rhapsody of the results. "The neat thing is, when you look right into a red laser, there's a blue spot in the middle."

Ed is holding a 6-outlet adapter and a plug. As he speaks, he inserts the plug. There is a small explosion.

"Uh oh, blew the circuit breaker," he says, disappearing through the hatch.

Down the hall, several stacks have gotten together to construct a 3-dimensional maze, 26 feet high, in a Blacker stairwell. "It's sort of a communal clue swamp," Montague says, explaining that anyone who wants to can use the maze to hide a clue to their stacks.

Nearby, on a veranda outside their bedroom, Pete Wyckoff and Alex Dukhovny are staring at 30 concrete blocks, set in a 6 by 5 array. A puzzle of squiggles is painted in bright red and aqua over the blocks. These squiggles, Wyckoff explains, when made into a transparency and set on an overhead projector with other squiggles in another puzzle, should yield words, which will direct . . .

The blocks weigh 15 pounds each, and Pete and Alex still have to secrete them at various sites around campus. It is 1:30 A.M. Outside, on Holliston Avenue, three guys with white string are marking the pavement in chalk, laying out huge letters, 12-feet high which, when painted in, will spell CENTENNIAL DITCH DAY. (Caltech being 100 years old, not Ditch Day). Part of solving the stack will be painting the letters and obtaining an aerial photo of the phrase.

Ditch Day dawns Wednesday cool and gray, with a heaviness in the air that hints of rain. At 7:30 A.M., the campus is largely quiet. The Hispanic workers who prune and tend to the Venusian

Ditch Day prepares Caltech students for the working world by teaching them to slavishly carry out arbitrary demands.

flora are beginning to arrive, chatting before they take up their rakes and brooms. Just another day in paradise.

Yet. There is a giant white weather balloon, slowly rocking on the lily pond. A mysterious aqua concrete block is perched nearby. Closer examination of the balloon reveals a cryptic symbol—a blue and a green triangle—marked on the side.

There, suspended from a string, hovering high above the courtyard between the Mabel and Arnold Beckman Laboratories of Behavioral Biology and the Donald E. Baxter MD Hall of the Humanities and Social Sciences, is a beer can.

Every casual glance falls upon some strange object—a note, a package, a sign. In a men's room on the fourth floor of Millikan Library, a series of smudges and streaks on a mirror—something normally dismissed as the fault of bad janitorial work—gains sudden importance from a yellow Post-it note proclaiming DITCH DAY—DO NOT CLEAN!

A stroll across the empty campus reveals Ditch Day's deep emotional appeal for Caltech students. Nobody goes into science because they think the world is too orderly and complete. They yearn for a world of significance, for what Pynchon calls "another mode of meaning behind the obvious," and for today, they've got it. A world transformed into a crystal of paranoid complexity. Clues peek out from under bushes, puzzling envelopes are taped to walls—so much conspiracy it crowds itself. Fresh purple footprints, newly painted, vector past the fountain in front of Beckman; a manila envelope, neatly labelled, "Senior Ditch Day material, please do not remove," flutters on a wall. A piece of black tagpaper taped to the ground is covered in gold hieroglyphics, with a purple square of overlapping tissue paper and a black square, sealed with maroon wax.

Shortly before 8 A.M., a trio of seniors, each carrying a backpack, sprints by, heading off campus. Most will spend the day at beach parties, pool parties, or barbeques. They had better—like a holdover from the class wars of the 19th century, any senior caught on campus on Ditch Day between 8 A.M. and 5 P.M. is tied to a tree.

It is no empty tradition. In 1990, senior class president Cliff Kaiser was duct taped to a tree so tightly he got sick and nearly passed out. (And it wasn't even Ditch Day, but underclassmen fooled—actually pretending to be fooled for the purpose of duct taping Cliff—by a senior bluff tactic).

In 1985, when senior Dan Schwartz tried to thwart Ditch Day by refusing to leave campus and holing up in his room, underclassmen relocated Schwartz's brand-new BMW to the roof of the Central Plant building, then arranged for the campus police to find it and give him a parking ticket.

At 8 A.M., a stereo clicks on, automatically, blasting the Doors' "People are Strange" with expensive stereo clarity from an upper floor. Fleming House president Tim Maddux begins furiously ringing the house bell, to wake anyone who is still sleeping through the commotion. Underclassmen clatter out of their rooms and confront the senior stacks.

"This is like the Bible Stack-o-Doom!" screams Jessica Nichols, a red-cheeked sophomore with a Fleming T-shirt and a Wagnerian voice. She sits before a brand new, pricey NeXt computer displaying a three-dimensional cube covered with multicolored squares. "God bless America! I don't even want to do this three-D crossword puzzle stuff!"

She reads out loud from a sheaf of five pages of instructions for the stack, which is called the "Hyperstack of Miracles." The tasks range from the difficult and unpleasant to the seemingly impossible.

The stack scenario begins: "Just recently it was reported by a scholarly journal that three scientists/engineers discovered a way to transport themselves into another universe. . . ."

Others rush in.

"The Dobie stack is awesome," someone shouts, and in moments the "Hyperstack of Miracles" is abandoned in the rush to the Dobie Gillis stack, a tribute to the 1950s sitcom, wildly popular on campus thanks to cable reruns.

Other noteworthy stacks include "Crack House" ("Caltech professors are up in arms over the clandestine drug dealing going on right inside their labs. . . ." begin the instructions) and "The Myth of Osiris," which not only involves construction of a 15-foot pyramid, but mastery of hieroglyphics.

In the courtyard, a group of underclassmen gather around an innocent-looking white envelope. The stack instructions read that the envelope cannot be opened, but must be set aflame. After much hesitation, someone touches a match to a corner of the envelope. It explodes.

"Sulfur!" somebody cries. A scorched clue comes fluttering to the ground.

"That was excellent, man."

Ed Vail's stack is labelled "Ed & Sylvia's Stack O'Transmogrification." There is a sign-up sheet, and four people have signed up. The doorway leading to Ed's room is completely closed off with a black plywood wall. To the right is a gray fuse box, and mounted midway up the wall is a gray plastic boxy device that looks like the control panel for an alarm system. The undergrads quickly guess that both are merely ornamental.

Eleven events are listed on the wall. The first is to go through the doorway. Someone peers into the darkness.

"I don't like it," says Xavier Bengoechea. "All right. I'm going in." It is 8:19 A.M.

Marc Lopez and Troy Bassett gaze at the door. Time goes by. "He's been in there a while," says Troy, uncomfortably. Marc looks at the fuse box. "Do you think this does anything?"

Ten minutes pass. Someone sets off the fire alarm. It has a reedy, blown sound. Xavier doesn't come out of the Transmogrifier. Nobody pays attention to the alarm.

By 9 A.M., Ditch Day is in full cry. A group of students run by, tracing a string snaking through trees, up walls, into windows. Freshman Shreyas Vasanawala and juniors Willy Watson and Jon Lange try to untangle three strings leading to a file box. The untangling is complicated by the fact that the strings are attached to tennis balls and, according to instructions, must be untangled by juggling the balls. It takes forever but—remember the Code— none of the three even suggests they untangle through any method but laborious juggling.

"Throw the one in the middle," says Willy, who is working the strings loose while Jon and Shreyas take turns with slow juggles. "What pattern, inside or outside?" asks Jon.

Most of the activity is centered around the Olive Walk. Eight underclassmen in pink GO-GO'S STACK T-shirts (most good stacks will provide cool T-shirts as souvenirs) set up mike stands and a drum kit in front of the bookstore. Their stack instructs them to make a Go-Go's video, which they do, complete with loopy

Joyous Caltech students, freed from the library, indulge in physical activity.

dashes toward the camera, arms held straight out, airplane style. A phalanx of 16 people, all dressed in Mad Max outfits with shoulder pads, goggles and odd headgear, brandishing high powered squirt gun rifles, comes by at a military trot and sounding off.

"See that soldier turning green?" the leader shouts.

"See that soldier turning green!" the gunners shout.

"Someone pissed in his canteen!"

"Someone pissed in his canteen!"

They pass Alex Lin, of Lloyd House, who is standing on a block of concrete, chipping away at it with a midget jackhammer. Caltech is no doubt the only school where a student can go to the physical plant department, request a jackhammer, and be loaned one. Inside the concrete is a threaded rod, the "control rod" from a nuclear reactor stack they are trying to disarm. A radio reporter tries to interview Lin over the sound of the hammering.

Pirates in red bandanas, waving swords, race by. They are Danny Chu, Henry Choi, Pete McCann, and Dave Skeie, who wears a black T-shirt reading SLEEP ALL DAY. PARTY ALL NIGHT. NEVER DO HOMEWORK. NEVER GRADUATE. IT'S FUN TO BE IN BLACKER HOUSE.

Back at Blacker, they quickly prepare two pirate flags out of construction paper provided by Pete. After some argument over artistic skill, the scissors are handed to Danny Chu to cut the shape of the skull. "You're the resident MD," someone says.

"OB/GYN," he says, beginning to cut out the bones.

The flags done, they open up clue number five. "Oh shit, we're behind," Danny says, and they take off running toward Mudd Laboratory. Their colorful gear catches the eye of a television cameraman, who briefly gives chase, moving surprisingly quick for a guy shouldering all that heavy equipment. Caltech students generally hate the media attention given Ditch Day— signs along the Olive Walk read REPORTER FREE ZONE and warn that violators are liable to be hit with water balloons. A letter several days later in the school newspaper will complain of being referred to as "raving nerds" in the *Los Angeles Times* and "geeks" on television. Ditch Day is a time for serious, technically minded students to let their hair down, and it's embarrassing to have strangers watch them do it. To spite TV reporters wishing to use the Olive Walk as a visual backdrop, one stack has students string big CALPOLY banners from the lightposts.

The pirates' instructions are to steal a Dai—campus slang for the tiny pickup trucks, some of them Daihutsus, driven by the grounds crews—from the lot where they are kept behind Mudd Laboratory. A Dai is quickly discovered and even more quickly hotwired, and soon the pirates are roaring through campus, waving their swords. Henry climbs atop the cab and stands, precariously. The instructions to move the Dai just one building away are ignored, and the truck is triumphantly driven to Blacker, through the arch and into the courtyard. Back home, they check their next clue. It involves breaking and entering. Danny runs to get his set of lock picks.

The quartet of women working on "The Myth of Osiris" hieroglyphics are making good progress. The pyramid is done. They've got their cool black MYTH OF OSIRIS T-shirts on. Their arms are covered with ankhs and *udjats* written in a golden ink, and they are wearing scarabs around their neck—a reward for

Larceny. Vandalism. Grand Theft Auto. It's all good clean fun at Caltech.

solving a certain task. Rebecca Green lugs a huge quarto volume of *Art of the Ancient World* as they traipse from clue to clue—all beautifully done, with colored tissue paper and sealing wax.

One clever aspect of the stack is that some clues can be learned by directly translating the hieroglyphics, but others use them in a different fashion, which the group quickly figures out.

"Forget the Egyptian, do it phonetically," Green urges as they work on a clue whose literal translation is meaningless but whose transliteration sounds like: "We-keep-u-seef." They immediately guess campus security, and race to the office. Sure enough, there by the sign, another clue.

Despite a few extraordinarily well-planned stacks, the grand designs of many seniors, so bright the night before, are often nowhere to be seen in the actual stack, abandoned in the press of time. Keith Akama's stack has no heat-sensitive plate, no remote-control car. Rather the entrance to the u-trap is covered by chicken wire and four sliding metal panels. The scenario is more faux Tolkien—"The year of our Lord 1287, during the final campaign . . ." Mechanical engineering freshman Don North says he is not scared of entering the water, per se. "I just hope they remembered not to use electrical currents," he says. Caltech students worry about electrocution the way students at other universities worry about venereal disease.

While North and his classmates contemplate the soggy instructions retrieved through the u-trap, a passing student grimly informs them, "I have bad news. Drop day is today." The students ponder this for a moment.

In Blacker courtyard Troy and Marc—two of the underclassmen working on the transmogrifier stack—are whipping up 20 gallons of purple Kool-Aid in a plastic garbage can.

"We're small," explains Troy, dropping foot-wide cubes of clear ice into the purple liquid. "We've been transmogrified." The next clue instructs them to sell 50 cups of the Kool-Aid for 5 cents a cup. They run off to make a sign. "Hey, small dudes!" exclaims a passerby.

It's 11:10 A.M. At the Olive Walk, a crowd has gathered around those solving the "Stairway to Heaven" stack, dedicated to forming a cult religion around their god, "Fred the Dog." They are at step eight of their karmic journey—venting rage—and are accomplishing this by dropping objects in a cooler of liquid nitrogen and smashing them on the ground. (For the uninitiated, liquid nitrogen freezes ordinarily unbreakable objects, such as rubber balls, so profoundly they can be easily shattered). A Master lock explodes into shards while TV news cameramen struggle to set up their equipment. They have to settle for a shot of a student kneeling by the smoking liquid and explaining it has a temperature of 77 degrees Kelvin, or 200 degrees below zero, Celsius. (Being a Caltech student, he's right on the money. Nitrogen boils away at -195.8 degrees C and freezes solid at -210 degrees C).

Someone drops a quarter into the liquid nitrogen and it begins to bubble. "Hey, is this legal?" nervously asks a TV guy.

TV attention is diverted from the nitrogen to a tree by Fleming Hall. "Bob, can we shoot a little of these people in the trees, whatever they're doing," a news face shouts. The cameras gather around a group of students hanging in the branches of a small tree. The students, wearing blue construction paper cone noses and tails of orange, red, and yellow crepe paper, make a sort of "bow wow wow" noise. They are from the "Dobie Stack," and are performing the mating ritual of the Ragianni Bird of Paradise.

Of course, not everyone on campus is involved with Ditch Day. Caltech has over 1,000 graduate students, a pair of whom get on the elevator at Millikan Library. They ride together in silence, for a while, facing the front of the elevator. Then one speaks, in a flat, mechanical voice.

"I walked around campus," he begins, still staring ahead. "It's pretty funny what people are doing." His companion says nothing. The door opens. They walk out.

After lunch, the sky is cloudless, bright and hot, and entropy begins building in the air. The first stack cracked is at 1:30 P.M., and teams working on other stacks begin to sag with fatigue.

Three girls from the hieroglyphics stack sit staring morosely at a new clue. "What's that boot thing?" says Rebecca Green, pointing out a certain hieroglyphic character. "It doesn't make sense at all. It just doesn't make sense." They are looking for the next clue, somewhere between Dabney and Fleming, but just can't find it. "Have you tried hyperspace?" a geeky-looking character suggests, perhaps sincerely, perhaps as a pick-up line. The girls ignore him.

A "Stairway to Heaven" acolyte with a fire hydrant cutout hanging around his neck rushes up and drones. "Here—I have to give out 100 pennies by three o'clock or God will kill me," politely handing over a shiny new penny. Less than a minute later, a girl approaches, offers a penny, and says exactly the same thing.

The most interesting spot is Blacker courtyard, where a variety of novel stacks are being acted out. Mike Ricci's "BEGA-Death Beach Party" stack asks the underclassmen to saw off the roof of his beater Capri. The ugly bronze-brown finish is painted into wild beach multicolors as students round off sharp metal edges with rasps. Three of the five metal letters are returned to the Capri to spell out "CAR." Max Baumert's "Senseless Violence Against Road Runners" stack evolves into a giant, guillotine-like cleaver made of heavy timbers, soon put to work crushing watermelons and ice blocks and computer terminals and anything else at hand.

One of the big losers is senior Sam Dinkin, whose "Bridge Problems" stack, presenting 52 bridge problems, so irked underclassmen that they scorned the bribe and counterstacked, dragging the contents of his room out onto the Athenaeum lawn. To top it off, Dinkin tries to return to campus early, and is duct taped to a tree.

Those who have solved their stacks begin to line the Olive Walk, indulging in their bribes. One stack, solved early, involved lobbing potatoes at distant targets, including the beer can suspended in the air by Millikan. The stack's bribe offered a 12-pack of Coors, a 4-pack of light wine coolers, and 2 cheesecakes. The bribe is considered just barely adequate.

"We thought about counterstacking," says Jessica, the Wagnerian-voiced freshman.

There is at least one classic finesse stack. At Page House, Ajay Cheeda left a single mathematical puzzle that involved factoring a huge number into primes, which then formed a cryptogram that had to be deciphered to finally yield the combination to Cheeda's room. A group of underclassmen, led by Dave Lande, cracked the stack so quickly, they had time to counterstack the room by

The poor man's Miata. Eager frosh uses menacing power tool to cut roof off of woebegone 1977 Capri.

changing the combination on the door lock (which Cheeda worked out almost immediately). "I suppose he and Dave are just too smart to outwit each other," a student quipped.

In a dark hallway in Ricketts, some seedier-looking Techers are slumped on the floor, enjoying the benefits of a generous bribe—Piper-Heidsieck champagne, Glenfiddich scotch, marijuana, chocolate chip cookies, and egg rolls.

The pirates have broken their stack—Dussin ended up running a power line into the pond, but the juice somehow shut off (perhaps explaining why nobody was killed). By the time the pirates got there the key had fallen. But it was a moment's work to hammer the concrete into pieces. They inventory their bribe's goodies: British Pusser's rum, a mango, Fiddle Faddle, Doritos, Lowenbrau, and Chee•tos. Pete wasn't taking any chances.

Shortly after five, the seniors begin to filter back in. Keith Akama seems disappointed that the underclassmen were able to breech his u-trap and race through the clues and tasks he left for them. But he really doesn't want to talk about it. "They got in, for the most part," Akama says, curtly.

Told that his stack worked, in general, Dussin raises his arms to the sky and exalts. "It did? Yes, yes, I am happy" and dances away.

The bribes are gathered in the rec room of Fleming—soggy vistas of cream pies and cupcakes and brownies and chips and beer—and there is a party of a sort, handicapped by the lack of ice and the lack of some sort of intangible party spirit. One is reminded of an unescapable truth about Caltech—nobody got in on the strength of their social skills.

The Fleming cannon, an old breach loader and perhaps the only still-operable cannon on a college campus, is loaded with a blank charge and fired for the benefit of "Action 2 News," which has lingered around all day. (The cannon, incidentally, was liberated 20 years ago from nearby Southwestern Academy in San Marino. It wasn't quite a prank—at least not on the Academy, which was looking to get rid of it anyway. It may have been something of a prank on nearby houses, since Fleming House residents cleaned and restored the Franco–Prussian War-era weapon and fire off massive salvos to celebrate big events such as finals week and commencement. The concussion sometimes shatters nearby windows).

There is a burst of excitement as Harry Gray, Arnold Beckman professor of chemistry, strolls down the Olive Walk accompanied by a young female friend. This is the same Harry Gray whose face students once skillfully superimposed on a cheesecake photo of a naked man holding a well-placed clipboard. The photo, dubbed "Caltech Chemmate of the Year," was pasted in 1,000 copies of the 1973 Caltech catalog sent to prospective freshmen. He is a popular guy, and the students go wild, applauding and chanting his name.

They hoot and holler for a few minutes, but quickly load up on Ding Dongs and pie then drift off to their residence halls for dinner. The party soon breaks up. Well before sunset, the Caltech students are back in their rooms, hitting the books, or slumped over broken-down couches, watching the local news on giant-screen TVs, waiting to see how Ditch Day played, hoping for the thrill of seeing themselves on television.

1

SPECIAL CASE #2
Lady Liberty Lights Up
Lake Mendota

They're taking student government as a joke!
—Sue Krull, 1978
Wisconsin student

ive days after arriving on the sprawling Madison campus of the University of Wisconsin, Leon Varjian, who enrolled in just one class, was already hard at work—collecting signatures on petitions to change UW's name to the University of New Jersey, so graduates could say they had attended a prestigious Eastern school.

Besides, he reasoned, New Jersey was the only state without a "University of . . ." school. It should have one. Wisconsin, on the other hand, already had 26 branches of the University of Wisconsin. It could spare one.

Without doubt many who passed Varjian, sitting at his little card table on the mall, with his droopy mustache and long hair, must have smirked to themselves and thought: "Loser. Nutcase."

Little did they know. Before the school year was out this odd man, passionately pursuing his quest, would gain control of the student government. He would funnel its considerable budget into a whirlwind of pranks, stunts, games, and feats of frivolity.

He would bask in the glare of national publicity and form a legend that still glows, radioactively, in Madison to this day.

Varjian did not do this alone. Central to Varjian's story is a person who, passing his card table, did not dismiss him as a mere lunatic. This was Jim Mallon, a tall, thin communications arts junior from Rochester, Minnesota, who was to act as a deadpan counterweight for all of Varjian's unbridled energy. Mallon immediately recognized the beauty of what Varjian was doing. He signed the petition.

"To me, it was great theater," remembers Mallon. "He was treating it seriously as a leftist cause—the card table, the petitions, the maps of New Jersey and Wisconsin—but it had an absurdist premise."

"We instantly recognized each others' genius," Varjian said, at the time. "The melding of two creative sparks."

From a field of pink flamingos to relocating the Statue of Liberty to campus, twice, these two sparks would use their position and access to funds to create something even rarer than a single great prank—an atmosphere of great pranking. A Golden Age.

Working out of the Student Government Association Office—their office—Mallon and Varjian created a prank government called the Pail & Shovel Party, attracted supporters, and carried on the entire charade for two years, despite continuous opposition from grim-jawed Junior League types.

Varjian, whose manic personality gathered most of the attention, was not your average new student, trembling with anticipation at being freed from the parental overlords.

When he arrived on campus, in the fall of 1977, he was 25 years old, battered from a 15-month stint in the working world.

The University of Wisconsin-Madison was his third holding pen of higher education. At New Jersey's Montclair State, in 1972, he set up the Miss Montclair Steak Pageant, a spoof of the university's beauty pageant.

Graduating with a degree in mathematics, he moved to Indiana University at Bloomington, where he sponsored the Banana Olympics, which included a banana toss, banana relays, banana water races, and the search for a banana hidden in a haystack.

It was at Indiana that his behavior shifted from the merely whimsical to the truly unhinged. At Halloween, he pranced through the streets of Bloomington in an orange cardboard pumpkin suit.

"I think it was the change in the air—it affected my brain," Varjian said during the blaze of publicity that attended his stay in Wisconsin.

Flush from the pumpkin suit success, and others, such as the coronation of a rubber-masked Nixon on the university library steps, Varjian ventured into politics, running for the mayor of Bloomington on his Fun City ticket in the 1974 election.

One can only speculate how the political climate of the country might have been changed for the better had Varjian won. As it was, he pulled 16 percent of the vote, carrying 2 of 15 precincts, and ran third in a field of four. Not a bad showing for a man who proposed erecting a circus tent over Bloomington's municipal building so the politicians would feel at home.

Ironically, Varjian's lighthearted play for mayoral office almost torpedoed his later attempt to submit to the pedestrian working world. After receiving his master's in mathematics from Indiana in 1976, he took a job as a computer programmer with the U.S. Bureau of Labor Statistics in Washington, D.C.

This offended the finely-tuned sensibilities of Representative John Myers, a Republican from Indiana's 7th district. Myers felt that anyone guilty of ridiculing the electoral process shouldn't be allowed to toil at a dreary, number crunching government job. He sent a two-page letter to the bureau commissioner, berating him for hiring Varjian, whose "open mockery of government and his disdain for the system he will be a part of seems to warrant the attention of your personnel office."

But Myers's clout was not what he imagined, and Varjian kept the job until he saw what work was doing to his quality of life:

"It was awful," he said. "I couldn't stand it. You get up every morning, get on a bus and go to work with a bunch of pasty-faced commuters, sit behind a desk all day doing nothing and come home at night. I just couldn't take it."

Most people live their lives that way, but Varjian chucked his job in August 1977 and reached out toward the reassuring maternal teat of college life. He chose Madison—at random, he claims—without having seen the campus and with no particular academic program in mind.

He took one credit, to maintain his student status, while working part-time at the school's computer center on weekends.

The germ of the Pail & Shovel Party began as Varjian's brand of one-man street theater. About twice a week, he and his friends put on public displays such as the University of New Jersey petition campaign or snipping off a mattress tag marked "Do Not Remove Under Penalty of Law," then being arrested by confederates dressed as policemen.

One of Varjian's favorite ploys was called the "Blue Light Special." He would go to a discount store and buy $25 worth of the trashiest, most tasteless merchandise he could find, then hawk it on the street and see if he could get passersby to accept it for free.

Mark Borns, a member of the WSA senate, knew Varjian from his sidewalk performances, and thought he would be the ideal person to fill a vacant senate seat. He asked Varjian to submit his name for consideration.

The student senate debated Varjian's appointment for an hour and a half, finally approving him by two votes. Whatever else can be said about the somber, pre-Pail & Shovel Party student government, at least it had the sense to plant the seeds of its own downfall. No one can say Varjian misrepresented himself—he attended his nomination hearing in a clown suit.

Toward the spring of 1978, Varjian and Mallon hit on the idea of a mock campaign for student government, based in part on Varjian's membership in the senate.

While its opponents were to later portray the Pail & Shovel Party as a horde of Visigoths, gleefully sacking the sedate Rome of serious student government, that was not the case. Student politics—then, as always, in Madison, as everywhere else—were adrift in a sea of apathy. Every election, some 30,000 Madison students didn't even bother to vote.

That spring the campaign began with Varjian seeking the vice presidency ("that's where the power is" he said) and Mallon the presidency.

The campaign was one continuing performance-art piece on the corruption of government. They flung mud at their oppo-

nents—literally, hurling buckets of wet earth at life-size carica-
tures of other candidates, which they later turned around and
stabbed in the back, using rubber knives.

They built a party platform of Popsicle sticks, and made the
usual election promises—to convert the school budget into pennies and dump it on the UW Library Mall, then let all the students go at it with pails and shovels. They would replace parking
meters with bubble-gum machines and buy the Statue of Liberty
and move her to Wisconsin. They promised to flood the football
stadium and hold mock naval battles. They would provide free
long-distance phone calls, erect a 50-foot tall Mickey Mouse Pez
candy dispenser and change all students' names to Joe Smith "so
that professors in large lecture courses would know everyone by
name."

The Pail & Shovel Party made no effort to hide what they were
all about.

"Honesty, integrity, responsibility . . ." began a campaign flyer
distributed that May. ". . . Pail and Shovel doesn't believe in any
of them!"

To their great surprise, they drew a following and, to their
delight, opponents.

"Our campaign was just a comedy routine," said Jay Kennedy,
a member of Varjian's inner circle. "Slowly we began to realize
it was a threat to somebody—the fact that somebody saw us as a
threat was funny, to us, and spurred us on."

"The student government at that time consisted of the self-
appointed descendants of the superstar leftists of the sixties,"
says Mallon, today. "They were humorless, self-serving people in
various incestuous cliques between the government and the
newspaper. It was very closed, very humorless and extraordinarily serious—about as dry and boring and distant from main-
stream students as it could have been. . . . It occurred to us, two
days before the election, we might win."

They did win. In May's two-day student election, only 12
percent of the students voted, and the P & S ticket got 33 percent
of the vote, enough to beat a field crowded with 10 other tickets.

Simply having the most votes did not guarantee Varjian and
Mallon would be able to assume power, however. The candidates
they had defeated complained about their unorthodox campaign
tactics to the school election board, which held a circus-like hear-

Geniuses at play.

ing to settle the question. Largely owing to the efforts of an eccentric Madison lawyer named Eddie Ben Elson (see box) Pail and Shovel managed to prevail, marking their success by hanging a banner reading UNDER NEW MANAGEMENT from the Union Building.

In the fall student senate election, the P & S took 29 of 36 senate seats, providing the rubber stamp the two would need to implement their policies and fight off constant attempts to impeach them.

The monthly WSA meetings became more interesting. Each one was given a theme. One month was a Halloween costume meeting. Another was a singing meeting, where debate had to be rendered in song.

At a meeting to "air some dirty laundry" P & S members drank beer, wore laundry baskets over their heads, tossed dirty clothes, strung clotheslines across the podium and blew soap bubbles.

EDDIE BEN ELSON

The Pail & Shovel Party would have never survived the blizzard of legal challenges leveled against it were it not for the good offices of Eddie Ben Elson, "the Looney Lawyer" of Madison, Wisconsin. A local legend, Elson campaigned for mayor in 1969 on a platform that included painting police cars psychedelic colors. He lost. The next year, he ran for Dane County district attorney. To show he had nothing to hide, Elson announced his candidacy in the nude, from the stage of a strip club called the Dangle Lounge. He lost again.

His motto during the campaigns was "Only Obey Good Laws," and posters bearing the slogan have become collectors' items.

Despite his antics, Elson had a serious side. An early defender of the rights of the mentally ill, he had a hand in overturning Wisconsin's involuntary commitment law in 1972, and was constantly testifying at Congressional inquiries into the subject.

Taking on the cause of Pail & Shovel was a natural for a man who, among other things, defended the attorney general's Irish Setter for running unleashed (among his various defense strategies was threatening to demand a jury of the dog's peers—12 other dogs—and requesting that the dogcatcher identify the dog from a lineup of Irish Setters).

"He was directly responsible for our success," remembers Mallon, who said after their first election, those still in power in the WSA tried to invalidate the election. Elson represented them at a hearing before the student board in UW's Great Hall, which was packed with close to 1,000 students.

Elson walked up to each of the five board members and screamed that each was personally liable for the actions they were about to take, and if they illegally invalidated the election then he, Eddie Ben Elson, would personally sue each of the board members, tying them up in court proceedings for years and ruining their lives. They voted to uphold the election results.

"He won the victory we had already won," says Kennedy. "They could have just said the election was invalid, and that would have been the end of it."

Eddie Ben Elson's own tale ends tragically, however. He killed himself in 1983. Over 500 people attended his funeral. 🐄

Of course, certain quick-witted students were fast to catch on to what Varjian and Mallon were really doing.

"They're taking student government as a joke," pouted Sue Krull, a junior majoring in agricultural education and a member of the senate. "I don't believe that students are so apathetic that they vote people like this in."

One of their early activities involved appropriating $200 for a "defense fund" to save a broken-down horse named Roberta from the glue factory (or more precisely, to save Senator Roberta from the glue factory, since Varjian and Mallon saw that the beast was named to the student senate).

They also hosted a toga party for 10,000 people, inspired by the movie *Animal House*. The party received enormous publicity and John Belushi called during the middle of the festivities to bestow his blessings.

Critics of Pail & Shovel were not irked by the pranks as much as the maddening belief that they were *wasting money*. Each student kicked in two bucks a year to finance the student government, and Varjian and Mallon used that pool—some $80,000 a year, as well as surpluses from previous years—to fund their activities.

The expenditures, breathlessly revealed by the journalism school pinheads at the student newspaper, the *Daily Cardinal,* included $600 worth of toys for their office, $100 in personal long distance phone calls, $125 for a telephone answering machine used for the "Dial a Joke" service, another $532 for toys for students to play with during registration, and $11,500 lost sponsoring a Little Feat concert.

If the eager investigative journalists over at the *Cardinal* expected Varjian and Mallon to dissolve into a puddle of shame when confronted with the evidence of their departure from standard WSA budgetary practices, they were in for a surprise.

"Sure we are squandering funds," said Varjian, responding to the allegations. *"Absolutely* true! We squander them on beer. We squander them on parties. . . . We squander them on all sorts of things. That's what keeps the Wisconsin Student Association *strong."*

Mallon and Varjian also brought less ribald—if equally controversial—fare to campus. They sponsored appearances by poet Lawrence Ferlinghetti, birth control enthusiast Bill Baird, consumer advocate Ralph Nader, along with writers, alternative energy experts, and artists.

In the beginning, their term was quiet. It took about six months for Mallon and Varjian to figure out how to loosen the purse strings of student government. Once they learned how to appropriate and spend money, the fun really began.

By the new year, they were confident enough to begin honoring a campaign promise even their staunchest supporters never expected them to fulfill.

They brought the Statue of Liberty to Madison.

The statue, constructed in a woodworking shop on Winnebago Street, was to have been set up in the dead of night, facing campus, on the ice of frozen Lake Mendota.

In reality, the construction took three days, which mitigated the surprise somewhat, but not the dumbfounded reaction of most who saw it.

Traffic snarled on roads leading to the statue, as gawkers slowed to take a look at the chicken wire, papier-mâché, and plywood mock-up of Lady Liberty, the head, 22 feet tall from the bridge of the nose up and the arm, 40 feet tall from the wrist to the tip of the torch.

"The neat thing was, you could walk right out and touch it," says Varjian, today. "It was spectacular to see, it really was. The pictures don't even capture the essence—the coldness out there, cold weather, cold air, the whiteness around it, and here's this greenish thing, and it's huge, just sitting there."

The submerged view—obviously done for reasons of econ-

omy—was taken by some Kremlinologists to be a political statement, à la the last scene from *Planet of the Apes*.

This Varjian denied.

He claimed that the statue was purchased from a financially-
strapped New York City, and the cable snapped while it was
being helicoptered into place, sending the statue crashing
through the ice.

*Some are born to greatness, others construct a giant replica of the
Statue of Liberty, jutting out of the ice on a frozen lake.*

While the general consensus was positive—the statue was
called "beautiful," and city fathers speculated it might become a
winter tourist attraction—student government types were again
incensed at the tab—$4,500. Tom Bilodeau, a student senator
and third year law student, took Varjian to court, charging that
the money had not been approved by the senate, in violation of
the WSA charter. A student coalition, headed by former WSA
members ousted by the P & S Party, began a petition drive to put
a recall referendum on the ballot.

Ironically, Mark Borns, who had brought Varjian into the

WSA and started the whole thing, was now one of the P & S Party's chief opponents, collaborating with the *Daily Cardinal* on exposés and rising in the student senate to read the fine print from budgetary bylaws.

Varjian countered that the money had been approved, as part of a general art fund he could spend at his discretion. He offered anyone who didn't like the statue the rebate of a dime—each student's share in the cost. Some 60 students gathered outside WSA offices chanting "We want dimes" and protesting the statue. Varjian eventually complied, writing each a check for ten cents.

The *Daily Cardinal* had a field day. While it had failed to even note the construction of the statue, the newspaper lovingly recorded the dime incident and other tiny protests that erupted in its wake. After polling 409 students—less than 1 percent of the student population—they reported massive unhappiness about the statue and claimed "only 10 percent said they would continue to support Pail and Shovel."

Mallon and Varjian weathered the storm. The complaint against them was thrown out on the grounds it hadn't been taken first to student court, which was packed with a trio of P & S judges.

Real legislators, apparently without better things to do, took notice. State Senator David Berger (D-Milwaukee) began drafting a bill that would require the university chancellor to approve all student expenditures beyond $500, but the measure was dropped when student leaders at other campuses complained that it would hopelessly snarl the administration of their own funds.

The dean of students, Paul Ginsberg, froze WSA assets while he examined the books, but decided that no laws or regulations had been violated, and granted the P & S a kind of grudging admiration rarely extended by administrators toward students who step beyond pay-your-tuition-and-get-out conformity.

"It's their money and we're not going to tell them how to use it," Ginsberg said. "The thing about this is, they're not misleading people. They made their platform very clear when they ran. Everyone has a chance to vote in these elections, and if they don't like it, it's up to the students to vote them out."

DAD GINSBERG

*P*aul Ginsberg was dean of students at the University of Madison for years, and oversaw the safety of hundreds of thousands of students. None of them gave him more trouble than Leon Varjian, who called Dean Ginsberg "Dad," since it was Ginsberg who signed their allowance checks. During their first meeting, Ginsberg who speaks slowly and deliberately, took out a pipe, lit it, stretched his arms over his head and said: "Hello Leon."

Varjian, without missing a beat, leaned back in his chair, pulled out a bubble pipe, stretched his arms over his head, and began blowing bubbles.

"He realized we were going to be more difficult to deal with than he thought," says Kennedy, who was there.

Despite the difficulty, Ginsberg became a supporter, in fact an admirer, of Pail & Shovel.

"I took to the Pail and Shovel because they brought smiles to people and they gave people permission to look at the world and say it's crazy," says Ginsberg, now living in retirement in Madison. "They frustrated the hell out of some people, and me at times, but they didn't hurt anybody."

Ginsberg, who refers to Leon Varjian as "one of the brightest minds I have ever encountered," added that one of the few souvenirs he keeps from his days as dean is a plastic pink flamingo.

Ginsberg's words of reason went unheeded, however. The statue was undone by a political process more time-honored than democracy. With the naked hypocrisy of those who talk up good government while in fact craving personal power, the P & S enemies, their legal options exhausted, chose a, uh, *preterparlimentary* move against the statue—they burned it down.

It happened in the early hours of March 2, 1979. No one is certain who did it, though an investigator hired by P & S pinpointed a certain fraternity. The *Daily Cardinal* was accused of having advance knowledge, since they happened to have a photographer at the scene, in the middle of the night, minutes after the fire was set. In fact, some say the *Cardinal* hired high school students to set the fire, though nothing was ever proved.

The head portion of the statue was completely razed, but the armed survived intact. The *Capitol Times* captioned a picture of the wreckage: "A sad scene on a bleak day—Miss Liberty's head is gone forever." Time would prove them wrong.

The next month, Varjian was dealt another defeat when he ran for a seat on the Madison City Council.

"I wanted to turn Madison into 'Cheesetopia.' After all, Wisconsin is the dairy capital of the nation," reasoned Varjian. "Why not turn Madison into the cheese capital? We could line the streets with cheese. We could build a statue of Elsie the cow to put on top of the Capitol building."

Alas, like Bloomington, Madison balked at such progressive leadership, and Varjian finished fourth in a four-way race.

"I guess Cheesetopia was just somewhat ahead of its time," Varjian sighed.

Varjian's city council defeat failed to dim his and Mallon's confidence on campus, however. Announcing their intention to lead the WSA "for life," the pair mounted a second campaign in the spring of 1979.

This campaign was just as wild as the first. Instead of promising just the Statue of Liberty, they promised *all* the major monuments of the world, and indeed did bring the Washington Monument to the mall—they hired a huge construction crane, from which they suspended a tiny five-inch bronze copper replica of the nation's most famous phallic symbol.

As always, their campaign was marked by a candor rare in politics of any sort.

"Are you nuts enough?" read a campaign flyer from the second election. "A year ago you turned over the reins of student power to a couple of mindless clowns. Now we are asking you to go for it all. We are asking you to reelect Mallon and Varjian, who started it all, the two who made wackiness, nuttiness, irresponsibility, craziness and self-motivation household words. Are you nuts enough for that?"

The answer was a resounding "yes." In May, 17 percent of the

OTHER SMARTY PARTIES

*T*he Pail & Shovel Party was neither the first nor the last to tweak the inherent hubris, futility, and pointlessness of student government. Among other noteworthy prank parties:

1. Dead Beet Party. Just a few years after it was created, student government at the University of Illinois—one of the first schools to pretend to give power to the students—was already an object of apathy and derision. In the spring of 1874, no less than three joke tickets ran for office—the Reporter, the Anti-Clique, and the Dead Beet parties—as compared to just two earnest parties. They did not wield power, but the student government collapsed anyway, under the weight of student ambivalence and the festering belief that student officers acted merely as "faculty spies." Which in fact they were. Before the end of the decade the attempt at government utterly failed, the faculty admitting that student government was "an agency chosen by us for the accomplishment of the disciplinary work incumbent on us as a Faculty" and had always received "a constant though generally silent supervision."

2. Gumby Party. Running under the slogan "Reason as a last resort," MIT juniors Kenneth H. Segel and Kenneth J. Meltsner were elected president and vice president, respectively, in March 1982. One of the most noteworthy events of their administration occurred in April, when the MIT Undergraduate Association passed a resolution granting Harvard College colonial status—based on its demonstrated inability to govern itself—and named an MIT sophomore as colonial governor. The following fall, during his speech to the incoming freshmen, Segel was kidnapped by "Commando Hacks" protesting Harvard's subjugation, and a banner FREE HARVARD was unfurled.

3. Monarchist Party. The University of Maryland at College Park not only elected James Risner, "King James," as he liked to be called, to the presidency of its SGA in the fall of 1988, but gave his Monarchist Party a majority in the university legislature. Risner, who sometimes attended classes in an ermine robe and a crown, promised during the election to build a castle

behind the main library and surround the campus with a beer-filled moat. On his first day in office, he commissioned a cost analysis to study the feasibility of the project, which included refrigeration units to keep the beer cold. He also announced plans to restore the university to its agricultural roots. "What we'd like to do is bring the cows back," he said. The student body, including the newspaper, generally supported the Monarchists, voting to change the school motto from what Risner called "something in Latin which no one understood" to "I'd rather be studying."

4. The Who Cares? Party. At the same time the University of Maryland was in the hands of monarchy, the University of Utah in Salt Lake City was in the grip of apathy. The Who Cares? Party leaders, a pair of longhairs named Mike Kaly and Grant Sperry, campaigned on promises to raise money by "panhandling, running strip bars, raffles and prostitution"—an unusual platform for a college that is 50 percent Mormon. They won an astounding victory, if you consider the 90 percent of the students who did not vote as supporters. The feat was compounded by the fact that Kaly and Sperry spent only $6 on their campaign—for colored chalk to scribble campaign slogans—as compared to other candidates who spent more than $1,000 in their unsuccessful campaigns for the offices, which not only controlled a $500,000 student budget, but included free tuition and a personal stipend of $250 a month. For their inauguration, the Who Cares? candidates rejected the costly traditional ball in favor of a simple Indian ritual.

5. Dow Jones and the Industrials. Chris Clark was a physics major at Purdue University. He also played bass with a band called Dow Jones and the Industrials. In the spring of 1980, they began to cut their first (and as it happened, only) album, and the question arose of how to promote the record.

As luck would have it, Purdue was gearing up for their student government elections at the same time, and Clark decided to run for SGA vice president as a way to tout his band.

Running on a platform borrowed from Pail & Shovel (his two major issues were "getting my hand in the till" and "arbitrary government," though he also promised to dress the football team in florescent pink-and-green) Clark was swept into office by a heavy turnout of voters.

Once in office, he hired his band as much as possible and held government sponsored beer parties and a "Jamaica Ganja Giveaway."

As with Pail & Shovel, some people were caught off guard by all this.

"We had promised to drain the treasury and blow it on fun stuff," remembers Clark, now a computer consultant. "People were surprised, toward the end, when the budget ran into the red."

While the highlight, as described in chapter three, was holding "Vegetable Awareness Week" to coincide with a visit by Ronald Reagan, they were also able to sell 5,000 albums and hold countless gigs, typically at some frat, where they poured invective on the brothers, who happily boogied to their music while oblivious to their message.

"The whole time we were bashing frats; we would just abuse the hell out of them, and they loved it," marvels Clark. "What could be more fun than finally having a platform to expose and ridicule people you really hate?"

Even Leon Varjian came down to bestow his blessings. Dow Jones paid his expenses for a weekend trip to Lafayette, where he presided over the "Win a Date With Dow Contest" and partied to his heart's content.

6. Silly Party. Northwestern. A descendant of the Pail & Shovel Party, since founder Andy Mozina is from Wisconsin and admitted being inspired by the goings-on up in Madison. The Silly Party's five officers were swept into power in April 1984, on the promise of making student government more fun. High points of the party's lone year in office were bringing a penguin to campus in February (fulfilling a campaign promise) and sending a pair of frogmen, in full wet suits and tanks, to several classes to mark April Fool's Day. Mozina, who also edited the NU humor magazine, *Rubber Teeth*, could also be counted on for a stream of bons mots. "I stand on my record," a campaign poster read, "and jump up and down."

students voted in the election—close to a record for enthusiastic participation. When the dust settled, Varjian and Mallon had won, despite wistful polls in the *Daily Cardinal,* with a 37 percent plurality, beating their closest opponent by 600 votes. That fall, Pail & Shovel senators kept 26 of 36 senate seats.

MORE CLOWNS, MORE MUD FOR WSA, mourned a headline in the *Daily Cardinal,* which marked the event by reversing their masthead to white letters on a black background, an old journalistic symbol for extreme tragedy.

"They hadn't done that since the invasion of Cambodia," says Kennedy. "Here we are, a group of clowns winning the student election, and it's equated to the illegal invasion of Cambodia."

In the fall, Pail & Shovel hit the ground rolling. The first day of classes, students were welcomed by over 1,000 pink plastic flamingos planted on Bascom Hill, the quadrangle in front of the dean's office. Students gaped in wonder. The birds may have been "blown north by Hurricane David," Varjian speculated.

The flamingos were a wonderfully ephemeral prank. They had been set up at eight in the morning, and at first formed a uniform field of pink—people said it looked as if Pepto-Bismol had been poured over Bascom Hill.

Almost immediately, however, the birds started disappearing. People would stop, admire the hill, and grab themselves a flamingo. By 2 P.M., the entire flock was gone, though individual members were spotted around campus for years to come—in windows of fraternities, on the roofs of dorms, everywhere.

"It was a fitting end," says Varjian.

Pail & Shovel again provided toys for students to play with during registration. They raised money to send "Vern the Mouse" to Iran to rescue American hostages. They ran an ad touting the WSA's pending first-strike nuclear capability, and for an organization called "United Alcoholics of America."

Toga II was even a bigger blast than the year before, forcing the university to relocate an appearance of the Dalai Lama for fear he would be swept up in the festivities (which included a Dalai Lama look-alike contest). At the evening's end, Mallon and Varjian discovered they had $20,000 in one dollar bills in "big leaf piles" at the Pail & Shovel office. Not knowing what to do with the money, they stuffed it, uncounted, into grocery bags, which they jammed into the night depository of their bank.

They also tried to take control of the *Cardinal* board, running a slate of P & S candidates who would, presumably, take the bile out of the reporting of their fanatical enemy. The *Cardinal* shrieked about press freedom, and the P & S slate was defeated.

In early February 1980, the P & S Party reprised their Statue of Liberty success of the previous year. They had at first planned to place something even more controversial on the ice. In November, the WSA had approved the concept of building a replica of the Chappaquiddick bridge in Madison. "Going along with the idea of bringing these famous monuments from the East Coast, I thought, 'Why not Chappaquiddick?' " said Tom Sontag, a P & S Party senator who thought up the idea.

But when the lake froze over the chance of striking back at the statue arsonists proved too great. Chappaquiddick fell by the wayside (sorry Ted) and plans were set in motion to build another statue.

This one cost even more—over $6,000—and was assembled by a crew of about 50 people in the Old Music Hall on the UW campus. To thwart arson, they claimed the new statue was fireproof. (It wasn't. Carved out of Styrofoam, it would have burned like a glob of Sterno). The P & S Party provided guards to protect the statue, and hawked postcards, which are sold in Madison to this day. Great plans were harbored for the statue. Jim Mallon said eventually they would create an entire New York skyline to go behind it, however "these things take time."

The statue remained in place until March 5—when the Department of Natural Resources regulations required that "fishing shanties" be off the ice. It was removed to Barneville, Wisconsin, where it supposedly remains.

By the time the statue was taken down, a war of sorts had broken out.

Earlier on, a P & S Party official, sergeant at arms Stu D. Baker, had taken to sending postcards to various campuses across the country, declaring "war" on them. In February 1980, hostilities erupted between the governments of the University of Wisconsin and the University of Missouri, which had elected its own absurdist student government.

> ## ''BOJ MOI! ETTA OTTAWA!''
> *L*ike Madison, Carleton University in Ottawa is situated on a lake. Well, really no more than a bulge in a canal, but they call the 10-foot-deep body of water "Dow's Lake." In the late 1970s, Carleton architecture students capitalized on the current concern about Soviet submarines (one had become trapped in a fjord in Sweden) by creating their own sub scare. Constructing a large-sized submarine conning tower, they anchored it off-shore in Dow's Lake one night, causing considerable surprise the next morning.

Tensions began rising when the Missouri Student Association sent out questionnaires, nationwide, seeking information on student governments. WSA responded with "a vicious letter."

A flurry of derisive, frequently obscene letters were exchanged between the governments—UW was called "sewage-sucking swine" and "toenail-chewing imbeciles."

"I guess they got tired of answering all our surveys, so they sent us a nasty letter and we sent them a nasty letter," said MSA president Garth Bare. The MSA officially declared war back on the WSA.

The war of words turned into a war of, well, shit, when a quartet of MSU students slipped up to Madison and spread 500 pounds of manure on the steps of the Memorial Union on Sunday, February 24.

"BOOM. Consider yourselves nuked," read a note, accompanying the waste. "Compliments of the four saboteurs from Mizzou."

"We just wanted to prove to Mallon and Varjian that they couldn't push us around," said Bare.

But just as a good prank is, by nature, a fleeting thing, so the P & S Party could not keep going forever. Even though Mallon and Varjian were still declaring themselves in office for life in March, in April they announced they would not seek a third term.

They offered no public explanation, at the time, but now say they both realized the joke had run its course.

"It was time to do something else," says Varjian, simply.

"It was a moment, those two years," says Mallon. "We had all reached the end of our senior years—I had two senior years. We couldn't spend our lives being student government leaders. There was no money in it. It pretty much kind of ended. Also, it was more legendary to go out big and mighty rather than let it wind down."

To the end, the *Daily Cardinal* was in the dark. In a brief editorial titled "Clowns Step Down," the newspaper summed up the Pail & Shovel reign with "In addition to wasting thousands of dollars from student fees on toys and other worthless indulgences, the Pail & Shovel regime is known to have a sizeable slush fund due to a health insurance fraud."

A variety of parties, including the Badger Party, the Great Expectations Party, the M & M Party, and the Campus Reformation and Appeasement Party tossed their hats into the ring. But serious student politics began creeping back, and as it did, the Wisconsin Student Government rejoined that great realm of things which no sane person cares to know anything about.

Sic transit gloria mundi.

CODA—LEON AND JIM

*M*allon and Varjian hovered around the periphery of campus life for a number of years. In the early 1980s, they produced a locally-popular cable show four nights a week, "The Vern & Evelyn Show," featuring comedy sketches hosted by a pair of mice, who spoke in falsetto voices provided by Mallon and Varjian. The CBS affiliate, WISC Channel 3 in Madison, featured a sanitized monthly version, "The Best of The Vern & Evelyn Show" and the pair assembled a 13-show package they hoped to sell into syndication.

But success proved elusive, and their friendship ruptured over disagreements about how to proceed with "The Vern & Evelyn Show."

There was one swan song prank. On April Fool's Day, 1982, Varjian led a squad of high-stepping, red-jacketed, giant radio-toting marchers in the "First Annual April Fool's Day Boom-Box Parade" through downtown Madison. There was no second.

Mallon pursued a career in television production and directed a low-budget horror movie he called *Muskie Madness*. It can sometimes be found in the grade-Z section of certain video stores titled as *Blood Hook*. Today he produces the much-acclaimed comedy cable show "Mystery Science Theater 3000," and, reprising his Vern & Evelyn days, supplies the voice of one of the puppets.

Varjian returned to his native New Jersey, cut his hair, and now teaches mathematics at a high school in Midland Park. Describing himself as "a retired public official," he insists he has no regrets about leaving Pail & Shovel behind and, in fact, says most of his friends do not even know about that chapter in his life. Still, he is proud of what he accomplished at Madison, and feels the experience made him a better teacher. "Getting up in front of a group of people and speaking, getting their attention, putting on a show," he says. "Isn't that what the best teacher you ever had did?"

COMMON PRANKS
All Hail the Noble Cow!

It was such an insult to be beat out by a cow that I refused
to accept any of the honors at all.
—Rosalind Morrison

The vast bulk of the world's creatures are not whales or
elephants, but basic organisms such as worms and slugs and
paramecia. Similarly, the majority of pranks are not the epic
events we've been highlighting so far—Rose Bowl Hoaxes and
Sacred Cods and Statues of Liberty—but rather small occur-
rences, hastily conceived and executed.

But just as it would be remiss to limit a study of life on the
planet to hulking, complex creatures, so a prank should not be
ignored simply because it is reproduced on many campuses over
the years.

As we saw in the chapter on early pranks, a well-done minor
prank can be a thing of beauty.

The problem is, if pranks as a whole are barely mentioned in
any sort of written record, then common pranks are practically
never documented.

The exception, of course, is Caltech. In recording their incred-
ibly sophisticated pranks, they have—almost as an after-

thought—also wrote down a few very basic pranks, pranks that are replicated thousands of times each year at colleges all over the country.

For instance, in 1932, several students at Caltech's Blacker House moved the entire contents of a student's room into the courtyard. The room was reconstructed completely, with clothes hanging on the rack, books on the shelves, the front door propped open and even the light fixture, hanging from a tree. The owner of the room, identified only as a senior named Jack, returned to Blacker and comported himself in the best way a person could under the circumstances—he spent the night in the "room," sleeping in the center of the courtyard and starting a tradition at Caltech of spending the night in your dislocated room before hauling it back to where it belongs.

Most college students are not nearly so meticulous when it comes to stealing somebody's room. As a freshman, I lived in a four-man room at Northwestern where one of our roommates had committed the unpardonable sin of coming from a wealthy family and going by his middle name, "Fitch." There was a fire exit across the hall from our door, and it was quick work to drag everything Fitch owned to the fire exit and hide it in the stairway. The only thing more frustrating than finding your bedroom set up in a public place is not finding your bedroom at all. He searched and searched, and we compounded the prank by pre-tending to not fully understand what Fitch was talking about, perhaps pushing the prank further into the realm of cruelty than pranks should go. Fitch certainly never forgave us, for this and other offenses, and we all felt genuinely bad about it later; re-morse being one of the risks run by those who commit pranks.

The polar opposite of hiding the contents of a room is leaving the contents where they are but hiding the room. Again, it is a prank found everywhere but actually chronicled at Caltech.

Chuck Conner, '75, was one of those freshmen who are some-what uneasy at living in such close proximity to others of his species. Several times, he mentioned to his dormmates that he had a reoccurring dream of someone going into his room and twisting off the tonearm of his stereo system's Zero-100 turnta-ble.

When Conner left campus in the middle of the week to visit his

APOCRYPHAL PRANKS

$\mathcal{S}$ome pranks, alas, have had their verification lost in the sands of time. Or they sound a bit too good to be true. Or their proof is still resting, hidden, waiting for some member of the great lay public to bring it to light. Then there are those that are outright lies. Anyway, these are from the files of the delightful yet untrue, or at least unproven:

1. Hugh Troy, the legendary wag of Cornell University, is depicted in H. Allen Smith's *The Compleat Practical Joker* as taking a rhinoceros foot wastebasket, weighing it and attaching ropes to either side so he and a friend could makes sets of rhino tracks in the snow. Supposedly, he created tracks to the edge of the ice on half-frozen Beebe Lake, leading a professor of zoology to declare the next day that a rhino had visited campus and plunged into the lake. Both Troy and the rhino wastebasket are proven facts; whether the incident actually occurred depends upon whether you trust the word of H. Allen Smith, a dicey proposal at best. Other Troy pranks have more support behind them—general consensus seems to be that Troy actually did purchase a park bench, then carry it around with confederates until police stopped them, whereby they grandly produced the receipt—a tableau they repeated several times, until the police quit stopping them, after which they snatched all the benches in the park.

Still, despite Cornell's constant proud references to Troy, there is little hard evidence of his having actually done many noteworthy pranks. "I think you are right to be skeptical about Hugh Troy," said Gould Colman, an archivist at Cornell. "I have never seen any documentation on him."

2. Sir Robert Peel, while at Christ Church, Oxford, as an upperclassman, supposedly played a practical joke on a freshman known for his poor scholarship. Peel sent the youth a message that the vice chancellor, having heard of his poor academic performance, wanted to test him privately in Greek Testament to see if it was true. Peel played the role of the vice chancellor. He put the trembling freshman through a grueling set of questions, severely denounced him for his blundering, and

told the freshman that he would probably be expelled. The unfortunate frosh, so the story goes, fled the college without waiting for the final result and was never heard from again.

3. Like young Peel impersonating the vice chancellor, the most dubious prank stories revolve around students pretending to be people who, upon reflection, they could never successfully pass themselves off as being.

In 1824, the Marquis de Lafayette was scheduled to visit Brunswick, Maine on his tour of the country and receive an honorary degree from Bowdoin College. At the last moment, Lafayette changed his plans and could not make it. Word was slow getting around in those days, as the story goes, and a Bowdoin sophomore was able to dress himself as Lafayette and drive into Brunswick in a chaise, acknowledging the ringing bells and cheering townspeople, kissing the ladies and ending his day in an alcoholic haze at a feast given in his honor.

The problem—ignored in Bowdoin lore repeating the story—is that the hero of the American Revolution was 67 years old in 1824, and no sophomore was going to be able to enjoy a lengthy dinner, never mind get within kissing distance of any ladies, without giving away the deception and ending up riding to the town outskirts tarred and feathered and straddling a rail.

4. In his execrable memoir of Northwestern life in the 1950s, *College Bred: Or a Four Year Loaf*, Lee Riordan spins a tale that is eerily similar to the Lafayette at Bowdoin story. He claims to have dressed as General Douglas MacArthur and ridden in a Lincoln convertible through the wild Evanston throng that greeted the war hero on his triumphant visit to the city, April 26, 1951. It would have been a neat trick—sliding in front of MacArthur's motorcade and picking up the Evanston police escort, soaking up the masses' adulation, then nipping away. To top it off, Riordan says, when the real MacArthur showed up, people thought he was an imposter and ignored him.

Riordan insists the story is true, but then he also insists that the driver of the car is now "a very, very high official in the Pentagon" and would never consider substantiating the story.

What makes Riordan's fabrication worth mentioning is that someone did, in fact, scoot in front of MacArthur. Only it wasn't

Riordan pretending to be MacArthur, it was Bill Jauss, '52, pretending to be Teddy Roosevelt.

"Somebody remarked that I looked like a younger Theodore Roosevelt," says Jauss, now a sportswriter. "I went to the home of the guy and he dressed me up in as Teddy Roosevelt."

Jauss and his friend got ahold of a convertible and put a poster reading OLD SOLDIERS NEVER DIE on the side. Moments before MacArthur whizzed by, they drove leisurely past the crowds lining Sheridan Road.

Not only does Jauss's story have a more true-to-life ring to it (Riordan's tale includes ecstatic sorority girls hurling their pins at him) but the April 29, 1951 *Daily Northwestern* reported the escapade, noting that Jauss-as-Teddy "scooped MacArthur" and was "waving his sword defiantly" as he drove up the street. It is safe to assume a bogus MacArthur would have been noticed as well.

5. Speaking of MacArthur, the general's name has long been associated with the most famous prank at West Point. Classmates at the time suspected it was MacArthur who was the mastermind behind a group that, after taps one night, rolled the reveille gun over to the West Academic Building and hoisted it to the tower. It took almost a week for workmen to get it down. He was also suspected in another gun prank, this one on April 16, 1901, when the gun was dragged to the superintendent's lawn and the muzzle pointed at the door. Later biographers, however, credit the pranks to other cadets.

6. Another dubious tale involves Robert Benchley, theater critic and beloved humorist, who maintained that, while he was studying at Harvard at the turn of the century, he and a friend crossed the river one day to wander through Boston's Louisberg Square area, an enclave of the rich. On a whim, Benchley and his friend went to the front door of a mansion and knocked. "We've come for the davenport," said Benchley to the maid. Invited in, they picked up a sofa and carried it out, crossed the square, and rang the bell of another mansion. When yet another servant answered, Benchley announced, "We've brought the davenport. Where shall we put it?" After depositing the couch, Benchley says, the two proceeded on their way.

7. Perhaps the most well-known untrue college prank is the story of how Eugene O'Neill got kicked out of Princeton for throwing beer bottles through the windows of then-college president Woodrow Wilson's house in 1907. While O'Neill was certainly a hellion and well capable of the act, the story was without question concocted 25 years after the non-fact by one of O'Neill's gang of writer friends. George Jean Nathan felt the need to liven up the image of his grim pal, and invented the legend for his *Intimate Notebooks of George Jean Nathan*, published in 1932. O'Neill denied the story for the rest of his life. "I *liked* Woodrow Wilson," he told *The New Yorker* in 1948. "I wouldn't have done a thing like that if I had been swimming around in a lake of vodka."

8. Comedian Jonathan Winters would have been a member of Kenyon College's class of 1950, but he never made it. Exactly why he never made it is a matter of dispute. The story is that Winters welcomed the Ohio springtime by painting himself and his bicycle green and riding nude down Kenyon's Middle Path screaming "I'm the Spring Fairy! I'm the Spring Fairy!" It is not, however, an indisputable fact. "There are people who will swear it did happen, and people who will swear it didn't," said Kenyon's Tom Stamp. Winters denies the episode, but then, it is the type of thing a person in their mature years—even a comedian—might feel inclined to deny, whether it happened or not.

girlfriend, senior Randy Lewis felt it was an apt time to dust off the old "disappearing room" trick.

First the room was filled floor to ceiling with crushed computer paper (an abundant substance at Caltech, even in 1972). Then the real work began. Bob Durst, '74, tells the tale:

> We attached a sheet of plywood to the door and proceed to plaster over that section of the wall where his room had been. First a layer of rough plaster, then finish plaster, and finally the entire

side . . . was painted. The Housing Office donated the paint since it was to be used for "house improvement." We then removed the baseboards from the floor and scrounged up a new section and put it in. As the final touch we took the light fixture that had been a foot or so from his door and mounted it in the middle of the section we'd just plastered over. We didn't wire it up, but that didn't matter since most of them didn't work anyway. Then we waited for him to return.

Chuck came home about midnight Sunday night. The halls, of course, were filled with curious classmates, and Chuck, confronting the blank expanse of wall where his room had been, took it like a man, beating his head against the wall and wailing "Why me? Why me?"

To twist the knife a little deeper, everyone denied knowing who he was or what he was looking for.

Chuck located a hammer and began prospecting for the door, but the relocated light fixture threw him off and he had trouble finding it. About the time he started breaking holes in the plaster campus security showed up, responding to reports of a deranged man vandalizing campus property. It was all sorted out, eventually, and the computer paper, dumped out Chuck's window and into Blacker courtyard, was torched about 2 A.M. for an impromptu bonfire.

Poor Chuck trapped outside his room naturally leads to thoughts of a common, antithetical prank—pennying someone inside their room. This difficult, yet still-common prank is probably done daily on campuses across the continent. For those who have never done it, a brief description is in order, this one from a senior at the University of Toronto who, worried his career could be derailed by a simple act of prankishness, asked that his name not be used.

"We pennied somebody in—it took a hell of a long time," he said. "You've got to have thousands of pennies, and you've got to have the right door. Basically, you need a newer door, since some of the older doors have really large cracks (between the door and the frame). The best door will have the hinges outside the door, since then they can't get outside themselves."

The technique, the student said, is to carefully wedge pennies in between the door and the frame, going all the way around the frame. This takes time, and so is usually done at night or—in this particular instance—when the owner had passed out and was dragged to his room to sleep it off (not that we are encouraging this sort of thing. Ideally, the afflicted student would have been taken to a qualified medical facility, then straight to prison for the rest of his life).

"It was funny" remembered the U of T student, who has also practiced a variant of pennying where a rope is used to tie the doornobs of every room on a floor together, making exit something of a communal problem.

Pranks such as pennying begin to get into a highly desirable quality found in pranks that I like to refer to as the "time bomb" effect. In most cases, such as pennying, the prank and the payoff are hours apart, but in some pranks the setup and conclusion can be days, even weeks apart. This increases the delightful anticipation of the prank and, not incidentally, makes it harder to get caught.

A good time bomb tale comes from a professor I bumped into in the cafeteria at Occidental College. The professor, Eric Newhall, told me how in 1963 he was taking a history of Western civilization class with a fellow freshman, Michael Davis, himself a prankster who had pestered Newhall and his friends to such a degree that revenge was in order.

The course had a 10- or 15-page syllabus of reading material, one of which was a thick book on art. Newhall took Davis' syllabus for the class and removed a page of reading assignments several weeks in the future. He then found a typewriter that matched the script and retyped the page, inserting an extra assignment—115 previously unassigned pages from the art text on the history of Arab art.

The day of the class corresponding to the altered assignment arrived, and the professor delivered his normal lecture. Davis, who did the Arab art reading, kept waiting for the material to be referred to. Newhall could barely suppress his glee as he watched Davis grow increasingly confused and irritated, finally shooting up his hand and demanding: "But what does this have to do with Arab art?"

It is a cute truism that certain aspects of college life remain

---

RIDICULOUS RULES REDUX

The general liberalization of society has taken a toll on ridiculous college rules. But every now and then a new one pops up.

As the nation was getting ready to shake off the constricting skin of Prohibition, Northwestern University, situated next door to the Women's Christian Temperance Union in Evanston, Illinois, decided to stand up against the tide of popular opinion in a particularly idiotic fashion.

On December 16, 1932, the school banned beer. Not the foamy amber substance—that was already forbidden.

They banned the word.

"Beer has nothing to do with students, no matter what is done about it in Washington," said William R. Slaughter, advisor to campus periodicals. He ruled that neither the term "beer" nor "any word associated with it" could appear in Northwestern publications. Later, he vigorously denied having banned the word, but it is unclear whether the Associated Press was perhaps duped by a student hoax, or Slaughter actually did ban the word, but buckled under the ridicule that followed the announcement and beat a hasty retreat.

---

constant. Clay tablets from students in ancient Babylon are forever being discovered that end with whatever series of triangular scratches meant "send money."

Certain pranks that were common in earlier centuries are still common. Presidents no longer have horses, but certain schools retain their bells, and students still go after the clapper.

At Princeton, the bell in Nassau Hall rang on the hour, and for a full minute at the beginning and end of each class period. The first recorded instance of the bell being stolen is in 1864, and in 1985 students were still scaling the ivy clad walls with regularity in the dead of night. So much regularity, in fact, that the administration had the chance to become skittish at the thought of how decades of winking approval might suddenly become putty in the hands of some slick lawyer, his paralyzed client dourly parked in the corner of a Kafkaesque courtroom. Couldn't have that.

So they banned clapper stealing, and dreamt up a clapper hunt; the sort of dumb event that administration-types always assume will be embraced by the students. An old clapper was hidden on campus, and freshmen given clues to try to find it.

"Of course," remembers a Princeton freshman from the time, "no one thought this was very much fun."

What was fun was when two classmates dressed up as maintenance workers and entered Nassau Hall during regular working hours, approached a secretary and told her they were there to "fix" the bell. They fixed it with a hacksaw, removing the clapper and keeping the tradition alive until 1991 when quavering Princeton, tired of downing Maalox and looking over its shoulder, got rid of the clapper.

Just having had a bell did not make Princeton the most traditional college, bell-wise. The bell at Virginia's all-male Hampden-Sydney College is still rung by the janitor. (And it will continue to be run by the janitor for the foreseeable future. When the administration announced plans to install an automated bell system in 1988, student outrage scuttled the project).

Along with bells, chapel continued well into the 20th century, and with it chapel pranks. At Kenyon College, where daily chapel was mandatory until 1962, some students in the 1930s put flour into the pipes of the chapel pipe organ, causing the opening notes of the morning hymn to explode with a cloud of flour.

Cows are another continuing butt of college pranks. Anyone who has read Gary Larson's "Far Side" is aware that Larson has tapped into the intrinsic humor possessed by cows. Perhaps it is because their docility and blank-eyed dullness is so very human. Perhaps something else.

College students have always known this. As we have seen in chapter one, the earliest cow pranks involved their relocation. This did not stop. Both MIT and Harvard—neither school particularly associated with animal husbandry—have modern stories of cow removal.

On May 27, 1928 a Cambridge patrolman, Albert Waite, was startled to find four MIT students picking grass. Upon investiga-

PAINTED THINGS

*I*n the animal kingdom of college pranking, perhaps the lowest order still identified as pranks is the phenomenon of painting an object on one's own campus. Not to be confused with drenching the statue of your opponent's founder in your school colors, painting a place on campus is more a forum of communication than a prank, and only deserves mention because so many schools take such unfounded pride in the number of times a fence, or a rock, or a shoe gets painted by frat houses promoting their formals.

A few better-known pigment receptors:

1. The fence; Carnegie Mellon University.

2. The rock; Northwestern University: A former drinking fountain, the Rock metamorphisized into a meeting area and paint bulletin board. An amazingly big deal at NU, underscoring its lack of a pranking tradition. To drive home the servility of the student body, the administration moved the Rock a dozen feet from its normal post to keep students from dripping paint on the sidewalk.

3. Each class at the all-female Sweet Briar College in Sweet Briar, Virginia have their own paintable object: the freshmen paint a hitching post; the sophomores paint a rock; the juniors paint a bench, and the seniors paint a set of stairs.

4. The cannon; Tufts University: In spring 1989, a faculty member received a marriage proposal via the cannon.

5. The Student Administration Council Dome; University of Toronto: Just three stories tall, it seems high enough when you're snaking along a four-inch ledge with a bucket of paint in each hand. 🐄

tion, he learned the grass was to feed a brown-and-white cow that was residing on the roof of an MIT dorm. The dorm, on Ames Street, was five stories tall. As it is with all cows, it was a lot easier to get her up the stairs than down. The cow was coaxed, pushed, pulled, and carried down the five flights to the ground, where hundreds of students were waiting. "Pandemonium broke loose," the *Boston Herald* reported the next day. "The crowd howled in glee and cheered and yelled." Officer Waite, policeman of a gentler age, took the cow in tow and walked her a mile to the city stockyards.

Harvard's episode happened sometime in the 1930s (the clippings in the *Lampoon*'s scrapbook are undated, but have a Depression-weary feel to them). Editors of the magazine led a red-and-white cow into Harvard Yard and padlocked her to a small tree in front of Sever Hall. Around the cow's neck was a notice, "Property of Charles Townsend Copeland," who was Harvard's Boylston professor emeritus. As such, he had a traditional privilege of grazing a cow in the yard, a right unexercised, it was estimated at the time, for 150 years. Just as the authorities were puzzling over what to do with the cow, a truck from a nearby slaughterhouse pulled up and the angry driver demanded the return of the animal. Asked to comment by the press, the *Lampoon* issued the following bit of philosophy: "Fame today— hamburg tomorrow, such is life."

For some schools, cows were the best they could do. A history of Taylor University, a small college in Indiana, refers to a cow appearing on the second floor of the Administration Building in the fall of 1933 as "perhaps the most famous (or infamous) prank of the period." Considering what their peers in Cambridge, Ithaca, and Princeton were doing at that time, one must mourn for the Taylorites.

Big Midwestern universities have their roots in agricultural land grants, and take their cows more seriously. A classic cow prank that crops up at Ag schools, from time to time, is a heifer being elected homecoming queen.

If at all possible, involve a cow.

A prime representative of the genre is the case of Maudine Ormsby, homecoming queen of 1926 at Ohio State University. Supported by the College of Agriculture, Ormsby, a prize holstein, initially placed a respectable second.

The homecoming committee learned of Maudine's species during a check of the student directory, to contact the homecoming candidates for picture-taking purposes.

Maudine was disqualified from the final balloting for the crime of being a cow (how thankful we all should be that such appalling speciesism would never be tolerated on today's enlightened campuses). The Ag students raised a protest, but what saved their cause was that all the human candidates were disqualified owing to dishonest campaign tactics. That left Maudine, who was the wrong phylum, but at least had not cheated. The homecoming committee decided to chose a queen at a special session. Amazingly, they threw up their hands and selected Maudine.

The ball back in their court, Ag college officials had to nix the participation of Maudine in the parade festivities, since the cow—which had set world records in milk production—was too valuable to parade around. Her place in the homecoming procession was taken by two undergraduates inside a cow outfit. There was an attempt to inject some human cheesecake into the parade by naming a certain Rosalind Morrison as the unofficial queen.

But she had her pride, and refused. "It was such an insult to be beat out by a cow that I refused to accept any of the honors at all," she said, 30 years after the fact.

Maudine was not the last barnyard creature bedecked with human honors at OSU. In 1940, when all the candidates for May Queen were eliminated on technicalities, the OSU May Queen was a mare named Jean Scot.

In 1979, a purebred holstein cow named Bessie was elected Miss Auburn in a write-in campaign after "a wave of pro-Bessie sentiment swept across campus," said the *Auburn Plainsman*. Bessie trounced her closest competitor, a brunette named Cindy Murphy, 2,385 votes to 1,009—the largest margin in the history of the contest.

The originator of the Bessie campaign, Betsy Butgereit, sagely noted that support for the cow was more a raspberry at the frats than any great show of devotion to cows.

"It was so successful because independents saw it as a way to make their voices count in what has previously been a Greek-oriented race," she said.

But Bessie was disqualified when the election board ruled her campaign posters had been too large. Murphy—who was already the reigning Miss Auburn—took her contested reelection in stride, agreeing to be photographed presenting her bovine competitor with a cowbell engraved "Bessie, Miss Auburn 1979–1980. A moo beginning."

"A lot of people have said to me, 'Why do you want to encourage this sort of thing?' " she mused. "But I think it's just intended to be a joke."

Perhaps the most notorious cow incident of recent years took place at the University of Virginia, where pranksters hauled a calf to the top of the dome of their Rotunda on May 5, 1965. The calf panicked, and had to be tranquilized before it could be brought down. The shock must have been too much for its nervous system and the calf died shortly after returning to earth. Animal lovers around the world howled in protest.

Like cow pranks, the simple riot has also survived into modern times. While the student protests of the 1960s forever linked student rebellion with political action, traditionally student rampages were motivated by nothing more profound than misplaced sexual energy or the changing of the seasons. Typically, when-

CAN THE ''FREE BEER TECHNICAL LIBRARY'' BE FAR BEHIND?

*E*very so often, an administration will misstep and allow the students to name something, and the students will be bold enough to capitalize on the situation.

1. Jimi Hendrix Dorm; The State University of New York at Stony Brook: SUNY definitely has a Jimi Hendrix dorm, but nobody at Stony Brook seems to know how it got that way.

2. Tammany Hall; Northwestern: In an effort to get students to stop killing themselves at the Foster-Walker Complex, a hive of four buildings containing tiny single dorm rooms famous at Northwestern for inducing madness, the administration permitted students to name their residential halls. One of the more historically minded chose the moniker of the corrupt New York City government of the late 1800s. Dorm T-shirts were printed up with a Thomas Nast caricature of Boss Tweed and the immortal slogan: WHADDAYA GOING TO DO ABOUT IT?

3. The Alferd G. Packer Grill; University of Colorado at Boulder: An equally historically minded group at the UC-Boulder got control of the process naming the food service in the student union and named it after Packer, the inept Colorado guide who, during a cruel winter in 1874, survived for 55 days on the flesh of the people who had hired him to lead them through a remote pass. The name gave rise to Alferd G. Packer Day, with raw-meat eating contests and, sometimes, a life-size chopped liver mould in the shape of a man.

4. At MIT there are several strangely named buildings. Two dorms have been dubbed "New House," for obvious reasons, and "Next House," since there already was a "New House." In 1968, an old residential hotel was purchased and converted to a dorm. It was dubbed Random Hall, a joke for the mathematicians, named in honor of Arthur J. Random, who does not exist.

5. In the spring of 1972 a student government referendum at Northwestern University asked whether to keep the nickname of

their football team "Wildcats," or change it to "Purple Haze."
"Many nicknames are types which are normally associated
with aggressiveness and Wildcats certainly is one," said Jim
Bendat, the '71 graduate who originated the idea. "Haze, like
a mist, is a very peaceful thing."

He also pointed out there were 13 other colleges with teams
nicknamed the Wildcats, as well as a precedent for team name
changes at NU—prior to 1924, the football team had been
called "The Fighting Methodists."

The students voted 1,691 to 1,179 in favor of Purple Haze.
But the administration, slyly illustrating the powerlessness of
students even to determine their own cartoonish football mascots, chose to ignore the vote.

"The issue has hardly made a dent on my consciousness,"
said President Robert H. Strotz whose consciousness, truth be
told, was rarely dented by anything other than the sound of big
alumni donations ca-chunking into NU's bulging coffers. "I think
there are so many more important things in this world to worry
about."

ever the thaw hit in the spring, or students returned to college in
the fall, outbursts and pranks were de rigeur.

"The spring riot season got off to a whopping start," *Life*
magazine noted on May 11, 1953, describing how 1,000 Princeton students spent "three ebullient hours" setting off fireworks,
invading a movie theater, knocking over garbage pails, and blowing train whistles.

"The prankster season opened here Monday with the removal
of two 600-pound anchors from Northwestern University to the
University of Chicago and the walling up of an auto near North
Park College," the *Chicago Daily News* reported on October 26,
1964.

The avuncular chuckle sounded by *Life* and the *Daily News*
was typical the way these student outbursts were viewed by the
public, at least those who were not directly inconvenienced by
undergraduate revelry.

Students of today will note that no one was shot by jittery policemen, no symposia were necessary to sort out Gordian knots of student emotion—in fact, disruption was expected and universal.

A variation of the riot is the panty raid, which is basically a riot of the male students directed toward the women. Panty raids are not really very interesting—few can be thought of as clever; in fact there is a numbing sameness about them. Quite a few were simply destructive, cruel and offensive to even those with more robust sensibilities.

Yet, along with goldfish swallowing and phone booth stuffing, panty raids linger in the collective memory and are associated with pranks. So a quick history is probably in order.

The first coed college was Oberlin, which admitted women when it opened in 1833. More and more colleges went coed as the century progressed, often sticking women in auxillary "Ladies Institutes." But social custom was such that for coeducation's first 65 years not even the most boisterous male student would dream of harrassing his female counterparts, let alone steal her undergarments.

That changed. The earliest panty raid I could find took place in October 1899, when a Halloween nightshirt parade at the University of Wisconsin went out of control. About 400 male students, dressed in pajamas and nightshirts, marched over to the Ladies Hall. The idea was to serenade the women, but the parade got "out of hand" and some students broke into the laundry room and made off with 204 articles of clothing, worth an estimated $500, "as trophies of the escapade."

The raid had considerable repercussions. "No man," an incensed President Adams declared, "has any right to be called a gentleman who will still keep an article of ladies' wearing apparel as a trophy." The women, taking a page from Aristophanes, resolved to have "no social relations with the men of the University until the faculty or men of the University have satisfactorily dealt with the offenders . . . and until all losses sustained at that time have been made good."

Most of the clothing was returned, eight of the paraders were suspended, and five expelled.

Another early panty raid—at Mt. Union College in the winter of 1916—had a particularly ironic twist to it, in that the raid was precipitated by women students. While the school's fraternities were off-campus at their Pan-Hellenic banquet in downtown Alliance, a group of Mt. Union's female students snuck into the fraternity houses and stacked the rooms in some fashion that is lost to history.

The men, returning home, rushed to Elliot Hall, the women's residence, and lay a siege, clabbering for retaliation (not, however, for panties, or whatever it was women wore in 1916). At this point, the police laid a fire hose and threatened to douse the men unless they desisted.

Denison College reports mass raids on the women's dormitories in 1936, 1942, and 1946, producing what may be the best moment in panty raid lore: As hundreds of shouting boys surrounded Stone Hall, President Shaw raced to the scene to assess the situation. The besieged head resident of Stone, seeing Shaw hurrying toward the door, reportedly exclaimed, "Oh no, Dr. Shaw, not you, too!"

The panty raids that linger in the public mind, however, took place in the spring of 1952, when some sort of panty raid madness gripped the country. It began when 2,000 boys at the University of Missouri swept through, not only the girls' dorms on their own campus, but went on to hit those at nearby Stephens College as well.

Within a week, there were panty raids at Michigan, Nebraska, Miami, Iowa and other schools.

Not to belabor the issue, but there are a few panty raid highlights worth noting:

- at the University of Toledo the women raided a men's dorm and made off with boxer shorts.
- at the University of Massachusetts the boys, not content to removing panties from dresser drawers, took to stripping them from their owners' bottoms, and the police had to step in.
- at the University of Ohio, the Athens police used tear gas to break up a raid, and at Berkeley a rampage caused $10,000 damage to a girls' dorm.

The most interesting thing about the panty raid fad is not the events themselves, but rather what they say about life in the 1950s. You don't need to be a psychologist to find deeper meaning in hordes of young men howling outside women's windows, while the women shout encouragement and toss underwear at them (Which leads to another important point. As often as not, women were enthusiastic participants in the raids, egging on their besiegers and often drawing university censure for their provocations).

The entire phenomenon was pretty much killed by the one-two punch of political protest and sexual freedom. Massing the students against the war looses its oomph if the next night the students are massed for panties and, beside, if a guy can get ahold of women's underwear by nicely asking his girlfriend to hand him a pair, he'd look pretty silly soliciting it from strangers. (The current attitude on the subject is best summed up by the cover of the October 1991 issue of the *National Lampoon,* portraying well-armed sorority women gunning down panty-nabbing freshman and headlined: PANTY RAIDS ON CAMPUS TODAY: BAD IDEA.)

Onward. We have seen some of the delight that MIT takes in dandying up its Great Dome. Many other schools, while not showing the same perseverance or technical skill, manage to come up with some noteworthy building adornments.

Many times the peculiarity of a building itself will prompt pranks. The tower of Hammerslag Hall at Carnegie-Melon has a series of step-backed tiers, like a wedding cake. As a festive trapping of commencement in the late 1980s, somebody dressed a pair of life-size mannequins like a bride and groom and placed them on top of the hall, to complete the effect.

The University of Virginia rotunda clock in 1967 became a Mickey Mouse face, and in 1971 Vice president Spiro T. Agnew's mug beamed down from the clock. (Caltech's now-demolished Throop Hall boasted the same two faces on its clock—Mickey in 1965 and Spiro in 1971).

Science Hall at the University of Wisconsin-Madison is a solid, turn-of-the-century structure with a novel fire escape—a metal-encased tube that spirals around itself for four floors of pitch darkness. Leaping headfirst into the tube and braving the giddy, chilling corkscrew journey (not to mention enduring the lecture at the bottom if a university employee catches you) is a UW tradition.

AVOID THOSE HIGH TUITION BILLS

An old prank, repeated at many schools, is the fictional student. Princeton has had many—the earliest on record being Joe Gish, invented by several members of the class of '05 and given away when five of his creators accidentally signed chapel cards for him on the same day.

The great thing about a fictional student is he can be as elaborate as you wish, appearing only on paper for a while, suddenly assuming a tangible form, then laying low again. When one group tires of him (or her), another can take up the responsibility for breathing life into the spectral soul.

The grandly named Ephriam di Kahble lived in high style at Princeton in 1935. He had a rented, furnished room, and took out ads seeking tickets to the Dartmouth–Princeton game.

At Iowa State, in 1937, several instructors were actually persuaded to grant A's to the imaginary Cuthbert Gleep.

In the fall of 1931, several Caltech students crafted the name of Helmar Sciete for a specific goal—capitalizing on the particular pronounciation difficulties of their professor, Fritz Zwicky. Sciete was duly registered for one of Zwicky's courses but the professor, a resourceful man himself, avoided the tongue twister by skipping Sciete's card when calling the roll then, at the end, asking if there was anyone present who had not been called.

Sciete's progenitors were not quite ready to give him up, however. Come finals, they cooked up a little plot to rub their homunculus into Zwicky's face a bit. For the final, Zwicky wrote the questions on the board, then left the room (remember the Code). One of the conspirators copied the five questions, then passed them out of the room to a group of grad students—all of whom had taken the course. They whipped off perfect answers and included their own sarcastic comments, such as "This is a very stupid and trivial question—why waste examination time on such tripe?" and "Can't you think of anything new?"

The name signed to the exam, of course, was Helmar Sciete.

Caltech is responsible for yet another notable fictive student, the lovely Cyndi LePage.

The dorms at Caltech are exceedingly small and close-knit, and have their own distinctive personalities. In an attempt to make sure incoming freshmen fit into the dorm they eventually live in, there is "rotation week," where students visit various houses before being assigned. To facilitate a good match, they fill out "interest sheets" that are posted in all the houses. These include a photo and, not too surprisingly, these photos are scrutinized quite closely by upperclassmen looking for babes.

In 1984, Sean Moriarty, '85, and Warren Goda, '86, realized they could have some fun by creating their own, too-good-to-be-true freshman, whom they named Cyndi LePage in honor of Page House. Cyndi was a lovely blond gymnist from Ft. Lauderdale who dotted her I's with circles and listed her hobbies as "horseback riding, collecting figurines, having good times with friends."

With the help of a faculty sympathizer, they got Cyndi listed on the official rotation list, and they recruited a group of student confederates to pick up her name tag at mixers and report sightings. So effective was the ruse that some people who were not in on the prank swore that they saw the elusive Miss LePage, who was almost admitted into a residence house, even though nobody had met her. 🐄

"I don't know why we liked to do it so much," said a graduate. "It was a challenge and it was illegal and it was fun. And what the heck, you only go around once in life, right?"

The common prank that has the most sting is the hoax. The nice thing about a hoax is it flushes its own victims. It poses the question: "Who's a dupe?" and half the fun is watching the hands shoot up.

A good hoax doesn't have to be a grand, Hugo N. Frye type of thing. A pair of University of Kansas seniors pulled a nifty little hoax in the fall of 1989, and all it took was a clever idea, some pocket change, and a comb.

Carol Jong and Loretta Bass were good students who passed through KU without creating much of a splash. They found themselves waiting in line to have their senior photographs taken for the yearbook, pondering their rather uneventful transit through the giant university.

Jong had the idea, as she posed, remembering a cousin who posed for two yearbook pictures, one under the name Roland Garros, the famous aviator for whom the French Open's stadium is named.

Her friend Loretta thought it was a great idea.

Two days later, Jong and Bass entered a women's bathroom at Strong Hall and disappeared, emerging transformed into engineering students Bertha Heffer and Ethel McDown. For $3 apiece, the credulous yearbook photographer recorded their picture for the *Jayhawker.*

Over the next five weeks, Jong had eight pictures taken and her roommate, nine.

Jong ended up with her picture in the yearbook seven times, in each department, under such disguises as Buffi J. Baker (business); Violet Couleur (fine arts); Anne U. Rissom (allied health), and Dorrie N. Collum (architecture). Bass was less successful, since a friend on the yearbook staff noticed the duplications and plucked out her pictures.

Still, the picture that ran in her rightful spot was Bass's fictional computer science major "Meg A. Byte."

When the yearbook was released in May 1990, there was a burst of publicity, all taken in stride by the good-natured yearbook staff, ever ready to see the humor in a situation. "It makes us and the university look pretty silly," grumbled a *Jayhawker* editor.

Yearbook hoaxes are rare, simply because the yearbook is guarded by a zealous yearbook staff, whose interest is focused on a single volume. Newspaper hoaxes are more common since, in the crush of producing a paper every day, there is more opportunity for subterfuge.

Hoaxes should not be confused with parodies. The difference is that a hoax is designed to fool people—perhaps only momentarily—while a parody is more of a joke based on reality, but not

CAMEO PRANKSTER—KURT VONNEGUT

In his recent book of essays and memoirs, *Fates Worse Than Death,* Kurt Vonnegut says he was inspired to become a prankster by no less than the legendary Hugh Troy. Vonnegut also attended Cornell, and Troy would often pop back to school to regale undergraduates, including the future novelist, with his possibly-true tales.

Duly inspired, Vonnegut says he perfected his own trademark prank. He would go to a large lecture class where an exam was being held, take a copy of the exam, tear it up into small pieces, toss them into the face of the professor, then stalk out, slamming the door behind him. The trick was, of course, that he wasn't enrolled in the class.

designed to pass for it. For instance, in 1934 the *Harvard Lampoon* produced a cutting parody of tabloids with its *Daily Record.* The screaming headline NAB EINSTEIN, YALE PRESIDENT, HITLER, HARVARD STUDENT, IN LOVE NEST RAID ON EAST LYNN APT. may have been funny, but was never mistaken for the real thing.

Not so another *Lampoon* effort in 1968, directed at the *New York Times.*

On March 7, 1968, the *Lampoon* flooded Cambridge with 2,000 fake copies of the *Times.* It was a very well–planned-out mission. The year before, on March 7, 1967, the plotters set aside 2,000 copies of the *Times.* Removing the front page, they substituted their own new version.

Most fake newspapers err on the side of burlesque, but the 1968 *Times* is masterfully subtle. The stories are alarming—with headlines such as CASTRO SEIZES U.S. NAVAL BASE AT GUANTANAMO—but not implausible. The only photo on the page is that of the Parthenon, over the headline ANCIENT PARTHENON TOPPLES AS QUAKE ROCKS GREECE. A professor of classics purportedly wept at the news.

There were some ludicrous touches—a small story in the lower left-hand corner about the walrus in the Central Park Zoo speaking, or an announcement that the *Times* would begin printing comics—but you had to stop and read the thing to catch them. In all, it made for a neat package that caused a lot of momentary puzzlement (though there is no evidence to support the story of the weeping professor).

The perennial victim of the *Lampoon* is the *Harvard Crimson*. From their first fake *Crimson* in 1901, the Poonsters have been beating the *Crimson* like a drum. There are too many great fake *Crimsons* to even list them all, so a few highlights will have to suffice:

- That very first 1901 parody also set the precedent for taking advantage of the *Crimson*'s habit of not publishing on holidays. The newspaper had announced there would be no paper on Memorial Day, but of course no one remembered that when they looked down and saw a familiar-looking paper waiting for them. Perhaps most infuriating for the *Crimson* staff were the splattering of typographical errors the *Lampoon* intentionally spread over the issue.
- On November 10, 1963 a fake Crimson blared PARIETAL PRIVI-LEGES WITHDRAWN UNTIL MARCH—ABUSES, PUBLICITY FORCE BOARD TO PROHIBIT WOMEN. The news created understandable concern (for those who exist only in the immediate present, "parietal privileges" is oldspeak for having girls in your room) and the effectiveness of the prank was multiplied when the *Lampoon* came out with a second fake the next day, humorlessly dismissing the fake of the day before and darkly warning of repercussions. The double fake would be utilized again and again by the *Lampoon* to great effect; nobody expects a newspaper to be faked two days running.
- The double-fake was used in 1972 in the *Lampoon*'s most famous newspaper hoax. On February 20, the fake blared CHINA TRIP CANCELLED—KISSINGER REMARK OFFENDS CHOU, NIXON RETURNS TO U.S. Enhancing its believability, the article never revealed what Kissinger had said that was so offensive.

  That night, the *Lampoon* staged a fake arrest of its president, S. Eric Rayman, in the Adams House dining room. The campus buzzed with the news, and the next day, a second *Crimson* fake reported the arrest, explaining it was for "conspiracy to embarrass and humiliate the United States" and suggested an international incident had erupted out of the first fake.

Headlined LAMPOON'S CRIMSON PARODY PROVOKES INTER-
NATIONAL INCIDENT the second fake's lead story began "Word
came back from China that the People's Republic was incensed at what they termed 'a flagrant example of the depraved state of capitalist mentality.' "

The fake also provided a gripping account of the arrest of
the *Lampoon* editors.

"The *Lampoon* published its first *Crimson* parody in four
years yesterday, and two of its members may go to prison as
a result. . . ." began the story.

The crowning success of the two fakes came on the third
day, when he traumatized *Crimson* staff felt the need to banner
"This really is . . ." over their masthead.

• Perhaps the most wondrously-nasty *Lampoon* hoax came the
next year, on January 23, 1973 when the magazine tried to
deflate their rival's centennial by suggesting it had already
occurred. CRIMSON MISSES 100TH ANNIVERSARY, announced
the fake, whose lead story began, "The *Harvard Crimson*'s
one-hundredth anniversary, originally thought to be today,
actually passed unnoticed several months ago, a *Crimson* editor revealed last night" and went on to describe how a hereto-
fore unknown issue of the newspaper, dated May 17, 1872,
had just recently come to light.

Of course, Harvard is not the only college in the country to
offer newspaper parodies. We have seen a few other notables
in the sports chapter. The normally turgid University of Chicago provoked headlines in 1960 when the campus newspaper, *The Maroon,* published an article about the dismissal of an
assistant professor—identified as Theodore Salisbury—for
writing the screenplays of pulp crime and sex movies such as
Macumbo Love. (He is "well known as the rising author of
screenplays for what one Hollywood director has called 'the
boob market,' " the article revealed).

It was supposed to be a satire on the recent real-life dismissal of a University of Illinois professor for advocating free love
in a letter to the editor of the *Daily Illini,* but nobody got that,
and elements of the U of C community rallied to Professor
Salisbury's defense. Until, of course, it was revealed that the
author of *Macumbo Love* did not exist.

9

A STUDENT'S GUIDE TO PRANKING

You can't expect a boy to be depraved
until he has been to a good school.
—H.H. Munro (Saki)

*O*f all the pranksters in this book, perhaps the most vexing case is Dick Tuck. Famous for his determined hounding of Richard Nixon, Tuck has attached his name to some delightful pranks—the time he arranged for an old lady to embrace Nixon the day after his 1960 TV-debate drubbing and say "Kennedy got the best of it last night, but don't worry dear, you'll do better next time." The time he signaled for Nixon's campaign train to pull out of the station while the candidate was delivering a speech from a platform at the back. The time he tricked Nixon, during a visit to San Francisco's Chinatown, to have his picture taken under a huge sign which said, in Chinese, WHAT ABOUT THE HUGHES LOAN? alluding to a scandal dogging Nixon at the time.

So well-known was Tuck for his deeds, that when the Watergate scandal first broke, Nixon's henchmen initially blustered that it was merely a Tuckish prank.

It would be wonderful to say that Tuck is an exception to the Hugh Troy syndrome—legendary pranksters whose feats melt away when examined closely. Sadly, that is not the case.

The reason Dick Tuck falls within this book's scope of interest at all is that he traces his Nixon-baiting career to Nixon's run for California's Senate seat in 1950, when the Trickster waged a brutal campaign against Helen Gahagan Douglas.

A junior at the University of California at Santa Barbara, Tuck was a campaign worker for Douglas. He was also in the history class of professor Harry Girvetz, who was contacted by Nixon's campaign headquarters—Tuck says—looking for an advance man to coordinate a campus appearance by Nixon.

Girvetz, Tuck says, asked him if he would take the responsibility. Tuck accepted.

"I picked the largest auditorium I could find," Tuck told a newspaper in 1973. "There was nobody on campus at the time and this place must have seated 2,700."

Tuck also chose a time of 4 P.M. on a Thursday afternoon. Since most classes were held on Mondays, Wednesdays, and Fridays, the campus was largely deserted. "We went to the beach Tuesdays and Thursdays," said Tuck.

"Of course, only about forty people showed up. Then I held it up so latecomers could arrive. Well, Nixon and everybody there began getting impatient."

While waiting for the latecomers to arrive, approximately half the people who had shown up left. Nixon impatiently insisted that they get going.

"Finally, the meeting started and I got up to introduce him. During the introduction I proposed one hundred and three questions for Nixon to answer during his talk.

"And then I turned to him with a flourish and said: 'And now here's Richard Nixon, who will speak to us on the World Monetary Fund.' "

The appearance was a humiliating failure, and as Nixon was leaving, he called Tuck over and asked him his name. Tuck told him.

"Well, Dick Tuck," Nixon said. "you've just made your last advance."

A nice tag line to a great prank. The problem is, the entire thing is a lie; worse, one that Tuck has been repeating as true for the past 40 years.

After examining 30 years of credulous newspaper articles, all happily detailing Tuck's various exploits, I tracked down Tuck in New York, and he repeated his stories for me.

They sounded true enough—filled with detail and largely consistent. Then there were all those clippings. And I certainly wanted to believe him.

But the rally story started to unravel owing to Tuck's use of Professor Girvetz. No doubt mentioning a professor by name struck Tuck as the sort of small detail that adds veracity to a tale.

But he overlooked the fact that Girvetz was famous as a liberal Democrat—a building at U of C-Santa Barbara is named after him. The notion of Nixon's campaign staff, no matter how harried, contacting a famous Democrat to set up a campaign visit struck me as highly odd. The archivist at U of C was interested in my quest, and combed the student newspaper for news of the rally. Nothing.

I called Tuck back to see if he could provide me with more information—perhaps the date of the rally, or the name of a friend who attended. Suddenly, he was no longer the ebullient man I had spoken with before.

"Your desire for truth troubles me a little bit," he said. "I think the story is more important than the truth."

To give Tuck credit, under pressure, he finally admitted that not only was the disastrous University of California rally a fiction of his, but so was the train story and other pranks he is credited with.

In his defense, Tuck claimed that the truthfulness of a story is secondary to its effect—look at Santa Claus, he said.

But what he fails to see is that lack of truth completely undermine the value of anything presented as fact. It taints the moral of the story. The reason people embrace Tuck's pranks is not because they are wonderful, timeless tales. People love the punch line—tricky old anal-retentive Nixon, the wily puppet-master, reduced to a laughingstock, red-faced in the empty hall, flailing to finish his speech as the train pulls away.

Tuck's pranks appeared to play upon Nixon's defensiveness, egotism, and lack of humor. To see the importance of it being Nixon, imagine playing a prank on Jimmy Carter, somewhere in Africa, pressing a rag soaked in sugar water against the lips of a starving infant. Not quite the same image.

Remember, what brought Nixon down was not the Watergate break-in, per se. Rather, it was his lying to cover it up, shameless and on television, gazing into the camera and distorting the truth for his own benefit.

Kinda like Dick Tuck.

The reason I begin the final chapter with this lengthy discourse on Dick Tuck is because his sad story underscores the importance of the single most vital rule when it comes to committing a memorable prank:

Prank Rule # 1: You have to actually do it.

So much of a prank involves the right concept, that some people make the mistake of being hypnotized by the brilliance of a prank's idea, and end up never doing the deed.

This does not mean that every prank conceptualized should then be carried out. Lives have no doubt been spared by undergraduates shrugging off a brilliant-but-flawed prank idea.

When I was an undergraduate at Northwestern, I was peeved by professors who would reassign classrooms at the last minute, posting a note on the door of the regular classroom directing us, for some unfathomable reason, to another room across the campus. Quickstepping from one building to another, I cooked up the following simple prank: Make a sign reading: CLASS WILL BE HELD TODAY IN UNIVERSITY HALL, ROOM 306. Photocopy the sign 100 times. Head to campus about 7 A.M. one Monday and stick it on every classroom door.

It could have been a great prank. The problem was, I never did it. Maybe that's a good thing. Maybe enraged students, angry at having been funnelled up the tiny third floor of old University Hall, would have rioted. Maybe a couple of freshmen would have been crushed in the panic, like at that Who concert in Cincinnati. Maybe FBI handwriting experts would have traced the sign back to me. Maybe I'd be in Stateville Prison now. These things happen.

The positive thing about not doing a prank is that you can always tell yourself it would have been a good prank. Maybe the room change prank was a dumb idea—people would have laughingly torn the signs down, "What *idiot* put these up?" a pretty

Tri-Delt would shriek. "Who could be so mind-bogglingly stupid as to think anyone would fall for *this?*"

The important thing is, I don't go around telling people I went through with it. It boggles the mind, but people do that sort of thing. What happens is, they have a good idea, then are eaten away with guilt for not acting upon it. Lee Riordan probably saw Bill Jauss go by, dressed as Teddy Roosevelt, and thought, "Neato. But he should have dressed as MacArthur and picked up the police escort." Boom. Forty years later, he's making up friends in the Pentagon and—a grown man, mind you, over 60 years old—insisting he dressed as MacArthur and received the cheers of thousands. Sad.

Even more common than taking credit for a prank you didn't do is gilding the reality of an actual prank.

A lot of this is natural, telephone game sort of stuff. Pranks seldom work exactly the way they're supposed to, and the tendency is to gild the story a little when passing it along. For some, this may seem like an inconsequential matter. But to be a good prankster, and a good teller of prank stories, you need to have a sharp mind and a ready sense of the convoluted intricacies of life. Discerning between fact and fantasy is not exactly the most rigorous standard to hold up to yourself.

And Tuckish distortion is so cheesy. In Tolstoy's *War and Peace,* the biggest cowards, the guys who are trembling in a pickle barrel when the Hussars charge down the hill, are always the ones who survive the battle and immediately start bragging about how they were in the thick of things, cheating death a hundred times, saved only by the direct intervention of a benevolent God.

A failed prank can be a thing of beauty, too. Irv Sepkowitz's attempt at dumping manure on Tommy Trojan is certainly more timeless and noble—as a story—because Sepkowitz ended up picking fertilizer out of his teeth and not getting a speck on Tommy.

At Caltech, which knows a thing or two about pranks, they tell an interesting vignette in one of their *Legends* books. A bucket of water was balanced on top of a half-open door—the classic pail dump of cartoon fame—in a student's dorm room. The student saw the bucket, naturally enough, and carefully removed it from the top of the door. He walked into the bathroom, and was about to pour the water into the sink when he noticed light coming through the drain. The pranksters had removed the S pipe from the sink. The student had been a glance away from pouring the bucket of water onto his shoes.

To some, this is a failed prank. But at Caltech, they are savvy enough to realize that what is important is: 1) the neat, double-pump nature of the prank's concept and 2) the fact they tried to do it. There's no need to take a butter knife to the prank and smooth it into a success.

This might seem like a lot of intellectualizing to invest in an endeavor as light as pranking. But you get out what you put in, which leads to our second rule:

Prank Rule # 2: Think things through.

Originally, I included in this book a list of students killed in college pranks, tweaking them for their stupidity. But I found the list, like Benjamin Britt's shaving the president's horse, too deeply tinctured with malice for my taste.

The fatal pranks all shared a common thread. They were dumb. Whether climbing atop an elevator for a ride, setting off smoke bombs in the dead of the night, or doing push-ups in the middle of a busy intersection, they all contained some gaping flaw in conceptualization. A moment's thought would have saved their lives.

The fact that the participants were too drunk to reflect on what they were doing is another matter. What is important for budding pranksters to keep in mind before doing a prank is the importance of examining it from all sides. Avoiding death is just the first concern. Another is to predict what the results of the prank will be. Will the car explode? Will the enraged president expel you from school? Will the priceless artifact be damaged? These are the sort of questions you need to ask yourself, the most important being: Is this the sort of thing I am going to enjoy talking about over beers for the rest of my life?

This is why the common, Saran Wrap-on-the-toilet-seat sort of pranks usually fall flat. The "and then . . ." part of the prank just isn't interesting. Beginning your story "I snuck into Biff's room and placed Saran Wrap over his toilet seat," sounds promising enough, but the "and then" invariably is, at best, "he was surprised and some pee got on the floor." Not exactly *Gravity's Rainbow*.

How can you keep your pranks from descending into the mean spirited and the trivial? (Or, I should say, from too often descending into the mean spirited and the trivial. Sometimes, a little mean spirit and triviality are just what the doctor ordered).

That leads to the third rule of pranking.

Rule # 3: If at all possible, dispense justice.

When I was a freshman at Northwestern, the university marked homecoming week by blasting John Phillip Sousa marches from the top of Scott Hall between classes. This constant blaring of martial music offended my roommate Kier Strejcek, myself, and a few other guys. We took decisive action—sneaking into Scott Hall, we swapped the march tape for a tape of Jimi Hendrix playing "The Star Spangled Banner" at Woodstock.

The song played, perhaps, for 30 seconds before someone bolted up to the tape machine and pulled the plug. But that was enough. Somehow, I felt the imbalance between the mammoth, clanging boosterism of the school's power elite, and the private, pastoral murmurings of our individual human hearts had been adjusted the tiniest degree.

Rule number three is not a hard and fast one. A prankster should not try to be Batman. Sometimes a prank is worth doing just for the malicious glee. Many great Harvard pranks, such as giving the Ibis to the Soviets, are delightful just because they are so archly wicked. Justice doesn't enter into it.

But pranks are a good way to settle the score with those who otherwise would be beyond reach. The odds of delivering a few choice words to the college president over canapés are painfully slim. The only way to put Ronald Reagan in his proper context is do something like staging Vegetable Awareness Week around his visit.

The great thing about using a prank to correct a wrongdoing is that, oftentimes, the wrongdoer will weigh in with a reaction that reflects their original wrongheadedness and rounds the prank out with a nice finish.

In 1926, when the Boston police confiscated the *Lampoon*'s *Literary Digest* parody calling it obscene, the *Lampoon* reacted by launching a mock "Anti-Smut" campaign, which they labelled "an organized attempt to aid the police in their diligent prosecution of filth in Harvard University." They plastered the campus with stark posters (HELP THE OFFICERS TO KEEP YOU CLEAN read one, imploring DON'T BE DIRTY! DON'T BE DIRTY! DON'T BE DIRTY!) and held a rally.

What makes the prank truly wonderful is that the campaign was mounted with such dryness that it fooled almost all of Boston's censorious upper class, which never paused to question such a quick turnaround of Cambridge's flaming youth. The *Boston Telegram* congratulated both Harvard and itself with this Proustian nod of approval: "Moved to action by the vigorous denunciations by the *Telegram* of the moral uncleanness in the atmosphere of Harvard as shown by the publication of obscenity that nauseated the public in the *Lampoon* and *Advocate,* a committee of students has been formed to fight the filth and indecency by conducting an Anti-Smut Week beginning today and lasting until May 7."

The dull acceptance of Anti-Smut Week, along with all the various hoaxes and shams documented in this book, should combine in the mind of the clever collegian to form the basis of the next powerful prank tool:

Prank Rule # 4: People are gullible and will believe almost anything.

The *Lampoon* was never really going to restage the Battle of Hastings on October 14, 1966 as a way to "use up money rapidly accumulating from sales of its glossy parody on *Playboy*." The entire thing was a ploy to publicize their parody. But they certainly convinced United Press International of their intentions, and the wire story, detailing the number of men (2500) to perform in the reenactment and the number of elephants (4) ran in papers across the country. "It will be a lot of fun," Conn Nugent of the *Lampoon* was quoted as saying.

The key to a good hoax is to warp reality, but just a little bit. Newspaper fakes often fail because the comedy is so over-the-top and sophomoric that no one believes them for an instant. That instant's belief—that moment of confusion and shock—is the goal of every good hoax.

It helps a lot to make your hoax a multimedia event. Amherst's fabled prank group, Rubber Chicken Enterprises, delivered a great newspaper prank in October 1972, which illustrates the effectiveness of reenforcing a hoax from several directions.

As background, the campus was in the midst of a stormy debate on the merits of coeducation (that's right, kids. When mom and dad were in college, boys and girls going to school together was still a Big Thing. Thank goodness that issue was laid to rest, so we can give full attention to the more pressing matter of multiculturalism).

First, all students were sent a faked letter from the president, declaring that since he was unable to make a recommendation to the Board of Trustees, citing "pressures" of his office, Amherst would instead close for the remainder of the semester to allow a decision to be reached concerning coeducation.

That evening, a bogus edition of the *Amherst Student* was distributed, its banner headline screaming WARD CLOSES COLLEGE. The issue reprinted the letter, along with the "mixed reactions" of faculty members and an editorial mimicking the dry *Student* style, deadpanning that the decision to close the school "comes as a surprise to all of us in the Amherst community."

Like most hoaxes, it caused more surprise than belief, but one student reportedly was packing his bags when he learned the truth (of course, in pranks such as these, there is always the coda of the one gullible student, probably an imaginary one).

At Northwestern in the early 1980s, sororities raised money for charity by providing a tuck-in service. You gave five or ten bucks to cystic fibrosis, or whatever, and a Kappa Kappa Gamma in footie pajamas showed up at your dorm room at 10 P.M., gave you milk and cookies, read you a bedtime story, and tucked you in. This actually happened.

We at the Rubber Teeth Humor Network (no relation to *Rubber Chicken*—we published a magazine and produced a weekly radio comedy program) found it all rather trite and disgusting (though now, through the prism of a decade, I don't see why I didn't cough up the money and have the sorority girls drop by, perhaps several nights in a row. Who knows what could have developed?) We felt a prank was in order.

That prank was the Cuddle Up. Forming a fake sorority (most people can never keep all those Greek letters straight, anyhow) we announced that, on Valentine's Day, anyone donating a certain amount to charity would be visited in the evening by a sorority girl, who would climb into bed and cuddle for ten minutes.

To enhance the prank, we took out ads in the paper (featuring a smarmy, badly-drawn Ziggy character with his arms open wide) and set up a booth at the student center. The booth had a big CUDDLE UP sign and an open sign-up notebook with names in it. Over the back of the chair was draped a girl's jacket, and a sign that read BE BACK IN FIVE MINUTES.

On the day of the Cuddle Up, we delivered big red construction-paper hearts to certain people. The hearts, featuring Ziggy announcing "I'm being cuddled," were supposedly from anonymous donors, stating that a Cuddle Up had been purchased for them. The recipient was told to wear their heart during the day as part of the big Cuddle Up.

Some did.

The prank ended up in the newspaper, with the inevitable complaints from sororities that they were being made fun of. Hoots of protest from outraged, humorless victims make for a pleasing end to any prank, and introduce the next guideline:

Prank Rule # 5: Go after those who deserve it.

Target is very important when it comes to pranks. A prank against meek little Wubbly Meester, no matter how complex or grandly executed, is going to taste bad in the mouth over time.

One of my associates told me an intricate tale of a prank that took place at Georgetown in the early 1980s. A group of his friends were plagued by a snotty-nosed freshman who had the genuinely offensive habit of listening outside their doors.

To strike back at him, they formed a conspiracy to convince the freshman he smelled of peanuts. First, they began by casually mentioning peanuts in his presence. Then—over a period of weeks—they began expressing interest in eating, say, a peanut butter sandwich. Others were brought into the plot, so suspicion would not fall on any individual. They would sniff the air and inquire about peanuts, or demand to know if the freshman was hiding peanuts or had just eaten peanut butter.

This was all very disturbing for the freshman, who finally collapsed into apoplexy when a menacing Rastafarian was induced to approach him and start raving about peanut odor.

All in all, a slick conspiracy. The problem is the victim is too pathetic, a situation compounded by the us-against-you nature of the peanut conspiracy (actually a version of the Snark Hunt routine, where a bunch of people conspire to make an ostracized member of the group do or believe something ridiculous).

For a prank to be good, it needs a victim puffed with self-importance or arrogance. This is what makes the Carry Nation episode such a delight. Had the victim been Mother Theresa, the prank would have fallen flat. You need what the Greeks called hubris—overbearing pride, begging for a fall. (Richard Nixon is the definitional example of this, which explains why the unreality of Tuck's pranks is so hard to accept).

Zealotry in general provides wonderful prank fodder. People caught in the thrall of causes, fiery-eyed and taking themselves as deadly seriously as they can, are just waiting to have their balloons burst by a prank.

Consider the following announcement, which ran in an issue of the Harvard Divinity School's newsletter in February 1991:

> Someone changed the recycling sign in Rock entryway from "colored paper" to "paper of color." If this was meant as a joke, I don't think it's funny. If it was done because of a legitimate concern about language usage, please let me know by leaving a note in my mailbox.
>
> —Ellen Jennings, Recycling Coordinator

What makes the prank so funny is Jennings's oblivious reinforcement of it, her sad clinging to the hope that this is not someone mocking the current delicacy about nomenclature, but rather a sincere linguist trying to be precise. To top it off, she took what would have been a passing tweak and unwittingly immortalized it by printing it in the newsletter. Lovely.

Zealots, like dupes, also have the delightful tendency to flush themselves out of the woodwork, jamming their fingers into the spinning machinery of pranks and enhancing the overall effect.

A *Rubber Teeth* prank was rescued from mediocrity by the outraged intercession of the very group that should have applauded it.

Perpetually strapped for money, *Rubber Teeth* (which stood for "biting satire that doesn't hurt") had recently lost its university funding, and among the cash-raising stratagem considered by the editors was showing a pornographic movie—a surefire money-raising technique employed constantly by Northwestern fraternities.

But the editors decided that porn movies were an extreme and rather odious measure. We were, however, intrigued by the concept of porn movies, particularly the lurid and disgusting posters that the frats slathered all over campus to promote their screenings.

We decided to invent our own porn movie, which we called *D-Grade Women*—and produce a poster for it. Robert Leighton, a cartoonist and founder of the magazine, designed the poster, using photos of models from swimsuit ads in the back of *Cosmopolitan*.

If the name of the movie wasn't enough of a tip-off (get it? *D-Grade Women*—degrade women) we assumed the fact the movie was being shown every 70 minutes on the non-existent April 31, plus the rest of the jokes smeared over the poster, would be a subtle hint that we were not promoting an actual film.

Wrong. Women's groups, which generally turned a blind eye to the real porn movies shown weekly on campus, were enraged by the poster. Almost as fast as they were put up, they were torn down. (*Rubber Teeth* kept running off more and putting more up). There was talk of a boycott. The *Northwestern Daily* was flooded with well-thought-out letters like the following:

> . . . *Rubber Teeth* has stretched beyond satire and humor with its recent advertising campaign for the film *D-Grade Women* to be shown next week at Tech.
>
> The posters, spread around campus, depict women as objects of the violent male fantasy which assumes that women enjoy and invite exploitation and degradation. There is no question that the

film's advertising denies women any intellectual or emotional capacity. "They couldn't get A's . . . in ANYTHING" describes the women in this film, which dehumanizes sex to the point of having "cameras so close, you can't tell what you're seeing."

We question the mentality and humanity of men who are aroused by such a shallow and distorted sense of sexuality. We deplore this use of women in advertising (put out during Women's Week, no less) by a student organization which obviously has no sensitivity to the issues of violence toward women.

Rubber Teeth's tasteless and destructive humor, in this case, is unacceptable. Especially in an institution of "higher learning" which supposedly seeks to cultivate progressive values.

We strongly urge a boycott of the film screening.

> Adele Brown, Speech 1981
> Joan Grossman, Speech 1982

The letters were so bombastic our friends accused us of making them up, as part of the joke. But the letters kept coming, even after the nonreality of the film had been publicly established. (A second edition of the poster, with one of the models saying "Get It?" was similarly pulled down). Like all tempests, it eventually died away. *Rubber Teeth* got its funding, somewhere, and lasted for another decade at Northwestern before slowly vanishing, rather like its mascot the Cheshire Squirrel.

What makes fanatics react so strongly to pranks—even pranks such as *D-Grade Women,* which are supportive of their causes—is the solemnity of their self-image. You have to have a little humility to laugh at yourself, and being God's chosen messenger to rescue the world does not permit much room for humility. Pranks aren't funny. Nothing is funny.

A really special prank will be able to separate these zealots from the more rational. In the Veterans of Future Wars furor, the really amazing thing was that not all veterans groups attacked the students—a few were actually supportive, and distanced themselves from those groups pouring out frothing denunciation. (Not only were the Future Veterans funny, they were right. There soon was another war. Many of them were in it, some no doubt were killed. The government *should* have given them their bonuses).

If there is one person who might top a beyond-the-orbit-of-Pluto extremist in the ability to wax ridiculous over a simple prank, it's a beyond-the-orbit-of-Pluto extremist with academic credentials. Few pranks earn the frosting of a ringing, somber philosophical denunciation, but when they do, it's priceless.

At Amherst College, the lawsuit-fearing administration is joined in their assault on Sabrina by a handful of fringe feminists, who have managed—in an unbelievable leap of symbolic perversity—to contort theft of the statue into a women's issue.

"One thing that women students have in common with Sabrina is her fear of anger, her fear of her own fury," writes Amherst associate English professor Eve Kosofsky Sedgwick, in her huffy screed "Sabrina Doesn't Live Here Anymore."

Sedgwick argues that Sabrina, rather than being a statue that gets stolen a lot, is some sort of symbol for Greater Womanhood. Naked, unprotected, she is "a completely passive object of violence and mutilation" at the hands of "violent, threatening, and misogynist men." The solution Sedgwick offers to Amherst coeds, of course, is to become humorless, carping ideologues like herself. "Women, feel anger," she insists. "Think about what to do with the anger. If you know it's anger, then you're in control."

One wonders what she would have made out of the Doyle Owl.

It's important to note that, while it can be fun when zealots step forward to interject themselves into unrelated pranks, zealots generally make a poor choice of a prank target.

First off, their lack of humor and radio-beams-directed-at-my-head-controlling-my-thoughts worldview make them go nuclear if they think they are being targeted or victimized. I'm sure any student dumb enough to, say, make the palm-under-armpit farting noise in Eve Kosofsky Sedgwick's class would in a flash find himself kneeling on a rail before the assembled Amherst deans, babbling apologies and begging to be readmitted to the school.

And second, like Wubbly Meester, those unfortunates who cull down life's garden of pleasure into, for instance, total devotion to the Reverend Moon, or the Square Earth Society, or anthropomorphism, are rather sad, as a group, and deserve to be left alone.

If nothing else, pranks should enhance reality, not degrade it. They should make life funnier, trickier, more filled with the joyous and unexpected. Which leads to the final rule of pranking:

Prank Rule # 6: If at all possible, involve a cow.
This only incidentally refers the barrel-sided ruminant that has been cropping up in student pranks for as long as there have been colleges.

The sad reality is, it isn't possible all that much anymore. Unless he goes to Nebraska State University, the average student never gets a chance to even just slap the coarse, resonant side of a cow.

Which is a shame. Because after you've muscled a belligerent, 1,000-pound cow up a few flights of stairs, the normal challenges of day-to-day life don't seem so difficult anymore. After you've stood on the carpet of the dean's office, explaining why you thought it was a good idea to dress a cow in his best hat and coat and then tether her to the main gate, explaining the most convoluted political theorems is suddenly a breeze.

In the general absence of cows, however, we have to cling to the challenge they once presented, and convey that challenge to a new generation of students. Survey your campus and think of the great sacred beast of college humor. There have been pranks, sure, but were they at a cow level of difficulty? Have good pranks—possibly great pranks—gone unattempted because of mistaken notions of difficulty, when in fact they were not nearly as hard as slinging a lasso around a holstein's neck in a cowpie-dotted farmyard at midnight? Have you abandoned a pranking concept just because of a potential for self-humiliation that never even approached that of being discovered leading a jersey cow down some back alley of the campus?

These are tough questions that every undergraduate will someday have to ask himself or herself. The choice is clear. College only lasts for four or five years. Well, at the most eight. Nine if you have trouble with your thesis.

But however long it lasts, college offers up a final, precious chance at truly irresponsible living. A safe harbor to fine-tune your life before facing the windstorm that lies beyond. You can be a person who maneuvers the cows of life at will, heedless of farmers, fences, and flatulence.

Or you can be the cow.

EPILOGUE

*I*f this book were about bees, I could have consulted the countless bee experts and bee texts in writing this manuscript.

Because it is about college pranks, I had to beat the bushes, flipping, glassy-eyed through the indexes of college histories, cold-calling listless university public relations specialists, combing the *Reader's Guide.*

I'm not complaining. It was a lot of fun. It beats working, and I only wish I could have done it full-time for a few more years before having to disgorge a manuscript.

But such is life.

I am pleased because I've been able to present some great college pranks to a world hungering for such things. But I know there is greatness I have overlooked. Splendid pranks that are locked in the minds of certain members of the Great Lay Public.

Here is your chance. My puppeteers at St. Martin's and I hold out fond hope that this book will be followed by a sequel, filled with tales of your wonderful pranks.

Please write to me, being as specific as you can, including your phone number so I can call you and quiz you. I can't give any remuneration, other than to say that your prank will be rescued from the poisonous waters of oblivion and granted immortality of a sort.

I can be reached at:

> Neil Steinberg
> P.O. Box 10387
> Chicago, Illinois 60610-0387

Thanks. I'll look forward to hearing from you.

INDEX

PHOTOGRAPH CREDITS

ᴖ

Benjamin Crowninshield—courtesy of the Harvard University Archives; painted cannon—courtesy of the Photographic Archives of Vanderbilt University; Tommy Trojan steamcleaning, Tommy Trojan in a bag, captive Occidental Tiger—University of Southern California; the "Immortal 21," AXE RE-GAINED, giant stack of wood, scary bonfire—Stanford University News Service; Edward C. Read in the drink, Lampoon Castle riot—courtesy the Bettman Archive; Caltech Rose Bowl Hoax, "Hollywood" sign shenanigan—reprinted with permission from *Legends of Caltech* and *More Legends of Caltech,* published by the Alumni Association of the California Institute of Technology; Carry Nation party pics—courtesy of the Yale University Archives; John Kenneth Galbraith in garish Cadillac—Arthur Grace/NY Times Pictures; MIT weather balloon, Baker Hall piano recital sequence, cow raising, happy students with cow—courtesy the MIT Museum and the *Journal of the Institute for Hacks, Tomfoolery and Pranks;* the great pumpkined dome—E. Robert Schildkraut; Orwellian Conwell bust—Temple University; Sabrina unearthed, Sabrina held captive by alumni—Amherst College Photos; presentation of ibis to the Soviets—© 1953 (and kudos to) John Loengard; Ditch Day announcement, slip 'n' slide bowling, pirate guys, convertibilizing—Jonathan Alcorn; Varjian and Mallon at play—courtesy Norris J. Klesman; Statue of Liberty on ice—© Michael Kienitz; soon-to-be wet Canadian students—Hugh MacKenzie/University of Ottawa Archives.

Thank you all.